ANALYSING POLITICAL SPEECHES

Also by Jonathan Charteris-Black

Corpus Approaches to Critical Metaphor Analysis
The Communication of Leadership: The Design of Leadership Style
Gender and the Language of Illness (with Clive Seale)
Politicians and Rhetoric: The Persuasive Power of Metaphor

Analysing Political Speeches

Rhetoric, Discourse and Metaphor

Jonathan Charteris-Black
University of the West of England, UK

palgrave
macmillan

First published 2014 by
PALGRAVE MACMILLAN

Palgrave Macmillan in the UK is an imprint of Macmillan Publishers Limited, registered in England, company number 785998, of Houndmills, Basingstoke, Hampshire RG21 6XS.

Palgrave Macmillan in the US is a division of St Martin's Press LLC, 175 Fifth Avenue, New York, NY 10010.

Palgrave Macmillan is the global academic imprint of the above companies and has companies and representatives throughout the world.

Palgrave® and Macmillan® are registered trademarks in the United States, the United Kingdom, Europe and other countries

ISBN 978–0–230–27438–9 hardback
ISBN 978–0–230–27439–6 paperback

This book is printed on paper suitable for recycling and made from fully managed and sustained forest sources. Logging, pulping and manufacturing processes are expected to conform to the environmental regulations of the country of origin.

A catalogue record for this book is available from the British Library.

A catalog record for this book is available from the Library of Congress.

Contents

PART III   CRITICAL METAPHOR ANALYSIS

List of Figures

List of Tables

Preface

The aim of this book is to enhance the reader's ability to understand the variety of ways in which political speeches may excite and inspire as well as to recognize the various linguistic means used to misrepresent and manipulate. A political speech is an orderly sequence of words delivered by an individual to a physically present audience assembled for a specific social purpose. It also addresses a wider, remote audience via a range of communication media. Analysis of political speeches encourages engagement in public communication because possession of a linguistic and conceptual framework for investigating persuasion means that we do not *need* to be suspicious of a persuasive speaker. Suspicion arises from ignorance, and what we don't understand frightens us the most. Hope is a social necessity, and to achieve their purposes political speeches need to satisfy emotional, moral and social needs. In short, they need to persuade. The purpose of this book is to help readers understand how this is done.

It is hoped that the book will encourage readers to consider how traditional approaches to text analysis, such as cohesion and classical rhetoric introduced in the first part, may be integrated with 'critical' approaches in the remaining two parts. At the end of the book, readers should understand a range of critical and discourse theories that account for relationships between the linguistic features of speeches and the social and cultural contexts in which they are spoken. Someone who reads a cookery book is neither guaranteed a gourmet result nor will necessarily enjoy their food more; however, knowledge of the ingredients and the stages of preparing a meal is more likely to produce good results. Public speaking is not cookery, and readers are not guaranteed any improvement in their abilities as public speakers from reading this book, but it is hoped that by understanding a range of theoretical approaches to the analysis of speeches they may perhaps learn how to be more persuasive in their own speech-making.

In this preface I will first summarize in a little more detail what is meant by a political speech, and illustrate the main types of such speeches. I will then go on to consider what is meant by 'oratory' and its relationship with public speaking, before introducing some of the key ideas regarding success and failure in political speaking. The preface ends with an overview of the book. We start with a specific case: people in Western democracies, as they struggle to recover from seemingly insurmountable problems of indebtedness and media manipulation, may ask themselves 'Is oratory dead?' or

'Don't we need action rather than words?' Yet each time we are about to answer affirmatively, something happens to challenge this scepticism about spoken public language. In September 2011, a baby-faced 16-year-old boy called Rory Weal mounted the podium at his first Labour Party conference. He began innocently enough, 'This government appears to have taken a bit of a dislike to young people' but this was the opening sally of a forthright attack on Conservative government policies relating to young people – such as a large increase in university tuition fees and the removal of financial support for those attending colleges. He continued, 'I ask David Cameron: what does he advise when I can't afford to go to school any more?' The question evoked applause from the audience; there was something both moral and moving about a youth asking for advice about his future – even if such an appeal to 'ethos' sounded 'rhetorical'.

Politics is about trust, and trust is challenged by the current obsession with media manipulation and 'spin': we live in an age where conspiracy theories are considered to be as credible as cabinet ministers. But in some way the youth of the speaker and his oratorical flair suspended post-Blair scepticism about charismatic young speakers, and for a moment his audience could believe again. The press was, generally, full of praise[1] and alluded to a speech made by the foreign secretary William Hague when he was 16. Pundits contrasted the young speaker's fluency with the halting delivery of Ed Miliband, the Labour party leader. The boy was asked if he intended to enter politics and Ladbroke's put him down at 50/1 to be prime minister by 2040. As President Obama had already demonstrated in his 2007 election campaign, oratory is a sleeping giant waiting to be awakened when dark forebodings fail to satisfy our subliminal needs for reassurance and hope.

Political speech

I will define a political speech as a coherent stream of spoken language that is usually prepared for delivery by a speaker to an audience for a purpose on a political occasion. Broadly speaking, there are two main classes of political speech: the first is concerned with the making of political decisions; and the second with establishing shared values. We may think of the first type as policy-making and the second as consensus-building. The first type has been described since classical times as 'deliberative', whereas the second type has been called 'epideictic'. The speeches analysed in this book include three of each of these major types of speech: the policy-making speeches are Tony Blair's speech advocating war with Iraq (March 2003); Michael Howard's speech on immigration (September 2004); and David

---

[1] The exception was the *Daily Mail*, which researched his background and found that he had previously attended a private school and lived in a large house prior to his parents' divorce.

Cameron's speech on the European Union (January 2013), while the consensus-building speeches are Tim Collins' Eve of Battle speech (March 2003); John F. Kennedy's inaugural speech (January 1961); and Barack Obama's inaugural address (January 2009). I make reference to other speeches, such as conferences addressed by Michael Foot and David Cameron, which are consensus-building. Reisigl (2008a, 2008b) explores the interaction between rhetoric, political science and linguistics in 'politico-linguistics' and offers a detailed account of particular types of political speech.

The division between these two types of speech is not as clear-cut as this typology suggests, because a policy-making speech will also attempt to establish a consensus, and a consensus-building speech will also be setting out a framework for future policy. For example, Tony Blair's speech sought to establish a parliamentary consensus around the need to invade Iraq as well as advocating that policy; and Kennedy's inaugural address also fed into a policy for the USA to build alliances in the Third World. Perhaps the best way to conceptualize the distinction is in terms of their generality: a policy-forming speech necessarily addresses some specific aspects of policy about which a decision needs to be made in the near future: whether to go to war; on what conditions to allow further immigration; whether Britain should remain in Europe – and if so, on what terms. While the occasion of consensus-establishing speeches is very specific – the immanence of military combat, the election of a president – their content is, by contrast, more general. Presidential inaugural speeches, or Party Convention speeches, are necessarily broad-ranging, covering a wide range of policy areas such as foreign policy, economic policy and so on, and will view short-term decisions against the backdrop of their broader historical origin, the speaker's ideology and world view. This distinction relates, then, to the underlying contrast of purpose of these two speech categories: policy-making speeches need by definition to point towards a decision so that policy can be made – usually on the basis of a vote in the near future. Conversely, consensus-building speeches are primarily motivational: they serve to display the shared beliefs of speaker and audience so that a feeling of unity can underlie future policy.

Oratory and public speaking

We might ask ourselves if and how 'oratory' is different from 'public speaking'? According to the *Oxford English Dictionary*, oratory is 'the art or practice of formal public speaking', so apparently there is little difference. However, when we look at a corpus of language we find that 'oratory' is used alongside words such as 'persuasive', 'wit', 'brilliant', 'display', 'wonder', 'seductive' and 'art'. By contrast, 'public speaking' occurs with words such as 'competition', 'skills', 'debating', 'classes', 'courses'[2] and so on. Unlike oratory, public speaking is something learnt rather than something intuitive. This may explain why a search for 'public speaking' on the Amazon UK website scores 27,100 hits (offering many books of the 'how to do' type), compared to only 3,032 for 'oratory'. However, we have little evidence to indicate that the extensive range of self-help literature has led to any improvement in the quality of public speaking – it is just that more people aspire to speak publicly, as well as to make money from writing books about how to do it. I will use the term 'oratory' when referring to the status and origin of speech-making in classical rhetoric, and 'public communication' when referring to contemporary use. This is because a major difference between classical and contemporary situations is the opportunity offered through the media for the proliferation of a speech through multiple media – and the extent to which technology makes public speaking available for consumption.

Oratory is the art of formal public speaking – in which there is a clear speaker purpose that influences language use. A speech with the purpose of policy-making will differ from one whose purpose is consensus-building. In this respect there is nothing incompatible between the classical view of what a speech is and modern views in which language choices are governed by a consideration of the speaker's intentions. So, for example, a politician talking about future policy is likely to use modal verb forms such as 'will' to express conviction and convince an audience of the need for this policy.

An assumption behind the classical view of oratory was that it was necessary to develop skill in public speaking because of the importance of public decision-making; the effect of a speech on an audience could influence what were literally matters of life and death – either for an individual accused of a crime for which the punishment was death, or for the lives of soldiers if war was declared. The very direct form that democracy took in ancient Greece is rather different from our contemporary oligarchic systems of government, where citizens delegate to elected politicians their power to make decisions. For this reason, speech-making by 'ordinary' people has become closely associated with the consensus-building function – at weddings, funerals or commemorative events, because the policy-making function has been delegated to experts in the field of public or legal decision-making. None the less, there are still occasions when skill in influencing policy may be necessary on the part of the individual citizen, who may, for example, be fighting a planning application or an unfair tax demand, or arguing the case for, or against, the building of a road, a runway or a children's playground.

The purpose of this book is not to teach the skill of public speaking but to improve our understanding of how it works, though the two are partially

---

2   Evidence here is taken from the British National Corpus.

interdependent. We hope to develop critical faculties by explaining theories and demonstrating how they can be used to analyse seminal speeches. There are many new forms of public self-expression these days via the social media, such as blogging and tweeting, that provide evidence of the effect of a speech. At a time when interactive technologies are offering opportunities to access speeches, and access their effect, it is crucial that participants in democracies are able to make discerning choices and identify what makes speeches 'great' – and this leads to the question of what makes for a successful political speech.

Success and failure in political speaking

The iconic figures of Western politics have laid claim to power because of their success in communicating with large audiences: Winston Churchill and his combination of erudition and earthiness; Margaret Thatcher and her talent for rebuking her opponents and turning the rhetorical tables; and the charm and self-conviction of Tony Blair. Great American rhetoricians such as John F. Kennedy, Martin Luther King, Bill Clinton and Barack Obama have all inspired their followers by reviving different versions of the American Dream and offering hope to a suffering world. By contrast, Joseph 'Joe' McCarthy, Ronald Reagan and George W. Bush appealed to the need for strength and unity in a world filled with Evil and Terror. We can identify common themes in all of these speakers: an appeal to underlying mythic thinking about good and evil, the ability to establish political legitimacy by creating social and moral purpose, and to inspire through the creative power of language. The purpose of critical analysis is to understand how public communication contributes to the 'power' that arises from connecting with audiences, and we can do this as much by considering failure as success.

Political speakers should always have the audience in mind, and their choice of language will be influenced by their assumptions about that audience's current state of knowledge. The success of political slogans provides evidence of whether or not assumptions are shared with the electorate. For example, in the 1978 election campaign, the Conservative Party developed the slogan: 'Labour Isn't Working'. This correctly assumed that many people knew that there was a high level of unemployment, for which the Labour government of the time could be held responsible. By contrast, in the 2005 election campaign the Conservatives used the slogan 'Are you thinking what we're thinking?' – a rather indirect reference to immigration intended to highlight how it had become a taboo topic in British politics. Their failure in the election implied that they had made the wrong assumption because *at that time* the majority of people were not preoccupied by immigration (though they were soon to be). It also perhaps implied a dystopic futuristic world in which the agents of power already knew what we were thinking before we thought it. The subsequent escalation of immigration up the political agenda following the global financial collapse of 2008 demonstrated that in a sense they *had* read the future and were ahead of their time. But a misjudgement about the *current* preoccupations of the audience undermined the persuasiveness of their rhetoric.

Another example of such a misjudgement was when David Cameron coined the phrase 'Big Society' to refer to self-initiated social action by individuals acting in the public interest. While it was not used in the election campaign – perhaps because it did not clarify the assumptions it was making, it was subsequently re-introduced by the prime minister. The phrase sought to address people's belief that Conservative governments did not care about 'society' because of Margaret Thatcher's famous statement: 'There is no such thing as society.'[3] Perhaps Cameron also wanted to distance himself from Reagan's 'Small Government' – meaning a low degree of government control over business. Political advisers and speechwriters consider what their prospective readers and listeners know before deciding on an appropriate form for their slogans.

Increasingly, successful political speaking needs an understanding of the media through which a speech will be transmitted in order to attain maximum effect. While in ancient civilization it was assumed that oratory would be conducted in face-to-face settings, in the modern period symbolic resources have been enhanced significantly through the development of telecommunication media, and politicians often succeed or fail through their expertise (or lack of it) in the new media. For some in the audience it is the intensity of effect that comes from listening to the radio, for others it is more the intimacy offered by the visual close-up, and for others it will be through the symbolic effect of physical performance, engaging in some form of sport, or of dynamic display in what I have referred to as symbolic actions (Charteris-Black, 2007). As mentioned earlier, for this reason it is preferable to consider contemporary 'oratory' as public communication.

A present-day example of awareness of visual media occurred when the then Italian prime minister, Silvio Berlusconi, on being struck in the face and injured by a souvenir model of a building, got out of the car he was travelling in to display his injuries to the media – aware of how the event might have a negative impact on the 'character' of his opponents, whom he accused of whipping up hatred against him. As a media mogul, Berlusconi was aware of the power of the media to enhance his persona as someone who was an innocent victim rather than a perpetrator of elite power structures. Another example is the Russian politician, Vladimir Putin, who is photographed frequently in heroic masculine roles such as riding a horse while stripped to the waist, or swimming across a river. This leads us to

---

3 Interview, 23 September 1987, quoted by Douglas Keay, *Woman's Own*, 31 October 1987, pp. 8–10.

consider the vital question of how successful persuasion works in public communication.

We should not forget that, in a world increasingly dominated by technologically mediated communication – often by groups of performers, musicians, sports teams, or the use of dual announcers – the *individualistic* nature of a public speech retains a strong appeal. After all, globalization has brought to the fore a range of competitive self-promotional genres such as online personal ads and popular performances of singing and dancing ('The X Factor'), everyday living ('Big Brother') and getting a job ('The Apprentice'). The text behind a speech is often produced by a speechwriter who may be supported by a team; or a researcher, who has tried and tested its content on focus groups. While a speech is a socially produced text, when it comes to delivery, it is a live *performance* by a single individual – and, moreover, one that will be analysed by journalists, de-constructed by academics and judged by the general public. Part of the entertainment value of public speaking lies in observing how a particular individual responds to the demands of high-stakes, pressurized situations. Armed as a speaker may be with a set of notes or an autocue, he or she has to perform at the designated time in a highly constrained social situation in which he or she is the focus of attention.

Different individuals respond to this pressure in different ways: for some it is a long-awaited challenge, while for others it is a moment of pain and sacrifice leading to disastrous and humiliating failure. A good example of this occurred in a live TV performance in the early stages of the American presidential campaign in November 2011:

> Republican presidential candidate Rick Perry's campaign is facing meltdown after one of the most humiliating debate performances in recent US political history. His chances of securing the Republican nomination slipped after one painful minute in which he could not recall the name of a government department he is planning to kill off. Perry reeled off two of the three departments he wants to axe, but could not remember the third. Some Perry supporters declared his campaign over and suggested he head back to Texas to focus on his job as governor. (*The Guardian*, 10 November 2011)

The fluffed lines were posted on YouTube, to provide a permanent testimony to the importance of a feature identified in classical rhetoric as essential to success in public speaking: a good memory. Needless to say, the results were politically disastrous for this potential candidate for high office.

The minimum requirements for persuasion in public communication are fluency, a high level of confidence, sincerity, spontaneity and the ability to inspire trust. These are acquired over time by orators through proficiency with language, experience in its delivery and an awareness of how to perform in public. Fluency implies skill with language, swiftness of thought, and the ability to convey ideas – all leadership qualities. Similarly, confidence implies a strong sense of identity, which is also an attribute of leadership. Sincerity is the ability to speak (metaphorically) from the heart and is about having good intentions: when intentions are believed to be good, so much else can be forgiven. It may be that speaking from the heart can be simulated – since we cannot actually see this organ – and some of the most brutal leaders have demonstrated what is now described as 'conviction rhetoric'.

Spontaneity is about reacting to what is happening in the here and now, and being prepared to dispense with a prepared script. This expressive, performative dimension does not come from study and erudition. It could even be that the opposite is the case: the more we are analytical, the less we are spontaneous, losing the essential skill of interacting with an audience. Rory Weal appealed as much because of what he did not know as because of what he knew. So formal oratorical analysis – for example, studying lists of figures of speech as in the rhetorical schools of ancient Greece – may have exactly the opposite effect to the one intended, since by over-intellectualizing we may lose contact with the spontaneity and joy of the moment that can be the essence of great speaking. The key to successful performance is awareness of what is happening now, in real time, and when orators go off script or dispense with it altogether, they may be demonstrating their skill in creating dialogue with an audience, as well as their self-confidence. When the appearance of artifice and manipulation disappear, the ghost of the puppet master is no longer hovering over his mouthpiece, and an audience offers the most essential precondition for persuasion: trust.

Overview

What is distinctive about the approach taken here is that it does not restrict itself to a single theoretical approach. Just as rival schools of rhetoric – Gogias, Isocrates, Plato and Aristotle – emerged in ancient Greece, so a rich diversity of approaches have developed in the contemporary period. These range from the work of Norman Fairclough, drawing on systemic-functional linguistics (Fairclough, 1989, 1995, 2003, 2010); Teun van Dijk's extensive work on racist discourse (van Dijk, 2008) and Paul Chilton's (2004) and Ruth Wodak's (Wodak and Meyer 2009) analysis of ideology and political discourse. Richardson (2007) applies this framework to the language of the media. More recently, critical metaphor analysis (Charteris-Black, 2004, 2011) has received support from Goatly (2007), Musolff (2006, 2010) and Semino (2008). No single approach offers an authoritative view of successful public communication. The purpose of illustrating and evaluating different approaches is to gain the benefits of triangulation. Just as we learn about a sculpture by walking around it, so we learn about speeches by viewing them from multiple perspectives. It may ultimately depend on the characteristics of a particular speech as to which approach is the most insightful, but knowledge of more than a single approach improves the quality of our methodology.

The book is divided into three parts, which are organized chronologically. Part I of this book describes traditional approaches to oratory and discourse, as follows: Chapters 1 and 2 provide an overview of classical rhetoric and Chapter 3 examines the key concepts from traditional discourse analysis that developed in the 1970s and 1980s: 'cohesion' and 'coherence'; together, these three chapters cover some essential background in understanding how speeches work from classical and traditional linguistic perspectives. Part II describes critical approaches to discourse and public communication from the 1990s onwards. It is divided into three chapters – Chapter 4 discusses power, develops a model for analysing context, and presents a theory of persuasion. This is illustrated with further analysis of the speech by the young Rory Weale, discussed above. Chapter 5 examines how critical linguists draw on concepts such as modality and transitivity to analyse social agency. Chapter 6 offers an account of one of the most well-known critical linguistic approaches – the discourse-historical approach (DHA), and this is integrated with an account of argument theory. Part III provides a comprehensive account of an approach that has developed in the last ten years in which discourse is understood to arise from metaphor: Critical Metaphor Analysis. Chapter 7 provides an introduction to metaphor studies and considers some general methodological issues involved in researching metaphor; Chapters 8 and 9 then develop the author's own critical approach to metaphor. Chapter 10 illustrates how all these approaches can be employed to the analysis of a speech by David Cameron on the European Union.

Each chapter of the book starts by providing an overview of a theoretical approach to discourse analysis, with each theory being supported by figures and diagrams, and illustrated in model analyses of selected speeches. At the end of each chapter there is a list of recommended readings. The speeches chosen to illustrate particular discourse theories are seminal ones by British and American politicians and military leaders (both real and fictional) and are referred to as 'core texts'. All speeches concern contemporary issues of social, cultural and political importance, and illustrate effective persuasive strategies. Within the chapters there are structured exercises in which readers are invited to check their understanding of key concepts, often by analysing additional speeches. Comments on these exercises are provided after Chapter 10, and there is a glossary at the end of the book.

JONATHAN CHARTERIS-BLACK

Acknowledgements

Many of the extracts in this book come from the speeches of well-known orators. I would like to acknowledge both the orators and their speech-writers. In particular I would like to thank Tim Collins and his publisher Lucas Alexander Whitley Ltd for permission to use his Eve of Battle speech (core text 1). I would also like to thank Ruth Wodak and Michael Meyer and their publisher Sage for permission to use the discursive strategies in Table 6.5 (reproduced by permission of SAGE Publications from *Methods for Critical Discourse Analysis* by Wodak and Meyer © Sage, 2009) and Teun van Dijk for permission to use his diagram known as the ideological square (Figure 5.1). I would also like to thank Mark Davies for making accessible material in the British National Corpus and the American Corpus of Contemporary English and Palgrave Macmillan for permission to use Figure 4.5 that originally appeared in my book *Politicians and Rhetoric* (2011). Finally I acknowledge the various reactions of my students at the University of the West of England to the exercises contained in this book.

Every effort has been made to trace all copyright-holders, but if any have been inadvertently overlooked we will be pleased to make the necessary arrangements at the first opportunity.

This book is dedicated to students of English Language and Linguistics at the University of the West of England, Bristol. Many past students have contributed by engaging with these speeches in a way that has been enquiring, inspiring and, usually, insightful. It is hoped that future students will continue to do so.

PART I

Traditional Approaches to Rhetoric, Oratory and Discourse

Chapter 1

Classical Rhetoric: Artistic Proofs and Arrangement

1.1 Introduction: rhetoric, oratory and persuasion

Rhetoric is the formal study of persuasion; it includes both speech and writing. Oratory is the application of this knowledge specifically to speech-making. In classical civilization, the study of effective speaking and writing was viewed as an art. When referring to the act of transmission, our current preference is often for 'communication', as this has developed an inclusive sense that refers to both speech and writing. Developments in communication technology have led to a convergence between the styles of written and spoken language. Professions such as politics, the law, pubic communication and academia place great emphasis on the ability to communicate persuasively, and specify this as a skill required by entrants to these professions. Preparation involves practice in debating competitions that simulate authentic scenarios.

Given that, in ancient Greece, 'rhetoric' was the formal study of persuasive communication, why is it that 'rhetoric' has developed a largely negative meaning in contemporary English? For example, if we look in the British National Corpus (Davies, 2004) we find that the most common adjectives that precede 'rhetoric' are 'political', 'public', 'mere', 'radical', 'empty', 'official', 'populist', 'nationalist', 'revolutionary' others include: 'simplistic', 'violent', 'hostile' and 'tub-thumping'. A very common pattern is to contrast 'rhetoric' with 'reality', as in the following extract:

> Mr Baker: That is the trouble with the Labour party: one has to distinguish between its **rhetoric** and **reality** when it comes to law and order. This morning, the right hon. Member for Birmingham, Sparkbrook (Mr. Hattersley) said that he wanted to see more policemen on the beat, yet when he was a member of the last Labour Cabinet he cut the number of policemen and left the police force under strength. (House of Commons Debate, 23 June 1992 [emphasis added])

This illustrates a typical semantic pattern in which 'rhetoric' is equated with hypocrisy or falsehood, and 'reality' with truth. Here is another example of this contrast:

the unemployment figures as perceived locally greater than a similar number of people losing their jobs in Leeds or Selby or somewhere else, and so I think to some extent this the **rhetoric** has outrun **the reality** on that point. (Public county council planning meeting, 24 November 1993 [emphasis added])

Might this be a reflection of contemporary scepticism towards art, towards politicians, or towards both? Though both may be true, the origin of this opposition between reality and rhetoric has deeper roots – even as far back as a dispute between Plato and the Sophists over the merits of rhetoric. Plato believed that the purpose of philosophy was to discover truth that was independent of any special calculation of interest; he was suspicious of rhetoric because he thought it lacked any concern with a truth that was separate from the speaker's interests. An opposition therefore developed in the classical period between rhetoric and dialectic: dialectic gave equal weight to both sides of an argument, while rhetoric was concerned with persuasion from a particular perspective rather than presenting a balanced point of view. For Plato, rhetoric was therefore inherently deceptive, because it only showed a perspective that fitted with the speaker's point of view. By contrast, dialectic would arrive at the truth through the use of logic and evidence irrespective of whether it was rhetorically constructed. Plato would sympathize with the disdain towards rhetoric that is frequently shown in public communication, as in the following from a Trades Union Congress:

John Major himself, when they put adverts in every press in Europe, Come to Britain, our employees have no rights and they are cheap labour. So it's not **rhetoric, it's truth** ... The Thatcherite experiment was a failure, no nonsense, a failure. There was no economic miracle. Britain's industry is weaker now than it was fifteen years ago, and sure as anything Britain is a much nastier place to live in. Forget the **rhetoric** about the enterprise economy. Forget the bullshit about the Citizen's Charter. If you want to find the **reality** of Britain today, after fourteen years of Conservatism, go to a DSS [Department of Social Security] office, or a Job Centre, or a Citizens Advice Bureau, and look at the misery of a country that will not provide sustenance and dignity for its people. (Trades Union Annual Congress, 6 June 1993 [emphasis added])

Here, impassioned and self-righteous anger is expressed by the contrast between appearance and reality. Plato resisted the idea of persuasive appeals to interest groups because he believed in a permanent and abstract truth – one that would be to the benefit of all. The Platonic perspective has become the dominant one as, in contemporary language, 'rhetoric' is invariably contrasted with fact, and linked with disparaged social groups, such as politicians:

> And I think it's unfair of them, I think it's irresponsible of them to just criticise detailed budgets that are well thought out like ours, like ours always were. I have nothing, and to have nothing to offer the people of Lincolnshire as an alternative. It's just **rhetoric**, in a way, irresponsible **rhetoric**. (Lincolnshire County Council meeting, 14 January 1994 [emphasis added])

Aristotle restored the position of rhetoric as the counterpart of dialectic by arguing that persuasion was an essential part of civic life, and that rhetoric co-ordinated human action by allowing people the opportunity to debate options: this was preferable to having a specific option forced upon them, and therefore rhetoric contributed to democracy. He claimed that the origins of rhetoric are closely related to the origins of democracy since, if power was to be negotiated and distributed to the people, there would need to be those who were skilled in persuasion. Rhetoricians such as Aristotle and Quintilian recognized that different contexts required different methods of persuasion: influencing political decisions would not require the same methods as arguing legal cases or commemorating fallen heroes. Rhetoric therefore involved identifying, analysing and understanding the full range of the means of persuasion, and working out which were appropriate in particular circumstances. Both philosophers and rhetoricians needed to understand when language was being used to discover universal truth and when it was being used to manipulate or misrepresent. The development of rhetorical theory in ancient Greece was therefore motivated by the idea of a truth that varied according to time, place and situation, rather than Plato's idealized and permanent truth. Aristotle also assumed that rhetoric could be learnt, which is why he wrote *The Art of Rhetoric*.

Audiences are only persuaded when the speaker's rhetoric is successful. In classical antiquity, the definition of rhetoric was *ars bene dicendi*, the art of speaking well in public (Nash, 1989). This definition assumed that some people spoke better than others – the same assumption that underlies debating competitions, parliamentary debates and debates between candidates for president or prime minister. The most rhetorically successful speech is the most persuasive one, as measured by audience response – which in the long run in democracies is by voting. Rhetoric may be said to have failed when an audience expresses opposition to the speaker's underlying purposes. Western thought has oscillated between, on the one hand, the Platonic tradition – based on an abstract notion of truth – and, on the other, a 'rhetoric' that is concerned with how truth can be represented so that it persuades. Both Platonic and Aristotelian traditions survive.

Exercise 1.1

> Write a definition of rhetoric based on your own understanding of the concept using web-based and library sources.
> Undertake a search of the word 'rhetoric' in the Corpus of Contemporary American English (Davies, 2008). Note whether collocates of 'rhetoric' (that is, the words found in close proximity to 'rhetoric') are more or less negative than those in the British National Corpus (see start of chapter). Explain why you think this is the case.

1.2   Branches of oratory

Classical rhetoricians identified three branches of oratory: deliberative, forensic/judicial and epideictic. These can be differentiated by analysis of circumstances, so the typical context of deliberative oratory is in parliamentary or local governmental meetings; the typical context of forensic/judicial oratory is in law courts; and the typical context of epideictic oratory is in ceremonial events such as public commemorations, or funerals.

Deliberative oratory is delivered to a decision-making body with the general purpose of establishing the benefit or harm that may be expected from a certain course of action. Deliberative rhetoric considers different possible outcomes from different courses of action, and arrives at a recommendation as to decisions about future action. The orator seeks to recommend a particular argument, drawing on whatever means of persuasion are appropriate to win support for the action he or she is advocating. According to Aristotle, deliberative speeches typically consider one of the following subjects: whether to go to war or to make peace; defence; imports and exports. The general purpose (*skopos*) of a deliberative speech is to judge the course of action that would be most likely to enhance human happiness. Aristotle went on to propose that what are useful or advantageous are the measures for achieving happiness; these can be understood in terms of actions that contribute to socially valuable outcomes.

Forensic speeches are addressed to a court or legal assembly that requires judgements to be made about guilt or innocence in relation to past actions, such as a crime. The orator seeks to accuse or defend a suspect by drawing on evidence and arguments for either upholding or rejecting an accusation of guilt. Forensic rhetoric considers different possible interpretations of evidence to arrive at a recommendation as to the guilt or innocence of those on whom judgement is being passed. So a typical forensic speech is that made by the counsel for the prosecution in a courtroom. The purpose of forensic oratory is to arrive at a just decision in keeping with the law.

Originating from the Greek word for 'show' or 'display', epideictic oratory is addressed to an audience that is not required to make a decision but is assembled to honour or commemorate a particular individual, or individuals in an event such as a death or a marriage. The orator seeks to display his own eloquence in evaluating another by praise or criticism, and to arouse the emotions that are appropriate to the ceremonial occasion. We may think typically of funeral eulogies or speeches remembering the war dead as typical of this genre. But there are other types of epideictic speech, such as motivational talks given by chief executives to their employees, or by head teachers in schools, or speeches given by recipients of awards – such as Oscars.

The three branches of oratory vary in three ways:

◊ The types of response they expect of the audience – voting (deliberative), passing judgement (forensic) or applauding (epideictic).
◊ Their social purpose – for example, whether they are concerned with influencing policy (deliberative), ensuring justice (forensic) or celebrating someone's life (epideictic).
◊ Their time orientation – towards the future (deliberative), the past (forensic) or the present (epideictic).

It follows that the methods of persuasion need to be modified in keeping with what is most likely to be effective in the specific speech context. Consideration of effect or impact makes speech-making an art rather than an exercise in philosophical enquiry, and speech-making could both create a reputation for the speaker and influence the social world. Figure 1.1 summarizes the branches of oratory according to classical rhetorical theory:

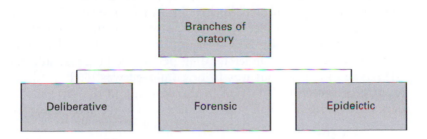

Figure 1.1   Branches of oratory

What is interesting about the identification and analysis of branches of oratory is how closely they relate to modern ways of thinking about how language is influenced by considerations of social purpose and context. The division between these branches could be modified to reflect blending between these genres, as a speech can be oriented towards a future course of action (deliberative) but at the same time honour the contribution of an individual (epideictic). However, overall these three branches of oratory have stood the test of time quite well, since they highlight how a speech event can be classified according to its social purpose, its audience, and the role played by this audience.

Exercise 1.2

Draw a table with three columns, giving each one a heading with one of the branches of oratory. Now position the following speeches in the table:

➤ An Oscar awards acceptance speech. (a)
➤ An objection to an application at a council planning meeting. (b)
➤ A pre-match address by a coach to his team. (c)
➤ A defence speech given by Tony Blair at the International Criminal Court. (d)
➤ A speech given at a college prize-giving. (e)
➤ A post-match address to the team by the coach. (f)

1.3   The proofs

Irrespective of the branch of oratory, Aristotle proposed a distinction between artistic and inartistic proofs. The inartistic proofs were not based in language at all but in sources of persuasion that existed before oratory, such as laws, or evidence from witnesses, evidence taken under oath, or even evidence from slaves obtained by torture. The artistic proofs were known as ethos, logos and pathos, and these were created through oratory. From these terms we derive the words 'ethical', 'logical' and 'empathetic', which provide insight into these appeals. As with the tri-partite classification of speech types, Aristotle's identification of three artistic proofs has generally been accepted by classical scholars and is still considered relevant in understanding persuasive language and rhetoric. The type of appeal that was to be employed was likely to depend on the type of speech, its position in the speech and the style that the orator was adopting. We shall now consider each of the artistic proofs in turn

1.3.1   Ethos: character

Initially, when an orator is seeking to establish a relationship with an audience, the appeal should be based on the character of the speaker: that is, his or her ethos – practical wisdom, goodwill and virtue – which together would contribute to his/her overall ethical credibility. For example, when an orator commences a speech by rejecting the eulogies with which he has been introduced, he displays the virtue of modesty. Or when an orator argues a case for a course of action 'because it is right' (as did Thatcher, Blair and Cameron) he is assuming a set of values that are shared with the audience. Demonstrating ethical credibility is necessary to establish trust, and trust is an equivalent in contemporary oratory to 'goodwill' in classical oratory. Both 'goodwill' and 'trust' are based in a belief that someone in a position of authority is concerned primarily with the interests of the people he or she is representing rather than his/her own personal interests, since only then will they be persuaded by his arguments. Politics is about building trust, and because of an increasing awareness of manipulation of public opinion through media presentation and the 'massaging' of consent, trust has become a rare commodity in democracies. Orators need to convince followers that they and their policies can be trusted. I shall illustrate this with reference to two contemporary examples: one from British and one from American politics.

When announcing his candidacy for the Labour Party leadership in May 2007, at a critical point near the beginning of the speech Gordon Brown made an appeal to ethos:

> For me, my parents were – and their inspiration still is – *my moral compass*. The *compass* which has guided me through each stage of my life. They taught me the importance of integrity and decency, treating people fairly, and duty to others. And now the sheer joy of being a father myself – seeing young children develop, grow and flourish – like for all parents, has changed my life. Alongside millions juggling the pressures of work, I struggle too to be what I want to be – a good parent. [emphasis added] (Speech announcing candidacy for Labour Party Leadership, May 2007)

By using the phrase 'moral compass' Brown represents himself as someone motivated by a desire to pass on the legacy of good parenting he has inherited from his parents. This is an appeal based on moral character, to imply that he shares the same values as the British people.

A major argument of Obama's criticism of the preceding presidency was that the Iraq War had cost so many lives and resources that it had led to a loss of trust by the American people in their elected leaders:

> When it comes to the war in Iraq, the time for promises and assurances, for waiting and patience, is over. Too many lives have been lost and too many billions have been spent for us to trust the president on another tried and failed policy opposed by generals and experts, Democrats and Republicans, Americans and many of the Iraqis themselves. It is time for us to fundamentally change our policy. It is time to give Iraqis their

country back. And it is time to re-focus America's efforts on the challenges we face at home and the wider struggle against terror yet to be won. (30 January 2007)

The need to regain trust then became a major theme of Obama's election campaign; for example:

We can seek to regain not just an office, but the trust of the American people that their leaders in Washington will tell them the truth. That's the choice in this election. (22 April 2008)

Making an explicit statement about his own moral character would have undermined the appeal of virtue, since immodesty is not compatible with humility. So his strategy was to *imply* that he had a better character than the present leader, because Bush could not be trusted. The same theme emerges in his Obama's first inaugural address on January 2009; the very first line is:

I stand here today humbled by the task before us, grateful for the trust you have bestowed, mindful of the sacrifices borne by our ancestors.

Notice that the trust between the people and its government has now been bestowed on him. What he recognizes is that trust must underlie the relationship between people and government:

And those of us who manage the public's dollars will be held to account – to spend wisely, reform bad habits, and do our business in the light of day – because only then can we restore the vital trust between a people and their government.

Trust would be restored through command of the national budget by saving the money spent unnecessarily on war but Obama implies that he also understands that trust can be withdrawn as easily as it is granted. Situations that lead rapidly to loss of trust are corruption scandals, when politicians siphon off public funds or make unjustified expense claims or use their positions to earn sexual favours. These are especially damaging for orators, since they imply that the speaker is acting in his or her own self-interest rather than in the interests of the group. Ethos or moral character is therefore a proof in which behaviour has to match language. A model orator (*vir bonus*) therefore necessarily needs to lead a morally virtuous life.

Exercise 1.3

Read the first and last two paragraphs of Barack Obama's inaugural speech (see the core text at the end of the chapter) and identify any appeals to ethos (the character of the speaker; his wisdom, goodwill and virtue). Discuss these values.

1.3.2   Logos: reason

Logos, or the appeal to arguments based in reason, was the second of the artistic proofs. As we shall see when looking at 'arrangement', argument was the only obligatory stage in a speech according to Aristotle. It is also central to the rhetorical canon of invention, since it is necessary to have ideas that are based on arguments grounded in reason. Logos represents a proposition so that it can be judged according to whether it accords with everyday experience. The most persuasive means of arguing is by a syllogism; this is a structure in which there is a major premise, a minor premise and a conclusion. For a conclusion to be accepted, both premises need to be things that the audience already accept as true. Figure 1.2 (below) illustrates a typical syllogism to support an argument on the financing of university education.

Acceptance of the conclusion is only possible if the audience accepts an ideal of social equality, and the proposition that a graduate tax is socially equitable. One way of attacking the logical structure of this syllogism would be to challenge the assumptions behind one of the premises. For example, the assumption that social equality is desirable could be rejected on the grounds that it encourages a lack of effort and a tendency to rely on others; this might lead to the counter-argument that universities should be financed entirely by the students. Conversely, someone could attack the idea that a graduate tax is socially equitable, because if everyone in society was to benefit from higher education it could be argued that it is more equitable to have a completely free system of education.

Classical rhetoricians preferred to use incomplete syllogisms by leaving part of the argument unstated, as this could draw the audience into making an inference in the conclusion. This type of argument based on an incomplete syllogism is known as an enthymeme. Figure 1.3 illustrates this.

Major Premise + Minor Premise + Conclusion

[**Major premise**] Universities need a socially equitable means of funding.
[**Minor premise**] A graduate tax is a socially equitable method of funding.
[**Conclusion**] People should support a graduate tax.

Figure 1.2   Structure of a syllogism

[**Premise**] Universities need a socially equitable means of funding.
[**Conclusion**] People should support a graduate tax.

Figure 1.3   Structure of an enthymeme

[**Premise**] Universities need a socially equitable means of funding.
[**Reason**] Taxation is socially equitable because the more you earn the more you pay.
[**Conclusion**] People should support a graduate tax.

Figure 1.4   Reason

[**Premise**] Universities need a socially equitable means of funding.
[**Reason**] Taxation is socially equitable because the more you earn the more you pay.
[**Analogy**] Graduates, just like everyone else in employment, pay tax.
[**Conclusion**] So people should support a graduate tax.

Figure 1.5   Comparison/analogy

Here the audience is implicitly invited to supply, or infer, the missing premise 'A graduate tax is a socially equitable method of funding'. The rhetorical effect is that the audience believes they have arrived at the conclusion on their own, rather than because of an argument supplied by the orator.

Logical argument can be strengthened by backing up one of the premises with a persuasive reason; so the enthymeme in Figure 1.3 could be modified as in Figure 1.4.

Here the reason explains the principle of progressive taxation to justify why a graduate tax might be viewed as socially equitable. Figure 1.5 shows another way of strengthening an argument – that is, by some kind of *comparison*.

The analogy here removes any distinction between graduates and non-graduates when it comes to taxation.

1.3.2.1   Refuting arguments
A common way to refute and reject an argument is by presenting an opponent's argument in the form of a counter-position as a preliminary to refuting it with a counter-argument. This also provides an opportunity to introduce an alternative position.

Here is an example of a typical way of refuting an argument:

1 *Present a counter-position*
   It might be thought that higher tuition fees and putting universities completely into a free market situation is the only way they can get sufficient funding.
2 *Refute the counter-position*
   But in reality that is not the case, because there are other ways of funding universities.

3 *Offer an alternative position*
They could be funded entirely through general taxation; through a combination of general taxation and lower fees; or by a graduate tax.

I shall illustrate refutation in an authentic context – a speech by Barack Obama entitled 'Renewing American Competitiveness'. He begins by contrasting an ongoing theme in American foreign policy – whether the USA should keep to itself (isolationism) or get involved with world problems (internationalism).

There are some who believe that we must try to turn back the clock on this new world; that the only chance to maintain our living standards is to build a fortress around America; to stop trading with other countries, shut down immigration, and rely on old industries (1). I disagree (2). Not only is it impossible to turn back the tide of globalization, but efforts to do so can make us worse off (3). Rather than fear the future, we must embrace it (4) … [3 sentences omitted]. But at critical moments of transition like this one, success has also depended on national leadership that moved the country forward with confidence and a common purpose (4). That's what our Founding Fathers did after winning independence, when they tied together the economies of the thirteen states and created the American market (5). That's what Lincoln did in the midst of Civil War, when he pushed for a transcontinental railroad, incorporated our National Academy of Sciences, passed the Homestead Act, and created our system of land grant colleges (6). That's what FDR did in confronting capitalism's gravest crisis, when he forged the social safety net, built the Hoover Dam, created the Tennessee Valley Authority, and invested in an Arsenal of Democracy (7). And that's what Kennedy did in the dark days of the Cold War, when he called us to a new frontier, created the Apollo program, and put us on a pathway to the moon (8). (16 June 2008)

1 *Present a counter-position* – (1)
He puts forward the counter-position: that America should turn isolationist.
2 *Refute the counter-position* – (2) and (3)
He rejects this position for two reasons: because it is does not correspond with reality and because economic isolationism would have the opposite effect to the one intended because it would lead to a lowering of living standards. To enhance the refutation he introduces two metaphors that describe going back in time: 'turn back the clock' and 'turn back the tide' to represent his opponents' policies as retrograde.
3 *Offer an alternative position* – (5) – (8)
He lists a number of historical analogies of situations when American leaders have made dramatic shifts of policy. This supports the argument

that the US should engage in economic and technological change – 'Rather than fear the future, we must embrace it.'

It is the supporting evidence provided by these historical analogies that adds depth and strength to his arguments. Historical analogies also contribute to positioning the speaker within a tradition of great American Democratic presidents – Lincoln, Roosevelt and Kennedy.

Exercise 1.4

Analyse the structure of this syllogism by identifying (1) the major premise, (2) the minor premise and (3) the conclusion:

> Going to university requires young people to take on a large debt.
> It is unwise for young people to go to university.
> It is unwise for young people to take on large debt.

> ➤ Re-write the syllogism in the form of an enthymeme.
> ➤ Add a further reason in support of the argument.
> ➤ Add an analogy to support the argument.
> ➤ Now write a refutation of the argument.

1.3.3 Pathos: emotion

Aristotle emphasized the importance of making appeals based on emotion, and described these as the artistic proof of pathos. Emotions could be aroused by evoking fear of injury, sympathy with an aggrieved party or anger arising from an insult. Aristotle's definition of emotion was that it was characterized by pleasure (for example, happiness) and by pain (for example, anger and fear). His view of emotions is that they are cognitive in nature because they have a cause such as a source of fear or anger, and because they lead us to make evaluations which in turn influence our opinions and judgements. He identified emotions as having an object and a ground (Fortenbaugh, 2007, p. 117), this means that they are directed towards something, so, to use a contemporary example, someone might be angry with the banks (the object) because of the profits that they make (the grounds for feeling angry). But emotions could also be aroused through humour; a good example of this was when Ronald Reagan was asked by Bob Hope what it felt like to be president. He replied, 'It's not a lot different than being an actor, except I get to write the script.' The arousal of emotion was a controversial issue in classical rhetoric, as rhetoricians debated the extent to which it was acceptable in developing arguments. Perhaps the most eloquent case arguing for the connection between language and emotion occurs in the speech Praise of Helen by Gorgias:

Speech is a great prince, with a tiny body and strength unseen, he performs marvellous works. He can make fear case, take away pain, instil joy, increase pity ... For just as various drugs expel various humours from the body ... Some speeches give pain, some pleasure; some fear, some confidence (Konstan in Worthington, 2007, p. 413)

As we have seen, Plato believed the purpose of philosophy was to discover the truth, and so he saw emotion as opposed to reason because it was likely to impair judgement. By contrast, Aristotle argued that because emotional responses could be influenced by reason – for example, when someone is upset about the irrationality of an argument – so it was also acceptable that rational argument could be influenced by the emotions, and so pathos was acceptable as an artistic proof. As Fortenbaugh (2007, p. 117) puts it: 'An orator of wisdom, virtue and goodwill advances reasonable arguments, and in doing so, he excites emotional responses that are appropriate to the situation.' Aristotle therefore held that cognition and emotion were not independent of each other, but interrelated: since thought could cause emotion, so emotion could reciprocate by contributing to an intelligent response to an argument. This recognition that emotional appeals could also be reasonable ones was an important development; using another contemporary example, a member of the Greek parliament might argue that it was necessary to accept financial austerity because the only alternative would be government insolvency. If the government became bankrupt that would lead to its inability to pay any public sector employee, let alone any form of welfare benefit, thereby causing even worse suffering than there was already. The emotion of fear that such a scenario would cause among public sector employees might be considered an acceptable proof of an argument (though it would be possible to use other types of emotional appeal in forming a counter-argument).

Exercise 1.5

First consider the circumstances of Barack Obama's inaugural speech (at the end of this chapter). By the time he gave this speech, Obama had full access to information about the state of the economy and was aware of the gravity of the 2008 financial crisis; he was also coming to power on the back of a huge wave of public expectation that had culminated in his election. He therefore needed to redirect political expectations to the reality of the economic situation by hinting at the financial 'cloud', but he also needed to establish himself as a young and vigorous leader who could respond to such challenges.

> What emotions are being aroused in the second paragraph?
> What metaphors are used?

➔

Now work through all the paragraphs in the speech and decide which artistic proof is predominant in each paragraph. If there is evidence of two artistic proofs, list them both. Decide from your analysis which is the most pervasive of the artistic proofs.

1.4   Arrangement in classical rhetoric

The five canons of rhetoric were invention, arrangement, style, memory and delivery. Initially there is a need to gain hold of the audience's attention through *heurisis* (discovery) and then to develop or 'invent' arguments in the way that is described in the section on logos. This section focuses on arrangement, or *taxis*. We may think of arrangement in terms of the distinct stages or parts of a speech, and how the sequence of these parts could influence an audience. It was at the planning stage of a speech that orators would need to consider the sequence of the various arguments they had identified at the invention or *heurisis* phase, and which artistic proofs would be most persuasive for each part. There were discrepancies among classical orators as to the number of parts into which a speech might be divided, and what types of appeal might be most effective in each of these. In the fourth and fifth centuries there was a division into four parts, however, and in the standard work on rhetoric in Renaissance times, the *Rhetorica ad Herennium*, there were six parts. In my account below I take a compromise position by outlining five parts.

While there is no generally agreed canonical order, according to Aristotle, speeches required a minimum of four parts: an introduction (known in Greek as *prooimion* and which I shall refer to as the 'prologue'), a narrative phase followed by a proof and a conclusion (or epilogue). The form of the narrative would vary according to the branch of oratory; for example, an epideictic speech would require only a narration, whereas a deliberative speech would require an argument, and a forensic speech would require proof in support of an argument. In forensic speeches there would also be a part where the opponents' arguments were rejected (refutation). More important than enumerating parts is the rhetorical purpose of each part and how this contributed to the overall argument, as I shall illustrate below.

1   The Prologue (prooimion)

The first part was a prologue, in which the orator sought to create rapport with the audience and to arouse interest. Some techniques, such as flattery or an appeal to goodwill, were directed towards the audience; others, such as a confession of inadequacy or of a lack of expertise on the part of the speaker, were directed more towards establishing the ethos or character of the orator. Frequently, an orator would establish empathy by demonstrating that he shared the same values as the audience by using the first person plural pronoun 'we' and by displaying his humility towards the audience. Interest could be aroused by emphasizing the importance of the topic of the speech or creating surprise; consider the opening to Obama's speech against the Iraq War given in October 2002:

> I stand before you as someone who is not opposed to war in all circumstances. The Civil War was one of the bloodiest in history, and yet it was only through the crucible of the sword, the sacrifice of multitudes, that we could begin to perfect this union and drive the scourge of slavery from our soil.

The decision regarding whether to go to war is probably the most important of all topics of deliberative speeches, and Obama, who had become associated with opposition to the Iraq War, starts by refuting the argument that he is opposed to all war. The directness of the opening arouses interest in the audience, and the statement of ethical position seeks to establish common ethical ground with his listeners. He shares with them a favourable disposition towards war in some circumstances and is not a pacifist, and refutes a possible counter-argument to the main argument of his speech that opposes the war in Iraq.

Or, consider this prologue from Obama's keynote address at the 2004 Democratic National Convention:

> On behalf of the great state of Illinois, crossroads of a nation, land of Lincoln, let me express my deep gratitude for the privilege of addressing this convention. Tonight is a particular honor for me because, let's face it, my presence on this stage is pretty unlikely. My father was a foreign student, born and raised in a small village in Kenya. He grew up herding goats, went to school in a tin-roof shack. His father, my grandfather, was a cook, a domestic servant.

This emphasizes his humility ('deep gratitude') of being allowed to speak at this occasion because of his background, and by implication his race – an expression of humility usually arouses positive emotions and has a primarily ethical appeal. In the remainder of the prologue he makes it authentic by offering an autobiographical account of his ancestry – this is likely to arouse curiosity and interest as to how the son of an African can be addressing the Convention and it also anticipates the next part, the narrative.

2   The Narrative (narratio)
The purpose of the narrative is to outline the main arguments by setting out the central facts of a case; the way these facts were laid out would frame whatever arguments might follow, so the orator uses the narrative

to establish key information in a way that will provide a springboard for his main argument. Unlike the prologue, which is usually oriented towards the orator, the narrative is directed towards the events that it is claimed have occurred or will occur, and which will form the topic of the argument. So in the Democratic National Convention speech we looked at above, after completing his autobiographical account, Obama continued:

> I stand here knowing that my story is part of the larger American story, that I owe a debt to all of those who came before me, and that, in no other country on earth, is my story even possible. Tonight, we gather to affirm the greatness of our nation, not because of the height of our skyscrapers, or the power of our military, or the size of our economy. Our pride is based on a very simple premise, summed up in a declaration made over 200 years ago, 'We hold these truths to be self-evident, that all men are created equal. That they are endowed by their Creator with certain inalienable rights. That among these are life, liberty and the pursuit of happiness.'

Notice how Obama frames his argument in support of Democratic policies within a epideictic 'grand' narrative that makes the transition from his personal life story – 'my story' – to 'the larger American story'; he then frames this larger, social story by quoting a section from the American Declaration of Independence, which it is assumed that all his audience will both recognize and support. He argues that such a transition is only possible in America because the country is founded on ideals of equality. He then continues his narrative by elaborating on the social aspects of the American dream:

> That is the true genius of America, a faith in the simple dreams of its people, the insistence on small miracles. That we can tuck in our children at night and know they are fed and clothed and safe from harm. That we can say what we think, write what we think, without hearing a sudden knock on the door. That we can have an idea and start our own business without paying a bribe or hiring somebody's son. That we can participate in the political process without fear of retribution, and that our votes will be counted – or at least, most of the time.

Notice how, rather than defining the American dream in terms of the Puritan work ethic – the myth of a shoeshine boy becoming president – so loved by free enterprise, he defines it as an ethical dream: the absence of corruption, and political (rather than economic) freedom. The narrative is concise, illustrating how he understands American social values and contrasting these with the alternatives of non-democratic societies. The primary appeal still seems to be to ethos, and this provides the springboard for an argument in the next section that emphasizes identification with social values, with its implication that constraints on individual 'freedom' may be justified when this clashes with a valued social outcome.

3   The Proof

Following the narrative (or sometimes integrated with it) is the 'Proof' – a part in which the orator identifies whether the argument will draw primarily on the artless or artistic proofs and which of the artistic proofs are most likely to be persuasive. The proof is at the very kernel of a speech and its nature varies according to the speech circumstances. In the speech we have been examining, Obama's proof of his argument that social need should override individual interest took the form of citing a number of cases that illustrated human interdependence:

> A belief that we are connected as one people. If there's a child on the south side of Chicago who can't read, that matters to me, even if it's not my child. If there's a senior citizen somewhere who can't pay for her prescription and has to choose between medicine and the rent, that makes my life poorer, even if it's not my grandmother. If there's an Arab American family being rounded up without benefit of an attorney or due process, that threatens my civil liberties. It's that fundamental belief – I am my brother's keeper, I am my sister's keeper – that makes this country work. It's what allows us to pursue our individual dreams, yet still come together as a single American family. 'E pluribus unum.' Out of many, one.

By personalizing the argument in this way he is appealing now to pathos, and he continues this argument that individuals do not exist as autonomous units divorced from each other with the following proof:

> Well, I say to them tonight. There's not a black America and white America and Latino America and Asian America; there's the United States of America. The pundits like to slice-and-dice our country into Red States and Blue States; Red States for Republicans, Blue States for Democrats. But I've got news for them, too. We worship an awesome God in the Blue States, and we don't like federal agents poking around our libraries in the Red States. We coach Little League in the Blue States and have gay friends in the Red States.

This setting up of contrasts – as well as appealing to both pathos and ethos – also rejects counter-arguments. Linguistically, it is based on a list of stereotypical social identities which he claims are used by 'pundits' that have the potential to be divisive: race, ethnicity, political or sexual orientation. In reality this is a straw man argument because he does not offer evidence that anyone *has* claimed that America is divided along grounds of race and ethnicity (but perhaps this is taken as given). Assuming that there are these divisions then allows him to reject them on the grounds that they are over-simplifications because Republicans can also be gay, and concerned about civil liberties. Obama knew that to be elected he had to unite a patchwork quilt of different social groups; so as to forge a sense of unified purpose among them he appeals to pathos and ethos but does this within the logical framework of rejecting counter-arguments.

4   The Refutation

The refutation can either be treated as part of the proof (as we saw in the discussion of Obama's proof) or as a separate part, where the orator tackles his opponents' arguments; this can involve naming the opponent, attacking his character or ethos, and presenting an opponent's argument prior to its rejection. Obama used an interesting strategy for refutation in the 2008 election campaign to refute the policies of his opponent:

> We already know what we're getting from the other party's nominee. John McCain has offered this country a lifetime of service, and we respect that, but what he's not offering is any meaningful change from the policies of George W. Bush (1). John McCain believes that George Bush's Iraq policy is a success, so he's offering four more years of a war with no exit strategy; a war that's sending our troops on their third tour, and fourth tour, and fifth tour of duty; a war that's costing us billions of dollars a month and hasn't made us any safer ... (2) We already know that John McCain offers more of the same. The question is not whether the other party will bring about change in Washington – the question is, will we? (3) (Pennsylvania, Indiana, 22 April 2008)

In (1) Obama rejects an appeal based on attacking his opponent's war record, because it was known that McCain had had a successful military career; instead Obama establishes his own ethos by showing himself to be above making cheap personal gibes. This allows him in (2) to put forward a counter-argument 'that McCain believes that Bush's Iraq policy is a success' followed by refutation based on the proof of logos. The general argument is that similar policies to those of George W. Bush would be continued by John McCain. He provides three reasons why the war is unsuccessful: (a) there is no plan for ending it; (b) it is expensive; and (c) it has not achieved its objective of ensuring security. In (3) he links his opponent very clearly with a widely discredited George W. Bush, by assuming that McCain's reluctance to withdraw from Iraq implies a continuation of Bush's policies. The Democrats offer more possibility of change because Obama has proved in the foregoing argument that McCain will simply continue with previous (discredited) Republican policies. Notice how, through repetition of McCain's name, he keeps the focus of his attack in clear sight, but it is an attack based on ethos and logos rather than on pathos.

5   The Epilogue

Lord Mancroft made an insightful and imaginative analogy to emphasize the skill required in the epilogue: 'A speech is like a love affair. Any fool can start it, but to end it requires considerable skill' (*Reader's Digest*, February 1967). Rhetorical theory proposed that the purpose of the epilogue was to bring the focus of the speech back to the orator by summarizing or recapitulating the main arguments and by an arousing appeal to the audience's emotions. This was especially important in situations where an audience might be taking a decision following the speech – for example, a vote in a deliberative speech, a verdict in a forensic one or applause in an epideictic one. Consider how Obama ends the Pennsylvania campaign speech:

> You can make this election about how we're going to make health care affordable for that family in North Carolina; how we're going to help those families sitting around the kitchen table tonight pay their bills and stay in their homes. (1)

> You can make this election about how we plan to leave our children and all children a planet that's safer and a world that still sees America the same way my father saw it from across the ocean – as a beacon of all that is good and all that is possible for all mankind. (2)

> It is now our turn to follow in the footsteps of all those generations who sacrificed and struggled and faced down the greatest odds to perfect our improbable union. And if we're willing to do what they did; if we're willing to shed our cynicism and our doubts and our fears; if we're willing to believe in what's possible again; then I believe that we won't just win this primary election, we won't just win this election in November, we will change this country, and keep this country's promise alive in the twenty-first century. Thank you, and may God Bless the United States of America. (3)

The purpose of this ending was to motivate Democratic activists in the final stage of an election campaign with the prospect of the longer-term idealistic benefits of a Democratic success. (1) and (2) are both summarizing key arguments he has made earlier in the speech. So in (1) he is referring back to a section of the speech that described the domestic financial difficulties of potential Democratic supporters. In (2) there is also reference to the prologue, where he described global, environmentalist concerns: 'the bickering that none of us are immune to, and that trivializes the profound issues – two wars, an economy in recession, a planet in peril'. Notice how, in the summary, he has selected the two issues that are most likely to arouse an empathetic response. This is reinforced in (2) by a reference to his own personal family biography, and there is an appeal to ethos in the metaphor 'a beacon of all that is good'. In (3) he continues an emotional appeal to idealism in the image of 'keep this country's promise alive'; this alludes to what Martin Luther King described in his 'I have a dream' speech as a 'promise' between the founders of the American state and its citizens:

> In a sense we have come to our nation's capital to cash a check. When the architects of our republic wrote the magnificent words of the Constitution and the declaration of Independence, they were signing a *promissory* note to which every American was to fall heir. This note was a *promise* that all men would be guaranteed the inalienable rights of life, liberty, and the pursuit of happiness. [emphasis added]

Consciously or unconsciously, Obama's appeal to this 'promise' is an appeal to historical continuity and patriotism that combines an empathetic with an ethical appeal.

Table 1.1 summarizes the parts in the arrangement of a speech and shows Artistotle's advice on the type of artistic proof that was likely to be most persuasive in each part.

Table 1.1   The arrangement of a speech

Part	Rhetorical purpose	Artistic proof
Prologue	Introduces the topic to the audience; establishes a relationship between orator and audience to make the audience well disposed towards the speaker, attentive and receptive.	Conciliation by appeal to ethos through character.
Narrative	Sets out the facts of the case from a perspective favourable to the orator.	Appeals can be made by ethos or logos.
Proof	Presents arguments in favour of the speaker's case.	Conviction by argument by appeal to ethos, pathos or logos.
Refutation	Rejecting opponents' arguments (could be incorporated with Proof).	Appeals could be based on logos or ethos.
Epilogue	Summarizes the most persuasive points in the previous parts so that the audience is left with a favourable disposition towards the speaker and his or her arguments.	Emotional appeals to audience (pathos) prior to an outcome.

Exercise 1.6

1. Analyse the parts of the inaugural speech. Try to identify transition points between parts and do not feel that the patterns will necessarily correspond directly with those shown in Table 1.1.
2. In the previous exercise you decided which artistic proof predominated in each paragraph. Use this analysis to discuss the predominant artistic proof in each part of the speech.
3. Evaluate the effectiveness of the speech with reference to the artistic proofs and the arrangement.

1.5   Summary

In spite of disparaging contemporary uses of the term 'rhetoric', the concept provides the basis for much of our current understanding of how persuasion operates in language. A classical framework for oratory still contributes to how speeches are classified in terms of three major types: deliberative, forensic and epideictic. These can be differentiated by analysis of the speech circumstances, taking into account the types of responses they evoke, their social setting and their orientation towards time.

Following Aristotle, persuasive appeals can be made on the basis of the three artistic proofs of ethos, logos and pathos. These are, respectively, appeals grounded in the speaker's morality, in his or her ability to form rationale arguments, and in his or her ability to arouse the emotions of the audience. Arguments can be analysed in terms of their logical structure by identifying syllogisms comprised of a major premise, a minor premise and a conclusion, though to stimulate inference on the part of an audience the minor premise may be omitted. Where this occurs it is known as an enthymeme.

The arrangement of a speech may be analysed into a sequence of parts, commencing with a prologue, continuing with a narrative, a proof followed by a refutation, and concluding with an epilogue. There are variations according to the branch of rhetoric, since, for example, a refutation is more likely in forensic oratory while this may not occur in an epideictic (that is ceremonial) speech. Speeches may be analysed by matching the artistic proofs with the parts of a speech, so, for example, appeals to emotion are likely to be especially effective in the epilogue, while the prologue needs to establish the speaker's credibility by appealing to the audience's ethos.

Core text: Barack Obama, inaugural speech, 20 January 2009

My fellow citizens: I stand here today humbled by the task before us,   1
grateful for the trust you have bestowed, mindful of the sacrifices
borne by our ancestors (1). I thank President Bush for his service to
our nation, as well as the generosity and cooperation he has shown
throughout this transition (2).

Forty-four Americans have now taken the presidential oath (1). The   2
words have been spoken during rising tides of prosperity and the still
waters of peace (2). Yet, every so often the oath is taken amidst gathering clouds and raging storms (3). At these moments, America has
carried on not simply because of the skill or vision of those in high
office, but because We the People have remained faithful to the ideals
of our forbearers, and true to our founding documents (4). So it has
been. So it must be with this generation of Americans (5).

That we are in the midst of crisis is now well understood (1). Our   3
nation is at war, against a far-reaching network of violence and
hatred (2). Our economy is badly weakened, a consequence of greed
and irresponsibility on the part of some, but also our collective failure
to make hard choices and prepare the nation for a new age (3). Homes
have been lost; jobs shed; businesses shuttered (4). Our health care is
too costly; our schools fail too many; and each day brings further
evidence that the ways we use energy strengthen our adversaries and
threaten our planet (5).

These are the indicators of crisis, subject to data and statistics (1). Less   4
measurable but no less profound is a sapping of confidence across our
land – a nagging fear that America's decline is inevitable, and that the
next generation must lower its sights (2).

Today I say to you that the challenges we face are real (1). They are   5
serious and they are many (2). They will not be met easily or in a short
span of time (3). But know this, America – they will be met (4).
(CHEERS)

On this day, we gather because we have chosen hope over fear, unity   6
of purpose over conflict and discord (1). On this day, we come to
proclaim an end to the petty grievances and false promises, the recrim-
inations and worn out dogmas, that for far too long have strangled
our politics (2).

We remain a young nation, but in the words of Scripture, the time has   7
come to set aside childish things (1). The time has come to reaffirm
our enduring spirit; to choose our better history; to carry forward that
precious gift, that noble idea, passed on from generation to generation: the God-given promise that all are equal, all are free, and all
deserve a chance to pursue their full measure of happiness (2).

In reaffirming the greatness of our nation, we understand that great-   8
ness is never a given (1). It must be earned (2). Our journey has never
been one of short-cuts or settling for less (3). It has not been the path
for the faint-hearted – for those who prefer leisure over work, or seek
only the pleasures of riches and fame (4). Rather, it has been the risk-
takers, the doers, the makers of things – some celebrated but more
often men and women obscure in their labor, who have carried us up
the long, rugged path towards prosperity and freedom (5).

For us, they packed up their few worldly possessions and traveled   9
across oceans in search of a new life (1). For us, they toiled in sweat-
shops and settled the West; endured the lash of the whip and plowed
the hard earth (2). For us, they fought and died, in places like
Concord and Gettysburg; Normandy and Khe Sahn (3).

Time and again these men and women struggled and sacrificed and   10
worked till their hands were raw so that we might live a better life (1).
They saw America as bigger than the sum of our individual ambitions;
greater than all the differences of birth or wealth or faction (2).

This is the journey we continue today (1). We remain the most pros-   11
perous, powerful nation on Earth (2). Our workers are no less
productive than when this crisis began (3). Our minds are no less
inventive, our goods and services no less needed than they were last
week or last month or last year (4). Our capacity remains undiminished (5). But our time of standing pat, of protecting narrow interests
and putting off unpleasant decisions – that time has surely passed (6).
Starting today, we must pick ourselves up, dust ourselves off, and
begin again the work of remaking America (7). (CHEERS)

For everywhere we look, there is work to be done (1). The state of the   12
economy calls for action, bold and swift, and we will act – not only
to create new jobs, but to lay a new foundation for growth (2). We
will build the roads and bridges, the electric grids and digital lines
that feed our commerce and bind us together (3). We will restore
science to its rightful place, and wield technology's wonders to raise
health care's quality and lower its cost (4). We will harness the sun

and the winds and the soil to fuel our cars and run our factories (5). And we will transform our schools and colleges and universities to meet the demands of a new age. All this we can do. And all this we will do (6).

Now, there are some who question the scale of our ambitions – who   13 suggest that our system cannot tolerate too many big plans (1). Their memories are short (2). For they have forgotten what this country has already done; what free men and women can achieve when imagination is joined to common purpose, and necessity to courage (3).

What the cynics fail to understand is that the ground has shifted   14 beneath them – that the stale political arguments that have consumed us for so long no longer apply (1). The question we ask today is not whether our government is too big or too small, but whether it works – whether it helps families find jobs at a decent wage, care they can afford, a retirement that is dignified (2). Where the answer is yes, we intend to move forward (3). Where the answer is no, programs will end (4). And those of us who manage the public's dollars will be held to account – to spend wisely, reform bad habits, and do our business in the light of day – because only then can we restore the vital trust between a people and their government (5).

Nor is the question before us whether the market is a force for good   15 or ill (1). Its power to generate wealth and expand freedom is unmatched, but this crisis has reminded us that without a watchful eye, the market can spin out of control – and that a nation cannot prosper long when it favors only the prosperous (2). The success of our economy has always depended not just on the size of our Gross Domestic Product, but on the reach of our prosperity; on the ability to extend opportunity to every willing heart – not out of charity, but because it is the surest route to our common good (3). (APPLAUSE)

As for our common defense, we reject as false the choice between our   16 safety and our ideals (1). Our Founding Fathers, faced with perils we can scarcely imagine, drafted a charter to assure the rule of law and the rights of man, a charter expanded by the blood of generations (2). Those ideals still light the world, and we will not give them up for expedience's sake (3). (APPLAUSE) And so to all other peoples and governments who are watching today, from the grandest capitals to the small village where my father was born: know that America is a friend of each nation and every man, woman, and child who seeks a future of peace and dignity, and we are ready to lead once more (4). (CHEERS and LONG APPLAUSE)

Recall that earlier generations faced down fascism and communism   17
not just with missiles and tanks, but with sturdy alliances and enduring convictions (1). They understood that our power alone cannot
protect us, nor does it entitle us to do as we please (2). Instead, they
knew that our power grows through its prudent use; our security
emanates from the justness of our cause, the force of our example, the
tempering qualities of humility and restraint (3).

We are the keepers of this legacy (1). Guided by these principles once   18
more, we can meet those new threats that demand even greater effort
– even greater cooperation and understanding between nations (2). We
will begin to responsibly leave Iraq to its people, and forge a hard-
earned peace in Afghanistan (3). With old friends and former foes,
we'll work tirelessly to lessen the nuclear threat, and roll back the
specter of a warming planet (4). We will not apologize for our way of
life, nor will we waver in its defense, and for those who seek to
advance their aims by inducing terror and slaughtering innocents, we
say to you now that our spirit is stronger and cannot be broken; you
cannot outlast us, and we will defeat you (5). (CHEERS and APPLAUSE)

For we know that our patchwork heritage is a strength, not a weak-   19
ness (1). We are a nation of Christians and Muslims, Jews and Hindus
– and non-believers (2). We are shaped by every language and culture,
drawn from every end of this Earth; and because we have tasted the
bitter swill of civil war and segregation, and emerged from that dark
chapter stronger and more united, we cannot help but believe that the
old hatreds shall someday pass; that the lines of tribe shall soon
dissolve; that as the world grows smaller, our common humanity shall
reveal itself; and that America must play its role in ushering in a new
era of peace (3).

To the Muslim world, we seek a new way forward, based on mutual   20
interest and mutual respect (1). To those leaders around the globe who
seek to sow conflict, or blame their society's ills on the West – know
that your people will judge you on what you can build, not what you
destroy (2). (APPLAUSE) To those who cling to power through corruption and deceit and the silencing of dissent, know that you are on the
wrong side of history; but that we will extend a hand if you are willing to unclench your fist (3). (APPLAUSE)

To the people of poor nations, we pledge to work alongside you to   21
make your farms flourish and let clean waters flow; to nourish starved
bodies and feed hungry minds (1). And to those nations like ours that
enjoy relative plenty, we say we can no longer afford indifference to

the suffering outside our borders; nor can we consume the world's resources without regard to effect (2). For the world has changed, and we must change with it (3).

As we consider the road that unfolds before us, we remember with humble gratitude those brave Americans who, at this very hour, patrol far-off deserts and distant mountains (1). They have something to tell us, just as the fallen heroes who lie in Arlington whisper through the ages (2). We honor them not only because they are guardians of our liberty, but because they embody the spirit of service; a willingness to find meaning in something greater than themselves (3). And yet, at this moment – a moment that will define a generation – it is precisely this spirit that must inhabit us all (4).   22

For as much as government can do and must do, it is ultimately the faith and determination of the American people upon which this nation relies (1). It is the kindness to take in a stranger when the levees break, the selflessness of workers who would rather cut their hours than see a friend lose their job which sees us through our darkest hours (2). It is the firefighter's courage to storm a stairway filled with smoke, but also a parent's willingness to nurture a child, that finally decides our fate (3).   23

Our challenges may be new (1). The instruments with which we meet them may be new (2). But those values upon which our success depends – honesty and hard work, courage and fair play, tolerance and curiosity, loyalty and patriotism – these things are old (3). These things are true (4). They have been the quiet force of progress throughout our history (5). What is demanded then is a return to these truths (6). What is required of us now is a new era of responsibility – a recognition, on the part of every American, that we have duties to ourselves, our nation, and the world, duties that we do not grudgingly accept but rather seize gladly, firm in the knowledge that there is nothing so satisfying to the spirit, so defining of our character, than giving our all to a difficult task (7).   24

This is the price and the promise of citizenship (1). This is the source of our confidence – the knowledge that God calls on us to shape an uncertain destiny (2). This is the meaning of our liberty and our creed – why men and women and children of every race and every faith can join in celebration across this magnificent mall, and why a man whose father less than sixty years ago might not have been served at a local restaurant can now stand before you to take a most sacred oath (3). (CHEERS and APPLAUSE)   25

So let us mark this day with remembrance, of who we are and how   26
far we have travelled (1). In the year of America's birth, in the coldest
of months, a small band of patriots huddled by dying campfires on the
shores of an icy river (2). The capital was abandoned (3). The enemy
was advancing (4). The snow was stained with blood (5). At a
moment when the outcome of our revolution was most in doubt, the
father of our nation ordered these words be read to the people: 'Let it
be told to the future world ... that in the depth of winter, when nothing but hope and virtue could survive ... that the city and the country,
alarmed at one common danger, came forth to meet it (6).'

America, in the face of our common dangers, in this winter of our   27
hardship, let us remember these timeless words (1). With hope and
virtue, let us brave once more the icy currents, and endure what
storms may come (2). Let it be said by our children's children that
when we were tested we refused to let this journey end, that we did
not turn back nor did we falter; and with eyes fixed on the horizon
and God's grace upon us, we carried forth that great gift of freedom
and delivered it safely to future generations (3).

Thank you. God bless you and God bless the United States of   28
America. (CHEERS and APPLAUSE)

Essential reading

Braugh, M. de (2007) 'The Parts of the Speech'. In Worthington, I. (2007) *A Companion to Greek Rhetoric*. Wiley-Blackwell, pp. 187–252.

Fortenbaugh, W. W. (2007) 'Aristotle's Art of Rhetoric'. In I. Worthington, *A Companion to Greek Rhetoric*. Wiley-Blackwell, pp. 107–23.

Gunderson E. (ed.) (2009) *The Cambridge Companion to Ancient Rhetoric*. Cambridge University Press.

Konstan, D. (2007) 'Rhetoric and Emotion'. In I. Worthington, *A Companion to Greek Rhetoric*. Wiley-Blackwell, pp. 411–26.

Reisigl, M. (2008a) 'Analyzing Political Rhetoric'. In R. Wodak and N. Krzyżanowski (eds), *Qualitative Discourse Analysis in the Social Sciences*. Basingstoke: Palgrave Macmillan, pp. 96–120.

Chapter 2

Classical Rhetoric: Style and Figures

2.1   Introduction: what is style?

'Style' is a notoriously elusive word to define. The word has a broad range of meanings that have largely positive associations in a wide range of creative areas of human activity such as art, architecture, fashion, literature and leadership – as well as in language use. The origin of the word is in the Latin 'stilus' – an instrument for writing on a wax tablet (with a sharp end for inscription and a blunt one for erasure) – which suggests that 'style' was used in relation to language before it was used in these other expressive domains. The largely positive connotations of 'style' are evident from considering its common uses in the British National Corpus (see Table 2.1).

Style refers to how distinct meanings are created; collocations such as 'new' and 'old' imply a contrast with what has gone before, and 'different', 'particular', personal', 'distinctive', 'individual' and so on imply distinctiveness. Style is therefore closely related to 'identity', being a manner of self-expression that marks an individual as distinct. Collocations such as 'Italian', 'French', 'English' or 'Western' are ways of creating distinctiveness through affiliation with a group identified by its location – though in such uses geographical location also represents the culture and history of people who originated in this location.

The difference between style and delivery is that style covers a range of modes of communication, whereas delivery is restricted only to the voice. When analysing style we might consider a range of semiotic modes such as physical appearance, dress, body language, artefacts or symbolic action. For example, Charteris-Black (2007) analyses how these modes are employed by a range of non-Western leaders. However, analysis of delivery restricts itself to language alone – though often in practice style and delivery go hand-in-hand. For example, Martin Luther King's style can be described as 'African American liturgical', and this blending of locations referred to the shared historical and cultural experience of slavery through which group identity was formed among Americans of African origin. His appearance clearly indicated that this was his ethnicity, and his delivery reflected an African-American tradition. For example, call-and-response

Table 2.1   Adjectival collocations of 'style' in the British National Corpus

1	NEW STYLE	167
2	OLD STYLE	88
3	GOTHIC STYLE	73
4	TRADITIONAL STYLE	60
5	DIFFERENT STYLE	59
6	PARTICULAR STYLE	57
7	PERSONAL STYLE	41
8	FINE STYLE	39
9	ITALIAN STYLE	39
10	CLASSICAL STYLE	38
11	MODERN STYLE	36
12	ARCHITECTURAL STYLE	33
13	AMERICAN STYLE	33
14	DISTINCTIVE STYLE	30
15	ENGLISH STYLE	29
16	FRENCH STYLE	25
17	CONTINENTAL STYLE	24
18	INDIVIDUAL STYLE	24
19	POLITICAL STYLE	23
20	ROMANESQUE STYLE	23
21	GRAND STYLE	22
22	SIMILAR STYLE	22
23	WESTERN STYLE	22
24	HIGH STYLE	21

exchanges were a feature of delivery that had frequently been used by black pulpit preachers to interact with listeners – by inviting them to participate. These exchanges would commence with familiar phrases from hymns or the Bible, to which the audience would respond and collaborate in a co-constructed rhythmical discourse. However, King also added his own personal style of delivery by the slow timing of his speech, the resonance of his voice and a distinct intonation pattern, each of which are instantly recognizable. Politically, the motive for the creation of an African-American identity was to create a sense of shared social purpose.

The rhetorical effects of delivery are achieved by combining features that make an orator sound unique with others that imply a shared set of values. So style is a complex interaction between personal choice and social meaning, and between the spoken mode and other means of communication. It is the semiotic effect attained by individual features of delivery and style that convey socially shared meanings. A further example of this would be the Shi-ite leader, Ayatollah Ali al-Sistani, who rarely talked above the level of a whisper. This style of delivery differentiated him from other ayatollahs in Iraq, who had a more aggressive, ranting style; it also ensured that the audience had to strain to hear him as well as giving the impression of saint-liness – spiritual values therefore formed the basis of a social meaning that was shared between leader and followers.

Another example of style of delivery is that of the white rapper Eminem, whose style features, such as the use of humour and multisyllabic rhymes, combined with features of delivery such as clear diction, complex rhythm, melody and syncopation (Edwards, 2009). While many of these features arose from imitation of previous rappers, Eminem combined these features in a unique way to demonstrate that he shared the same experiences as many of his audience – family breakdown, drug addiction and a shared identity of resistance to the mainstream. His style therefore marked him out both as part of a group but also as distinct: style is persuasive when it integrates personal and social meaning.

Exercise 2.1

> Check in the *Oxford English Dictionary* for definitions of the word 'style' and compare how these match with the evidence of its meaning in the British National Corpus. (You may also wish to compare the adjective collocates of style in the Corpus of Contemporary American English.)
> Analyse the style of the elected mayor of London, Boris Johnson – consider both verbal and non-verbal semiotic modes.
> Analyse the style of a speech, song or other text produced by a celebrity of your choice; see if you can distinguish between style and delivery choices. Discuss how judgements of occasion might have influenced these choices.

2.2   Style in classical rhetoric

Classical rhetoricians differentiated between style and delivery by treating 'style' as actual word choices and 'delivery' as the control of the voice and other performance-related aspects such as gesture and facial expression. As I suggested above, a contemporary interpretation of this is to restrict 'delivery' to spoken language alone and 'style' to a range of communication modes. In ancient Greece, the term for style was simply 'lexis' – style was equated with the selection of words (rather than other modes), and a major consideration was finding the right balance between clarity and elevation. Clarity derived from the complexity of word choices: ordinary words and simpler phrases led to a plain style, while less familiar words and more elaborate expressions led to an elevated style. Simpler words encouraged ease of comprehension, while more complex words, though less easily understood, encouraged admiration and wonder. The simple style was commonly known as the 'Attic' style, while the elevated style was known as 'Asianic' because of the influence of Asian rhetoric once the Greek states had expanded into Asia. There was also a middle style that integrated both plain and elevated language.

For Aristotle, style drew on the aesthetic resources of language – the choice of words and delivery – to ensure their maximum psychological effect. A persuasive delivery conceals the presence of a text that had been prepared in advance by the skilful use of memory, and is accompanied by appropriate non-verbal gestures and mannerisms. Choice of style would be influenced by the branch of oratory; forensic rhetoric required clarity and attention to detail, whereas a more elevated style would be suitable for epideictic rhetoric. Figures of speech with potential for elaboration such as metaphor would be more appropriate in epideictic rhetoric, while simpler figures such as antithesis and isocolons (about which more later) would be more appropriate in forensic rhetoric.

However, such generalizations are problematic, as rhetoricians such as Aristotle emphasized that the most essential consideration was the need to fit the style to the occasion so there is only a partial correspondence between stylistic choice and the branch of oratory. To use a contemporary example, an appeal to pathos might be made in a plain style when discussing the financing of state pensions, while an elevated style might be used at a commemoration ceremony for those who lost their lives in Arabic struggles for democracy in recent years. Evidence of this is that these democratic movements are collectively referred to using a more elevated choice of language – a metaphor – 'The Arab Spring'. This metaphor originated in the Western media and then became the standard way of referring to these events; in Arabic this is 'Arrabia al Arabi' (Arrabia = spring; al Arabi = Arab).

There was also the consideration of timing – *kairos* – which literally translates from ancient Greek as 'opportunity'; so finding the most opportune moment for a particular phrase would contribute to its success. Using more contemporary terms, we might think of it as the 'critical moment' – for example, a crisis of some kind – when a particular argument would be most persuasive. Considerations of *kairos* form part of the judgement as to what are the most effective circumstances in which to make a speech on a particular topic, as well as rhetorical judgements of when to introduce a particular appeal into a speech. For example, just prior to the 2012 US election, the devastating hurricane Sandy affected large areas on the east coast of the United States, including parts of New York. This gave Barack Obama an opportunity to make appeals to social empathy and to make a jibe at his main Republican rival, Mitt Romney, for having gone on record as favouring cuts to the disaster relief agencies that had been set up after Hurricane Katrina had devastated New Orleans in 2005. This made Obama seem a more empathetic candidate, as he had a view of government that required it to intervene in times of crisis; this timely criticism contributed to his success in the election, turning the tide of popular opinion that had been swaying towards Romney after his strong performance in the TV debates.

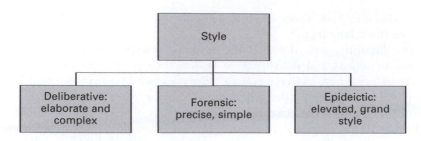

Figure 2.1   Style and branch of oratory

Figure 2.1 summarizes some general principles of style choice in branches of oratory, though the rules of style in classical rhetoric offer guidelines rather than a straitjacket.

Issues of style and timing are crucial in all types of public speaking, including speeches by individuals who are not politicians. This is particularly the case with motivational speaking to audiences who are facing imminent danger as a result of decisions taken by politicians, as is the case with 'eve of battle' speeches by those in positions of military command. As the executive arm of government, military leaders need to combine a range of aesthetic and psychological strategies to produce a style that is fitting to the occasion. An understanding of how speakers adapt their rhetoric to audiences that are under pressure because they are faced by a threatening event, for example an immanent battle, provides insight into how more non-military civilian audiences might respond to speeches given by politicians in times of crisis.

The speech we examined at the end of Chapter 1 – Barack Obama's inaugural speech – was given at a time when Western leaders were just becoming aware of the gravity of the effects of the 2008 financial crisis and as a result has the style of an eve of battle speech. This shows both in the choice of sombre weather metaphors: 'Yet, every so often the oath is taken amidst gathering clouds and raging storms' and in the 'call to arms' style that is intended to unify, motivate and raise morale: 'Today I say to you that the challenges we face are real. They are serious and they are many. They will not be met easily or in a short span of time. But know this, America – they will be met.' A combination of a mood of uncertainty (here from the metaphors) and the certainty that a challenge will be faced up to with courage, characterizes both speeches that address political crises and eves of battles because of the overlap between the psychological states of their audiences. It is therefore relevant to consider the motivational effect of style choices in two well-known examples of this sub genre: the speech by a British military leader in Iraq – Lt. Col. Tim Collins (Core text 2.1), and the other by Henry V in Shakespeare's play of that name (Core text 2.2).

Let's begin as usual with a brief analysis of circumstances: Collins gave his speech to his troops just prior to military engagement in March 2003, when British forces had embarked on a military campaign to remove the Iraqi leader Saddam Hussein from power. Collins was nicknamed 'Nails' by his men – a metaphor based on qualities of character such as being hard, unyielding and direct – so they would be expecting a tough and direct style. As indicated by the naming of the sub-genre, issues of timing are crucial in an eve of battle speech: it is designed to motivate, but also – in circumstances where there is a significant difference in the quality of weaponry and training available to the conflicting sides – to urge caution in the event of victory so as to win the hearts and minds of a defeated enemy. The objectives of military leaders in modern conflicts in the Muslim words are political as much as they are military – the aim of a global policeman in the 'war on terror' is to ensure success in the long-term ideological struggle as much as victory on the battlefield. Collins' speech is a fine example of how the style of a modern military leader is adapted to reflect these complexities arising from a combined military and political role in the field of conflict. The speech was delivered to the 800 soldiers of the 1st Battalion, Royal Irish Regiment, most of whom were young men with little previous experience, and apprehensive about the immanent conflict. It was given at a military base in the Kuwaiti desert 20 miles south of the Iraqi border. The speech was improvised – with minimal preparation and was recorded in shorthand by a journalist (see Core text 2.1).

Core text 2.1   Lt. Col. Tim Collins' 'Eve of Battle' speech

We go to liberate, not to conquer (1). We will not fly our flags in their country (2). We are entering Iraq to free a people and the only flag which will be flown in that ancient land is their own (3). Show respect for them (4).   1

There are some who are alive at this moment who will not be alive shortly (1). Those who do not wish to go on that journey, we will not send (2). As for the others I expect you to rock their world. Wipe them out if that is what they choose (3). But if you are ferocious in battle remember to be magnanimous in victory (4).   2

Iraq is steeped in history (1). It is the site of the Garden of Eden, of the Great Flood and the birthplace of Abraham (2). Tread lightly there (3). You will see things that no man could pay to see and you will have to go a long way to find a more decent, generous and upright people than the Iraqis (4). You will be embarrassed by their hospitality even though they have nothing (5). Don't treat them as refugees for they are in their own country (6). Their children will be poor, in years to come they will know that the light of liberation in their lives was brought by you (7).   3

If there are casualties of war then remember that when they woke up   4
and got dressed in the morning they did not plan to die this day (1).
Allow them dignity in death. Bury them properly and mark their
graves (2).

It is my foremost intention to bring every single one of you out alive   5
but there may be people among us who will not see the end of this
campaign (1). We will put them in their sleeping bags and send them
back (2). There will be no time for sorrow (3).

The enemy should be in no doubt that we are his nemesis and that we   6
are bringing about his rightful destruction (1). There are many regional
commanders who have stains on their souls and they are stoking the
fires of hell for Saddam (2). He and his forces will be destroyed by this
coalition for what they have done (3). As they die they will know their
deeds have brought them to this place (4). Show them no pity (5).

It is a big step to take another human life (1). It is not to be done   7
lightly (2). I know of men who have taken life needlessly in other
conflicts, I can assure you they live with the mark of Cain upon them (3).
If someone surrenders to you then remember they have that right in
international law and ensure that one day they go home to their
family (4).

The ones who wish to fight, well, we aim to please (1).   8

If you harm the regiment or its history by over-enthusiasm in killing   9
or in cowardice, know it is your family who will suffer (1). You will
be shunned unless your conduct is of the highest for your deeds will
follow you down through history (2). We will bring shame on neither
our uniform nor our nation (3).

It is not a question of if, it's a question of when (1). We know he has   10
already devolved the decision to lower commanders, and that means
he has already taken the decision himself (2). If we survive the first
strike we will survive the attack (3).

As for ourselves, let's bring everyone home and leave Iraq a better   11
place for us having been there (1).

Our business now is north (1).   12

Source: © Tim Collins, 2003. Reproduced with kind permission of
Lucas Alexander Whitley Ltd.

Generally, the speech is given in simple, direct language that character-izes the hard-talking style of a military officer addressing his men – in keep-ing with his nickname 'Nails'. It is impersonal, with only one use of a first-person pronoun ('my' in paragraph 5); the institutional authority and discipline that contribute to a military ethos are better evoked by an imper-sonal style than by the expression of raw personal emotion – though the situation was one where a mixture of excitement and fear of death would be likely. There are also some elements of an elevated style that fit with the speech's epideictic role in a ritual of military engagement; since time imme-morial it has been the norm for a commander to inspire and motivate his men prior to engagement to make victory more likely. Collins evokes a sense of Iraq's history – though without going into detail – and colours his language with references to the Garden of Eden, Abraham, Cain and so on; religious discourse is relevant in situations where there is the possibility of death. But we should note that references to the Old Testament imply a shared cultural tradition between Muslims and Christians – something that would have not have been the case had any reference been made to Jesus. The combination of ancient history and religion adds grandeur to ideas of national and regimental pride that are crucial to motivation in a military setting. The activation of religious schema seems a prelude to framing the rules of combat within broader humanist ethical principles. These are made explicit when he warns about the consequences for those who do not comply with such principles: 'It is a big step to take another human life. It is not to be done lightly' and 'If you harm the regiment or its history by over-enthusiasm in killing or in cowardice, know it is your family who will suffer.' His ability to address the long-term political consequences of mili-tary combat reinforce his absence of doubt as to the likelihood of victory: without being sure of victory there would be no reason to consider its consequences.

Stylistically, there is a mixture of plain and an elevated styles; this speech could be taken to represent Isocrates' so-called 'middle style'. This was characterized by smoothness and balance that arose from:

◇ consistency;
◇ the use of parallelism to create rhythmic balance; and
◇ the use of periods to create a complex sentence structure.

The speech has all these features – there is a very clear instance of paral-lelism within a sentence's structure in 10.1:

It is not a question of if
it's a question of when

It occurs again in (7 .1) and (7.2):

It is a big step to take another human life.
It is not to be done lightly.

A more complex use of periods occurs in paragraph 3, where there are a series of interlinked, co-ordinated, descriptive sentences (3.4–3.6) to provide an account of the complex emotions that will be evoked by experience of the Iraqi people. The alternation of shorter with longer, more complex sentences corresponds to the mixed emotions that the soldiers will feel. Another, more complex, example occurs in the matching grammatical structures illustrated by using the style features in 6.1 and 6.2:

The enemy should be in no doubt that we are *his nemesis* and that we are bringing about his rightful destruction.

There are many regional commanders who have stains on *their souls* and they are stoking the fires of hell for Saddam.

Here there is a rhythmic balance of structural elements, with two phrases linked by a co-ordinating conjunction. The speech has consistency of style in the sincerity of the tone with which he advocates ethical behaviour to ensure that the code of war is respected; there is consistency in its content through its emphasis on the significance of the event in an unfurling course of history and its tender recognition of the emotions and fears of young recruits. It is these features – as originally identified by Isocrates – that has led to the speech's seminal status in contemporary oratory. Its success dispels the idea that a large amount of time is necessary to prepare a good speech, though it also implies that extensive experience of both language and military combat are necessary to deliver one. Style choices are summarized in Figure 2.2.

We now need to consider in more detail the sorts of choices of lexis and grammar that allow us to analyse the style. We have seen in this introduction that 'style' is concerned with creating an impression of distinctiveness;

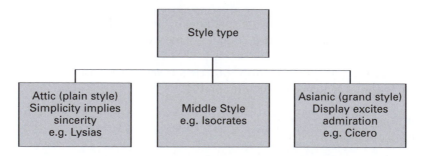

Figure 2.2   Style types in classical rhetoric

but when we move to examine a speech as a set of strategies employed by a speaker, we then need to consider what it is in language that gives rise to this impression. The selection of figures of speech is an essential component of style, and in the remainder of this chapter I shall describe a range of schemes and tropes, and the interaction between them, that give rise to the impression of style. This is not to assume that these strategies can necessarily be taught or learnt, but there was an assumption behind the classical schools of rhetoric that they could be studied and that this study would have practical benefits. I share that belief and I believe that readers of this book do too.

2.3   Figures of speech

Classical rhetoric distinguished between two major categories of figurative language: schemes and tropes:

◇ A *scheme* (from Greek *skhēma*, 'form' or 'figure') is a figure of speech in which there is some modification to the normal or expected sequence of words and so affects grammatical structure; the rhetorical effect is achieved by a rearrangement of word order that may also have an aesthetic appeal. Examples of schemes include chiasmus – the reversal of the order of words in adjacent clauses, as in Kennedy's famous 'Ask not what your country can do for you, but ask what you can do for your country'; and parallelism – the use of similar structures in two or more clauses.
◇ A *trope* (from the Greek *trepein*, 'to turn') is a figure of speech in which words are used with senses that differ (or 'turn away') from their literal senses, so the sense of words in metaphors, metonymys, allusion, irony, hyperbole and so on diverge from their normal, literal senses.

So schemes involve grammatical choice, and their syntax can be analysed for patterns such as repetition or word order reversal, while tropes involve the choice of lexis and can be analysed through lexical semantics for features such as polysemy (multiple meaning). Both schemes and tropes influence 'meaning' and contribute to persuasive effect, but schemes originate in syntactic patterning while tropes originate in lexical semantics.

2.3.1   Schemes

The following table summarizes a few of the most important schemes of the many identified by classical rhetoricians; I have tried to be selective, since rival schools of classical Greek oratory competed on the number of figures of speech they could identify, and these later formed the basis of handbooks

Table 2.2   Classical rhetorical schemes

Scheme	Definition A figure in which there is …	Example
anaphora	… repetition of a phrase at the start of a unit (anaphora leads to anticipation which involves an audience cognitively and emotionally)	*It's a promise that says* each of us has the freedom to make of our own lives what we will, but that we also have the obligation to treat each other with dignity and respect *It's a promise that says* the market should reward drive and innovation and generate growth, but that businesses should live up to their responsibilities
antithesis	… a semantic relation of opposition or contrast (time is quite often the basis of comparison in political rhetoric where this is a criticism of past performance and promise of a better future)	1. Now, I don't believe that Senator McCain *doesn't care* what's going on in the lives of Americans. I just think he *doesn't know* (contrasts caring and knowing, that is – feeling and thinking) 2. We need a President who can face *the threats of the future*, not keep grasping at *the ideas of the past* (contrasts past and future)
chiasmus	… the word order of the second part is the reverse of the word order in the first part (the primary appeal is the aesthetic one of balance)	*Some people use 'change' to promote their careers; other people use their careers to promote change.* (Sarah Palin) (the reversal is an implied criticism of Barack Obama, who was campaigning on 'change')
ellipsis	… omission of a word or phrase (assumes that the meaning is retrievable from context)	On November 4th, we must stand up and say: *'Eight* is enough' ('years' is omitted, but is retrievable as the audience know that George Bush was elected for 2 presidencies of 4 years each)
epiphora	… repetition of a phrase at the end of a unit (the repetition need not be identical)	This country of ours has more wealth than any nation, but that's not *what makes us rich*. We have the most powerful military on Earth, but that's not *what makes us strong*. Our universities and

Term	Definition	Example
isocolon	... use of two parts of similar lengths (contributes to balance)	our culture are the envy of the world, but that's not what *keeps the world coming to our shores* (as there are three repeated phrases this could also be analysed as a tricolon)
parison	... a comparison between two entities (both entities need not be mentioned as one can be inferred from the other)	*America, we are better than these last eight years. We are a better country than this.* (this could also be analysed as parallelism)
parallelism	... repetition of a syntactic pattern (syntactical repetition often also involves lexical repetition)	Tonight, *more* Americans are out of work and *more* are working harder for less. *More* of you have lost your homes and even *more* are watching your home values plummet (Comparison between present and past) You have shown what history teaches us – that at defining moments like this one, *the change we need doesn't come from Washington. Change comes to Washington* (the repeated pattern contrasts the words that have changed – 'from' and 'to')
repetition	... repetition of a word or phrase (repetition always adds emphasis and so intensifies meaning)	... was talking about the anxiety Americans are feeling, he said that we were just suffering from a 'mental recession', and that we've become, and I quote, *'a nation of whiners'. A nation of whiners?* (This is also a rhetorical question)
tricolon	... use of three parts of equal length (often signals the closure of a topic)	We meet at one of those defining moments – *a moment when our nation is at war, our economy is in turmoil, and the American promise has been threatened* once more (This preceded the example of parison above that was also a tricolon, so tricolons can be repeated)

on classical rhetoric. Those selected here are the ones that my previous analysis has shown to be the most pervasive (Charteris-Black, 2011). For each scheme, I have selected an example from Barack Obama's acceptance speech at the 2008 Democratic Party Convention in Denver (unless otherwise indicated), and put the scheme in italics (see Table 2.2).

The distinction between schemes and tropes is a valuable one, because the type of aesthetic appeal they make differs. Schemes contribute to the rhythm, balance and timing of sections of a speech; for example, the use of anaphora is often a strategy associated with a style of delivery in which the speaker begins slowly and then accelerates into a crescendo to create a powerful emotional effect. This has been described as a calm-to-storm delivery style and was used frequently by Baptist preachers and adopted by Martin Luther King. Watch Obama's acceptance speech for the nomination of the Democratic Party on YouTube and note how repetition of the phrase 'now is the time' and the resulting effect on speech pace and rhythm leads to audible audience responses:

Now is the time to finally keep the promise of affordable, accessible health care for every single American. (CHEERS) If you have health care, my plan will lower your premiums. If you don't, you'll be able to get the same kind of coverage that members of Congress give themselves. (CHEERS) And as someone who watched my mother argue with insurance companies while she lay in bed dying of cancer, I will make certain those companies stop discriminating against those who are sick and need care the most. (LOUD CHEERS and WHISTLING)

Now is the time to help families with paid sick days and better family leave, because nobody in America should have to choose between keeping their jobs and caring for a sick child or ailing parent. *Now is the time to* change our bankruptcy laws, so that your pensions are protected ahead of CEO bonuses; and the time to protect Social Security for future generations. And *now is the time to* keep the promise of equal pay for an equal day's work, because I want my daughters to have exactly the exact same opportunities as your sons. (LOUD CHEERS and WHISTLING) (28 August 2008)

You will have noted that the phrase is repeated at increasingly shorter intervals and this ratchets up audience responses in the form of cheers and whistles of increasing audibility. The use of timing, rhythm and intensity can be traced to how rhetorical features originating in African-American culture are merged with those of classical rhetoric such as anaphora and epiphora. This combination of schemes originating in ancient Greece with the interactional style of African-American oratory is highly motivating to followers: the repetition of formulaic phrases at various intervals signals to the audience the opportunities at which participation is actively encouraged. This is an empowering use of style because it creates a co-constructed speech event. Listen to the start of the Iowa Caucus night speech (3 January 2008) on YouTube (preferably with a script of the speech to hand) and notice what figure precedes an audible audience reaction; it starts with two consecutive anaphoric tricolons (in italics):

> You know, *t h e y   s a i d* this day would never come. (CHEERS)

> *T h e y   s a i d* our sights were set too high. (CHEERS)

> *T h e y   s a i d* this country was too divided; too disillusioned to ever come together around a common purpose.

> But on this January night – at this defining moment in history – *you have done what* the cynics said we couldn't do. (CHEERS) *You have done what* the state of New Hampshire can do in five days. (CHEERS and APPLAUSE) *You have done what* America can do in this New Year, 2008. (CHEERS and APPLAUSE)

Notice how his delivery *emphasizes* the anaphoric tricolons by drawing out the time it takes to say the repeated elements and how this evokes cheers. This sets up nicely a call-and-exchange routine through which audience involvement is sustained. By setting up a style of interaction through anaphora, Obama is drawing on the most appropriate aesthetic appeal – pathos – for a speech whose primary purpose is to motivate followers for the remainder of his election campaign. The rhythmic effect arising from these figures is further intensified when they occur in the epilogue of this speech leading to a calm-to-storm climax and evoking a powerful audience response.

> ... you'll be able to look back with pride and say that *this was the moment when* it all began. (CHEERS)

> *This was the moment when* the improbable beat what Washington always said was inevitable.

> *This was the moment when* we tore down barriers that have divided us for too long – when we rallied people of all parties and ages to a common cause; when we finally gave Americans who'd never participated in politics a reason to stand up and to do so. (CHEERS)

> *This was the moment when* we finally beat back the politics of fear, and doubt, and cynicism; the politics where we tear each other down instead of lifting this country up. *This was the moment.* (CHEERS)

Obama's rhetoric communicated commitment to a cause and prophet-like certainty that contributed to a consistent and coherent style. As particular speeches are adapted to specific occasions and audiences, it is the enduring features of style that form political identity; part of this was a preparedness to engage in forceful rhetorical combat – a characteristic that returns oratory to its classical origins, where it was employed in judicial and forensic debates as well as in deliberative ones. The combative style is evident in the use of another scheme – antithesis – a figure where two contrasting positions are juxtaposed: typically, one position is represented as legitimate while the other is illegitimate. I will illustrate this with reference to a speech he gave in June 2008 entitled 'Renewing American Competitiveness'. He began by contrasting an ongoing theme in American foreign policy – isolationism – with internationalism:

> There are some who believe that we must try to turn back the clock on this new world; that the only chance to maintain our living standards is to build a fortress around America; to stop trading with other countries, shut down immigration, and rely on old industries (1). I disagree (2). Not only is it impossible to turn back the tide of globalization, but efforts to do so can make us worse off (3). Rather than fear the future, we must embrace it (4).

In the first sentence, he puts forward a counter-position: that America should become isolationist (1). He explicitly refutes this position in (2) and then employs antithesis to introduce a counter-presentation in (3). In (4) he introduces an opposite position to the one stated in (1) – arguing that protectionism, associated with the past, should be rejected and replaced in the future with its antithesis – free trade. There are effectively two contrasts: between protection and free trade, and between the past and the future; the two are interconnected to strengthen the argument.

A warning about the use of schemes such as the tricolon is that they must be completed in order to be effective. An important part of delivery is memory, and if orators embark on three-part lists it is essential that they are able to complete them. A good example of the negative effect that poor delivery can have occurred in a televised debate for the Republican candidacy in November 2011 in which Rick Perry stated that he would close three government agencies – unfortunately he could not remember the third agency he would close down; this lapse of memory undermined his candidacy and ensured the safety of the agency concerned.

Exercise 2.2

Identify the schemes in the speech by Tim Collins given in Core text 2.1.

2.3.2   Tropes

Tropes influence an audience by turning the senses of words away from what is expected to draw attention to other possible meanings. Such use of language is valuable when the orator wants to evaluate positively or negatively or to intensify an appeal – usually to pathos – by drawing on the rich associative power of language. When directed towards the speaker they evoke positive emotions and values such as pride, honour, courage and solidarity, but when directed towards political opponents they evoke negative emotions and values such as fear, shame, estrangement and ostracism. Table 2.3 summarizes some of the most important tropes, with illustrations of each trope in italics.

When an elevated style is required, Obama typically uses metaphor, and he does so to contribute to the arrangement of his speeches: metaphors occur much more often in the epilogues of his speeches. Aristotle claimed that the epilogue has a high impact in deliberative oratory, since the last words the audience hears before taking a decision are the most persuasive. He proposed that the artistic appeal that is the most persuasive for the epilogue is pathos, since it is crucial to arouse the emotions when concluding a speech. Obama used a complex cluster of metaphors to do this at the end of his first inaugural speech, given on 20 January 2009:

> In the face of our common dangers, in this *winter of our hardship*, let us remember these timeless words. With hope and virtue, *let us brave once more the icy currents, and endure what storms may come.* Let it be said by our children's children that when we were tested we *refused to let this journey end, that we did not turn back nor did we falter; and with eyes fixed on the horizon and God's grace upon us, we carried forth that great gift of freedom and delivered it safely to future generations.* Thank you. God bless you and God bless the United States of America.

The metaphors (in *italics*) are from the semantic fields of weather ('winter', 'storms' and so on), water ('currents') and journeys ('turn back'). They arouse emotions of fear and courage that are connected to unify the audience towards a common purpose. These metaphors contribute to the aesthetic arrangement of the speech because they are from the same semantic fields as those that were used in the prologue:

> The words have been spoken during *rising tides of prosperity* and the *still waters* of peace. Yet, every so often the oath is taken amidst *gathering clouds and raging storms*. At these moments, America has carried on not simply because of the skill or vision of those in high office, but because we, the People, have remained faithful to the ideals of our forbearers, and true to our founding documents.

Table 2.3   Classical rhetorical tropes in Obama's first election campaign

Figure	Definition A figure in which ...	Example
allusion	... there is indirect evocation of another well-known textual or cultural reference	... we landed a man on the moon, and we heard *a King's call to let justice roll down like water, and righteousness like a mighty stream* (10 February 2007) (This alludes to Martin Luther King and the Bible)
autonomasia	... a person's name is replaced by an epithet (Similar to periphrasis but referring to a person)	And it is that promise that forty-five years ago today, brought Americans from every corner of this land to ... hear *a young preacher from Georgia* speak of his dream (28 August 2008) (Martin Luther King came from Georgia)
hyperbole	... a word or phrase is deliberately exaggerated to intensify the meaning (Origin Greek *hyper*: 'over'/'beyond')	We meet at one of those *defining moments* – a moment when our *nation is at war*, our *economy is in turmoil*, and the *American promise has been threatened* once more (28 August 2008) (Notice here that lexical choices such as 'defining', 'turmoil' and 'threat' combine in a tricolon)
irony	... there is a meaning that is the opposite of what is conveyed literally by these words (Differs from sarcasm in that the tone can be humorous rather than bitter)	John McCain said that George Bush's economic policies have led to '*great progress*' over the last seven years (22 April 2008) (Evidently not an opinion shared by the speaker)
litotes (= euphemism)	... there is a word or phrase that makes a deliberate understatement. (Origin Greek *litos*: 'plain'/'meagre')	Instead of reaching for new horizons, George Bush *has put us in a hole*, and John McCain's policies *will keep us there* (15 June 2008) ('In a hole' is also a metaphor, but the economic situation was more serious than implied by 'hole')
metaphor	... there is a shift in the sense of a word or phrase from its earlier, more concrete or more embodied sense	It's the answer that led those who have been told for so long by so many to be cynical, and fearful, and doubtful of what we can achieve to *put their hands on the arc of history and bend it once more toward the hope of a better day* (4 November 2008)

Term	Definition	Example
	(The new sense that occurs later in time will be more abstract, and less related to the human body)	(The metaphor is one of aspiration using a powerful visual image of an archer; the shooting of the bow represents political actions, hence something concrete and embodied refers to an abstract entity)
metonymy	... there is an attribute of an entity is used to refer to another entity to which it is closely related in our experience (Unlike metaphor, where the two entities related are experientially distant)	because we are not a collection of *Red States* and *Blue States*, we are the United States of America (3 January 2008) (Red is worn by Republicans and Blue by Democrats, so colour stands for political party – this could also be analysed as symbolic)
oxymoron	... there is a combination of words of incongruous or contradictory meaning (Often an adjective and a noun)	... And if you will join me in this *improbable quest*
periphrasis	... there is the use of more words than is necessary to express a meaning (It often produces a more formal register suitable for epideictic speeches)	Let me express my thanks to the historic slate of candidates who accompanied me on this journey, and especially the one who travelled the farthest – a champion for working Americans and an inspiration to my daughters and to yours – Hillary Rodham Clinton (28 August 2008) (This could have been phrased: 'Let me express my thanks to Hillary Clinton')
personification	... human qualities are ascribed to non-human entities (This is a type of metaphor – anthropomorphisms usually arouse more empathy)	Together, starting today, let us finish the work that needs to be done, and *usher in a new birth of freedom on this Earth* (10 February 2007) (Freedom is personified as a baby)
rhetorical question	... there is a question that is grammatically interrogative but for which the answer is already known and so not given	Senator McCain likes to talk about judgement, but really, *what does it say about your judgement when you think George Bush has been right more than 90 percent of the time?* (28 August 2008) (This is also ironic – Obama frequently combines the two figures)
synecdoche	... a part is used to refer to the whole entity (This is a type of metonymy)	... the same message we had when we were up and when we were down; the one that can change this country *brick by brick, block by block, calloused hand by calloused hand* (3 January 2008) ('Brick' and 'block' stand for building and 'hand' for the builder)

The matching of metaphor in the prologue and the epilogue shows the aesthetic appeal of arrangement, since in musical theory the coda is a section in which there is a return to the major theme. In language, this aesthetic appeal is created here by metaphor to produce an elevated style that is appropriate to the main theme of his speech, which is the need for a heroic narrative of nation.

It is interesting to compare this coda with the use of metaphor (in *italics*) in his acceptance speech for the Democratic party nomination:

> 'We *cannot walk alone*,' the preacher cried. 'And *as we walk, we must make the pledge that we shall always march ahead. We cannot turn back.*' America, we *cannot turn back*. Not with so much work to be done. Not with so many children to educate, and so many veterans to care for. Not with an economy *to fix* and *cities to rebuild and farms to save*. Not with so many families to protect and *so many lives to mend*. America, *we cannot turn back. We cannot walk alone*. At this moment, in this election, we must pledge *once more to march into the future*. Let us keep that promise – that American promise – and in the words of Scripture hold firmly, without wavering, to the hope that we confess. Thank you, and God Bless the United States of America. (28 August 2008)

Here there is an extended metaphor using words from the semantic fields of creation ('rebuild', 'mend') and journeys ('turn back', 'walk alone', 'march' and so on). These are oriented to the rhetorical purpose of the speech, which is to motivate and inspire. The epilogue has the purpose in an epideictic speech of arousing emotions that are appropriate to an occasion – in this case emotions of enthusiasm and social effort that are implied by a journey in the company of others. The use of journey metaphors alludes to the heroic rhetorical style of Martin Luther King that created a highly persuasive messianic myth (see Charteris-Black 2011, ch. 4):

> And if you will join *me in this improbable quest*, if *you feel destiny calling*, and see as I see, a *future of endless possibility stretching before us*; if you sense, as I sense, that the time is now to *shake off our slumber, and slough off our fear*, and *make good on the debt we owe past and future generations*, then I'm ready *to take up the cause, and march with you*, and work with you. Together, starting today, let us finish the work that needs to be done, and *usher in a new birth of freedom on this Earth*. (10 February 2007)

Here metaphors are drawn from the domains of journeys, sleep, finance and war, and there are personifications of 'destiny' and 'freedom'. The dense use of metaphor contributes to an elevated style intended to motivate hearers to the actions necessary to bring about the anticipated outcomes, so 'war' metaphors imply struggle and effort and sleeping is equated with inaction. Metaphor is therefore the prime rhetorical figure for evoking emotions appropriate for the political purpose of motivating social action.

Obama has been likened to the classical orator Cicero, and we might wonder why it is that his rhetoric evokes the rhetoric of ancient Greece more than, say, his predecessor George Bush, or many other American presidents? We have seen from the above analysis that one reason for this is that figures of speech are not employed just to add colour and interest to his style, or to fit with an ethnically defined rhetorical tradition, but also contribute systematically to an aesthetically pleasing arrangement by clustering in particular sections of the speech.

Exercise 2.3

> Identify the tropes in the eve of war speech by Tim Collins (see Core text 2.1).
> Identify the tropes in the speech from Shakespeare's *Henry V* (see Core text 2.2).
> Compare the use of schemes (which you identified earlier in the Tim Collins eve of war speech) and tropes in the two speeches.
> Consider how the use of schemes and tropes contributes to the time viewpoint of the speaker in each speech.
> Consider the linguistic means for communicating social relations in the two speeches.

Core text 2.2   Speech from Shakespeare's *Henry V*

1   This day is call'd the feast of Crispian.
2   He that outlives this day, and comes safe home,
3   Will stand a tip-toe when this day is named,
4   And rouse him at the name of Crispian.
5   He that shall live this day, and see old age,
6   Will yearly on the vigil feast his neighbours,
7   And say, 'To-morrow is Saint Crispian.'
8   Then will he strip his sleeve and show his scars,
9   And say, 'These wounds I had on Crispin's day.'
10   Old men forget; yet all shall be forgot,
11   But he'll remember with advantages
12   What feats he did that day. Then shall our names,
13   Familiar in his mouth as household words,
14   Harry the King, Bedford, and Exeter,
15   Warwick and Talbot, Salisbury and Gloucester,
16   Be in their flowing cups freshly rememb'red.
17   This story shall the good man teach his son;

18   And Crispin Crispian shall ne'er go by,
19   From this day to the ending of the world,
20   But we in it shall be remembered –
21   We few, we happy few, we band of brothers;
22   For he to-day that sheds his blood with me
23   Shall be my brother; be he ne'er so vile,
24   This day shall gentle his condition:
25   And gentlemen in England now a-bed
26   Shall think themselves accursed they were not here,
27   And hold their manhoods cheap while any speaks
28   That fought with us upon Saint Crispin's day.

2.3.3   Interaction between schemes and tropes

In this section I suggest that at the levels of middle and higher styles is often characterized by an interaction between tropes and schemes; this is effective, as it combines the resources of lexical semantics and syntax. I will also suggest interacting figures avoids the audience's attention being drawn too heavily to any particular figure and so has a more general rhetorical impact than one that relies exclusively on a single dominant and readily identifiable figure. Obama's rhetoric often uses antithesis (a scheme) in combination with a metonym (a trope), as in the following, where he contrasts 'Wall Street' with 'Main Street':

> It's not change when he offers four more years of Bush economic policies that have failed to create well-paying jobs, or insure our workers, or help Americans afford the skyrocketing cost of college – policies that have lowered the real incomes of the average American family, widened the gap between Wall Street and Main Street, and left our children with a mountain of debt. (3 June 2008)

The metonym here arises from a street standing for the activities that occur there, which in turn stand for the value system underlying those activities – so 'Wall Street' is a metonym for corporate values (via big business in the American metropolis), while 'Main Street' is a metonym for community values (via small business in the American small town). His own policies will reconcile differences between the two value systems:

> Put simply, we need tougher negotiators on our side of the table – to strike bargains that are good *not* just for Wall Street, *but also* for Main Street. And when I am President, that's what we will do. (16 June 2008)

The use of antithesis is also associated with a style of communication characterized by a very high level of certainty (see Chapter 5 for a discussion of modality). By simplifying issues into contrasting positions he is able to represent himself as being confident about his own position and as someone who can overcome conflicts between social groups in a way that appeals to ethos.

Obama's metaphors typically occur in combination with a wide range of schemes – antithesis, parallelism, anaphora, epiphora, isocolon and chiasmus – and in combination with other tropes such as allusion. An important contribution to his rhetorical success arises from the verbal interaction of metaphor with schemes and other tropes. It is rare to find isolated figures of speech, and his rhetoric is characterized by a high density of such features that are rhetorically coherent. Figurative clustering contributes to an elevated style that is persuasive because no single figure stands out as being readily identifiable when rhetorical features are rich and multiplex, making analysis more difficult, as in the following (metaphors in bold, repetitions in italics and metonyms underlined):

> the same message we had **when we were up** and **when we were down**; the one that can change this country _**brick by brick**, **block by block**, **calloused hand by calloused hand**_ – that together, _ordinary_ people can do _extraordinary_ things; because _we are_ not a collection _of_ <u>Red</u> _States_ _and_ <u>Blue</u> _States, we are_ the United _States_ of America. (3 January 2008)

There are metonyms for the Republican and Democratic states based on the political allegiances that the colours symbolize. There are also the synecdoches 'brick', 'block' and 'hand', that stand for the activity of building which in turn stands for productive activities in general (as building is a prototypical purposeful activity). The whole argument is structured by several antitheses: 'up' is contrasted with 'down'; 'ordinary' with 'extraordinary'; and 'red' with 'blue'. These antitheses themselves occur in a triplet and this is juxtaposed with a tricolon (syntactic repetition) of syntactically equivalent phrases beginning with 'brick by brick'. There are other repeated words such as 'States'. The section ends with a unifying appeal to patriotism and national identity. You will notice when listening to the speech that this section is followed by cheers, applause and even chanting.

As argued in the discussion of schemes, an important part of Obama's persuasive appeal is because he is able to integrate rhetorical features originating in African-American rhetoric with those of classical rhetoric – as we saw with the use of anaphora contributing to a calm-to-storm delivery. To sound convincing as a leader it was also necessary for him to demonstrate a high level of sophistication in his command of classical rhetoric; he does this by integrating a range of schemes and tropes, usually at high impact points in a speech. The following speech ending has parallelisms (in italics) and metaphors (in bold):

And so tomorrow, *as we take* the campaign South and West; *as we learn* that the *struggles of the textile workers* in Spartanburg are not so different than *the plight of the dishwasher* in Las Vegas; that *the hopes of the little girl* who goes to a crumbling school in Dillon are the same as **the dreams** *of the boy* who learns on the streets of L.A.; *we will remember* that there is something happening in America; that we are not as divided as our politics suggests; that *we are one people*; *we are one nation*; and together, *we will begin* **the next great chapter in the American story** with three words **that will ring** *from coast to coast*; *from sea to shining sea* – Yes. We. Can. (8 January 2008)

There are numerous syntactically equivalent phrases interspersed with metaphors. The parallelism arising from the schemes gives the speech a rhythmic balance that is aesthetically satisfying and, like the movement of tides, sets up expectations that are then fulfilled – culminating in the epiphoric 'Yes. We. Can.' There is a progression in the metaphors from a hope as a dream to history as a book and the phrase 'American story' blends together the 'hope' and 'history' conceptual frames; the metaphor of words that 'ring' is then added to this (it is also an allusion to Martin Luther King's 'let freedom ring'); like religious language, his oratory is steeped in metaphor, and this contributes to an elevated style suitable to convey aspiration.

It is the blending of rhetorical traditions of black and white that characterizes the formula that eventually became the slogan for his successful political campaign – 'Yes We Can'. The repetition of this phrase could be analysed either from the black rhetorical tradition as a 'call and response' routine or from the classical tradition as anaphora and epiphora – the repetition of a phrase at the start and end of sentences, respectively; in the speech epilogue the slogan (in capitals) is combined with parallelism (in italics) and metaphor (in bold):

YES WE CAN. (BREAK FOR CHEERING) YES WE CAN. (BREAK FOR CHEERING) YES WE CAN.

It was a **creed** written into the founding documents that declared the destiny of a nation.

YES WE CAN.

It was **whispered** by slaves and abolitionists as they **blazed a trail towards freedom through the darkest of nights.**

YES WE CAN.

It was sung by immigrants as they struck out from distant shores and pioneers who pushed westward against an **unforgiving wilderness.**

YES WE CAN.

It was the call of workers who organized; women who reached for the ballot; a President who **chose the moon as our new frontier**; and a King who **took us to the mountaintop and pointed the way to the Promised Land.**

YES WE CAN to justice and equality. YES WE CAN to opportunity and prosperity. YES WE CAN **heal this nation.** YES WE CAN **repair** this world. YES WE CAN.

(8 January 2008)

It is not entirely clear whether 'YES WE CAN' serves as an answer to an implied question (in which case it would be epiphora) or as preceding the actions in the following section (in which case it would be anaphora). In a sense it is a 'rhetorical answer' because, just as a rhetorical question does not require an answer, so his rhetorical answer does not require a question to be asked. The syntactically repeated elements of parallelism (in italics) create structural patterns into which the trope of metaphor can be slotted; the parallelisms introduce a mythic account of American history by integrating the founding fathers (white) with the struggle of slaves (black), the pioneers of the west and the space race (largely white) and the Civil Rights movement (black). The metaphors heighten the appeal to pathos through describing the various examples of the aspirations of whites and blacks.

It is a message that is communicated through both the content of the discourse, but also rhetorically, because of the combination of features from the classical and African-American rhetorical traditions. From the classical tradition there are a range of schemes and tropes, while from the African-American rhetorical tradition there is the 'call and response' interaction, and the 'calm to storm' delivery; there is the crescendo effect from the decreasing distance between the 'Yes we can's' in the final part of the speech. Rhetorical density and figurative clustering are hallmarks of Obama's elevated style and often occur at salient sections of the speech – the prologues and epilogues. The response they evoke shows that while the appeal is partly cognitive it is primarily emotional.

The blending of rhetorical traditions is especially convincing, because it is consistent, both because Obama refers explicitly to it and because it can be inferred from his elevated rhetorical style; above all, it is because it comes from a man who can lay claim to both traditions in his DNA. Any potential conflict between the two traditions is reconciled through the emphasis on a shared Christian faith that unites the 'white' and 'black' traditions, and evidence for this is in the choice of the word 'creed' in 'Yes we can. It was a *creed* written into the founding documents that declared the destiny of a nation.' It is a return to religious faith that is rhetorically the means for overcoming political and ethnic divisions – a fundamental purpose in American political discourse.

Exercise 2.4

➤ Is there any evidence of interaction between tropes and schemes in the Tim Collins speech? Identify the different figures of speech and the effect of such interaction (if identified).
➤ How far has your analysis of the figures of speech in the Tim Collins speech and Shakepeare's *Henry V* speech led you to identify similarities and differences in the style of the two speeches?

2.4   Summary

In this chapter we have discussed the concept of style and considered how it arises from semiotic forms of expression – mainly, but not exclusively, verbal ones – that create an impression of uniqueness but also accommodate to social identities. We have seen that classical rhetoric distinguished between three types of style: the elevated, the plain and the middle style, and these styles were evident in the extent to which figures of speech were used and also influenced the types of figure of speech that would be chosen. We have examined *schemes* that involve the arrangement or sequence of words and *tropes* in which the meaning of a word (or words) actually changes, as in metaphor. We have identified these in speeches by Tim Collins and in Shakespeare's *Henry V*. We have seen how Barack Obama drew on both schemes and tropes to create a blended rhetorical style that integrated features of both African-American and classical rhetoric. At all times we have emphasized the need to adapt style to speech circumstance, and in particular the purpose of the speech – whether to motivate or to celebrate, to attack or to defend.

Essential reading

Charteris-Black, J. (2007) *The Communication of Leadership: The Design of Leadership Style*. London/New York: Routledge, chs 2 and 3.
Charteris-Black, J. (2011) *Politicians and Rhetoric: The Persuasive Power of Metaphor*, 2nd edn. Basingstoke/New York: Palgrave Macmillan, chs 1 and 2, pp. 1–50.
Edwards, P. (2009) *How to Rap: The Art and Science of the Hip-Hop MC*. Chicago, IL: Chicago Review Press, p. 88.
Lancaster, S. (2010) *Speechwriting*. London: Robert Hale.
Leith, S. (2011) *You Talkin' To Me? Rhetoric from Aristotle to Obama*. London: Profile Books.

Chapter 3

Coherence and Cohesion in Discourse

3.1 Introduction – what is coherence?

In the first-ever televised presidential debates in 1960, a suntanned John F. Kennedy – concealing his ill-health behind his resemblance to a Greek god – came across as a stylish and vigorous leader. In contrast, Richard Nixon, with his tense facial expression and perspiration-stained, car-salesman suit, looked something of a loser. Kennedy's use of language reinforced the impression given by his appearance and manner that he was a valiant, vigorous and heroic leader, rather than a victim of illness. In this chapter I shall demonstrate how, through analysing Kennedy's inaugural speech (generally held to be the greatest of all inaugural speeches) using traditional concepts of discourse analysis such as coherence and cohesion can contribute to an understanding of its success. I shall interpret the speech with reference to its circumstances – especially its historical setting – and how these influenced assumptions about audience knowledge that contributed to its success. In the first section I discuss coherence and speech circumstances; I then analyse cohesion – considering first grammatical and then lexical cohesion. I shall argue that the close correspondence between coherence and cohesion contributes to an explanation of the status of Kennedy's address in the pantheon of great speeches.

3.1.1 Coherence and speech circumstances

Coherence is the impression a text leaves of being unified in some way – but not through explicit cohesive relations; it arises when a hearer or reader understands the writer's communicative purpose, as a result of shared background knowledge of the world or frames of reference. Though less measurable empirically than cohesion, coherence is no less influential in contributing to the meaning of a text. In the context of oratory we might say that coherence is the understanding that arises when there is a convergence between the audience's and the speaker's knowledge of the world. The knowledge that Kennedy assumed his audience had when he gave his first inaugural address was that the USA was struggling with the Soviet

Union for a position of global supremacy. To understand his speech we need to have some global-political knowledge of the type that Kennedy would have assumed among his audience, and this might be as follows: the Second World War had led to the break-up of the colonial government by European powers – in particular, Britain and France – as they could no longer resist the pressure for independence from the colonized powers. With Europe's resources directed largely into post-war reconstruction, there was an opportunity for a new dominant power to emerge. As part of this struggle, the USA and the Soviet Union were both seeking to develop networks of alliances with Third-World countries that had formerly been colonies. Neither aspiring superpower had a clear lead in terms of technological supremacy or military force, so were in competition with each other.

Within the context of American politics, neither Democrats nor Republicans were dominant, and both parties had relatively young leaders. Kennedy had emerged as the younger representative of a powerful political family, and needed a rhetoric that would establish him as a leader in his own right. Since the election had been won only narrowly, the speech, as with all inaugural addresses, needed to appeal to former political opponents as well as to supporters. It needed to reach out to Republicans as well as satisfying the expectations of Democrats. More than this, given the international setting described above, it also needed to reach out to an audience of potential supporters among the former colonies of European powers. In this respect the audience was international as well as national. With technological developments in communications, this global audience was coming within reach for the first time. The speech was perhaps the first truly modern piece of political oratory in its recognition of multiple audiences – and the particular challenge that they present to coherence, since it is evidently much easier to establish shared perspectives with a homogeneous audience. For this reason, it could be argued that it is the first genuine example of worldwide public communication.

The preceding paragraphs provide a brief analysis of the cognitive circumstances which should precede analysis of the text itself. The coherence of the speech relies on how far it fits with the reader's expectations and assumptions. The full text of Kennedy's speech is given at the end of this chapter; it is divided into numbered paragraphs and each paragraph is divided into sentences (while the text was written to be spoken, for ease of cross-reference I shall use the terms 'sentence' and 'paragraph'). The altruistic tone that characterizes the speech begins in paragraph 4, where Kennedy addresses 'every nation' with a proclamation 'Let ... know'. The propositions he makes have what is known as *illocutionary force*. This is the force behind a speaker's utterances that corresponds with his or her underlying intentions, such as a warning, promise or command – even though these so-called 'speech acts' may be done indirectly. Kennedy makes commitments to those countries that are potential allies of the USA (commitments that will later impose their own obligations), and Kennedy is offering an alliance with any nation that is prepared to resist the Soviet Union. The Soviet Union is not mentioned at all, but communism is referred to in 8.1, and the Soviet Union is implied by 'iron tyranny' in 7.1. This is because 'iron' alludes to the 'Iron Curtain' – Churchill's phrase referring to the division in Europe arising from the Soviet Union's occupation of much of Eastern Europe. This implied meaning contributes to the coherence of the speech – it gives clues as to intentions.

When considering process circumstances we should recall that the speech was also authored by Kennedy's speech writer, Ted Sorenson; he subsequently became famous for his authorship, but always emphasized Kennedy's own contribution. The commitments made by Kennedy (and his speech writer) are described as 'pledges' in paragraph 5, and the analysis of the speech circumstances explains the motive for the 'pledges' referred to in paragraphs 5.1–11.1. For the speech to become fully meaningful we need to know *why* pledges were being made and *to whom* they were being made; it is the analysis of the cognitive circumstances that contributes to the 'coherence' of the speech. It is worth noting that contemporary readers may no longer be aware of the Cold War, and so their interpretation of the text relies more heavily on analysis of the linguistic features of cohesion than would that of the audience for whom it was originally written. The original audience could rely more on cognitive circumstantial knowledge. Yet the speech has stood the test of time, and an audience of young people can still access the speech – and knowledge of its circumstances – because the coherence of the speech also *arises* from its cohesion; this is what requires analysis in the next section.

Exercise 3.1

➤ Write a definition of 'coherence', and explain how and why it arises.

3.2 What is cohesion?

Cohesion is a crucial concept in the traditional analysis of texts – both written and spoken – and is concerned with the linguistic means through which a speech gives the impression of being unified (Halliday and Hasan 1976). It contrasts with coherence, which is concerned more with the other types of cognitive and schematic knowledge that are identified when analysing speech circumstances. Different parts of a text can be related to each other by various lexical and grammatical relationships, which contribute to the impression of wholeness. When we analyse cohesion we identify what it is in language that forms the relationships between the different sentences of a text and create its interrelatedness. Without cohesion we would not be able to understand how two sentences belong to the same text rather than being random. The analysis of cohesion, as undertaken in the classic work by Halliday and Hasan, *Cohesion in English*, was concerned with providing a 'grammar' of texts, to enable a text to be analysed by analogy with the grammatical structure of a sentence to identify a unit above the level of the sentence – a text. The idea of cohesion can be illustrated first by considering a few extracts from the speech:

(4.1) Let every nation know, whether it wishes us well or ill, that we shall pay any price, bear any burden, meet any hardship, support any friend, oppose any foe, in order to assure the survival and the success of liberty.

(5.1) This much we pledge – and more.

We are able to relate 5.1 to 4.1, because 'this' (5.1) directs the reader to something to which reference has *already been made*; without the list of actions in 4.1 (pay any price' etc.) 'this' would not make sense, because 'this' is *only* interpretable with reference to something that has already been stated. The connection that is formed between the two sentences is known as a *cohesive tie*, and the type of cohesion where the hearer refers back to something that has already been mentioned is known as **anaphoric reference** (see below). Grammatically, 'this' is a demonstrative adjective and we can describe 'this' as an 'anaphoric demonstrative reference'. The linguistic means by which cohesion is created is usually analysed in terms of grammatical and lexical cohesion, and these will be examined in the following sections.

3.3   Grammatical cohesion

Grammatical cohesion was one of two main classes of cohesive relation identified in Halliday and Hasan (1976), as shown in Figure 3.1.

3.3.1   Reference

To understand grammatical cohesion we need to understand the concept of reference. Many words only take on a meaning in a text because of their relationship with other words that also occur in the text (as with 'this' in 5.1) and entities external to the text. The concept of *reference* is concerned with how these connections and relationships are established. To help with

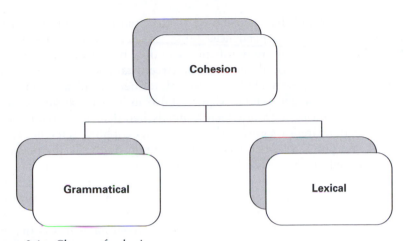

Figure 3.1   Classes of cohesion
Source: Halliday and Hassan (1976).

understanding this I shall first discuss the concepts of *exophoric* and *endophoric* reference, and then *deixis*.

Words that refer to entities <u>external to the text</u> are known as exophoric references, while words that refer to other words that occur elsewhere <u>within the text</u> are known as endophoric references. This distinction is illustrated by:

(1.2) For I have sworn before you and Almighty God the same solemn oath our forebears prescribed nearly a century and three quarters ago.

(2.3) And yet the same revolutionary beliefs for which our forebears fought are still at issue around the globe – the belief that the rights of man come not from the generosity of the state, but from the hand of God.

When 'forebears' occurs for the first time (in 1.2) it is referring to the founders of the American Republic – who have not yet been referred to in the speech – and so this is an exophoric reference, from the Greek prefix exō 'outside'. However, when 'forebears' is repeated in 2.3 it refers to the same word in 1.2 (we assume the 'forebears' referred to in 2.3 are the same people as the 'forebears' in 1.2) and so this is an endophoric reference. The term 'endophoric' originates from the Greek prefix 'endon' meaning 'within'. Other phrases in 2.3, such as 'revolutionary beliefs' and 'rights of man', have not previously been referred to in the text, and so are exophoric references, because they refer to ideas that are external to the text. Exophoric reference relies on schematic knowledge that we can describe as 'cognitive circumstances': in this case ideas that emerged in the

Enlightenment period that contributed to the French Revolution and the American struggle for independence.

Exophoric references are words that can only be explained with reference to the external social or political circumstances of the text – its discourse world. These include the list of former presidents and other members of the audience (1.1); 'victory' (also in 1.1) is exophoric, as it refers to the recent election in which Kennedy had defeated Nixon. 'Same solemn oath our forebears prescribed' (1.1) is an exophoric reference to the historical event in 1789 when George Washington first took the presidential oath. Exophoric reference is used in this speech to make the case for political allegiances with the recently independent countries in Africa and Asia; this is on the grounds of a shared interest in freedom from oppression – 'To those new States whom we welcome to the ranks of the free' (7.1); the USA has always seen itself as the prototype for freedom as it was the first nation to break away from British Imperial rule. In public communication there are appeals to various social groups to persuade them to shift their loyalties; representing former opponents as potential supporters through effective use of exophoric reference provided an incentive for them to become allies.

This section ends with two further examples of endophoric reference:

(20.1) All this will not be finished in the first 100 days.
(20.2) Nor will it be finished in the first 1,000 days, nor in the life of this administration, nor even perhaps in our lifetime on this planet.

'This' in (20.1) and 'it' in (20.2) are both endophoric references, because they refer to all the policy objectives and ideals that Kennedy outlined in the previous section of the speech.

3.3.2   Deixis

Deixis comes from the Greek word for 'pointing' and is a term used for words whose meaning arises by *referring to some aspect of the context in which they are spoken*. The speaker views him/herself as being at the deictic centre, and other entities are positioned in relation to *who* and *where* he or she is, and *when* he or she is speaking. Deictic references are the words the orator uses for *pointing* to the various aspects of the context in which he or she is located in time and space. The three primary elements to which the speaker at the deictic centre can refer are: people (persons); place; and time, as summarized in Figure 3.2.

Considering each of these in turn: 'people' means the human participants. Typically, this will be the speaker him/herself, supporters, opponents and other members of the audience; so 'person' deixis is typically realized

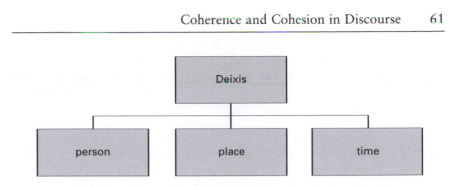

Figure 3.2   Types of deixis

through the pronoun system and *encodes the identity of participants* in the speech by pointing to individuals. So, when Kennedy says:

> (21.1) In your hands, my fellow citizens, more than mine, will rest the final success or failure of our course.

'In your hands' is person deixis, as it points to his audience: American citizens. Rhetorically, these empowering words imply that he is a democratically elected leader who will follow the will of the people. Earlier, he says:

> (11.1) Finally, to those nations who would make themselves our adversary, we offer not a pledge but a request

'those' is person deixis and refers to the governments of countries that are allied with the Soviet Union rather than the USA. Analysing 'those' as person deixis assumes that 'nation' really stands for leaders or governments of a geographical area – that is, it is a *metonym*. If we analysed 'nations' as a geographical location, we would classify it as place deixis. Throughout the speech, Kennedy uses the first person plural pronoun 'we' (as in 11.1) to point to a range of different people: himself, his political party – the Democrats, but also to American citizens, as he is also the head of state – a role he makes clear when he addresses them as 'my fellow Americans' in 25 and 'citizens of America' in 27. These are all examples of person deixis, and the first person plural 'we' (as in 11.1) is always a significant pronoun in persuasive language as it is deliberately unclear as to whom it refers exactly; 'we' gains power through this imprecision and invites hearers to ally themselves with the speaker. Followers are loosely defined in political speeches since, ideally, if rhetoric is successful, this group expands to include those who were previously opponents.

'Place deixis' means all the spatial relations that are referred to in the speech and is typically realized by demonstrative adjectives – words such as 'here', 'there', etc. – that *encode spatial relations* relative to the location of the speaker; but it can also be words or expressions that point to a location. For example consider the following rhetorical appeals:

(9.1) To our sister republics south of our border, we offer a special
pledge: to convert our good words into good deeds, in a new
alliance for progress, to assist free men and free governments in
casting off the chains of poverty.

'South of our border' uses a compass point 'south' and spatial location
'border' to point to the Central American states, which Kennedy viewed as
potential allies; circumstantial knowledge tells us this was against the
danger of Cuba, which since the Castro revolution was allying itself with
the Soviet Union. Sometimes place and person deixis work in combination:

(8.1) To those peoples in the huts and villages across the globe struggling to break the bonds of mass misery

There is deictic reference specifically to 'peoples', who are defined by their
location 'in the huts and villages', and it is interesting that the choice of
'huts' and 'villages' relies on the cognitive knowledge that American citizens
live in houses and towns, so the reference is to those living in Third-World
countries. 'Across the globe' reinforces this interpretation through place
deixis; notice again the imprecision of the location; the rhetorical appeal
does not restrict itself to a particular geographical area, but could be
anywhere there is poverty.

Time deixis *encodes time relations* relative to when an utterance is
spoken, so words such as 'now' and 'then' point to a time:

(1.2) For I have sworn before you and almighty God the same solemn
oath our forebears prescribed nearly a century and three-quarters
ago.
(2.1) The world is very different now.

'Now' and 'ago' are both instances of time deixis as they contrast the present time with the past; relying on the historical knowledge of what
happened 175 years before. His audience may infer that he is referring to
the American Declaration of Independence. Kennedy hopes to ally these
fathers of independence to his cause. He continues:

(3.1) We dare not forget today that we are the heirs of that first revolution.

'Today' is time deixis that reinforces the continuity between a time of heroic
struggle – the 'first revolution' – and the present, when he is speaking. Time
deixis is rhetorically important, because many of his audience will know
that 'the first revolution' refers to the struggle for independence from colonial Britain. This identifies 'America' as a nation that has also been colonized – an important rhetorical move to win support from those nations

that had been colonized much more recently. As noted above, America sees itself as the founding father of freedom. Deixis in all its forms – person, place and time – contributes to underlying rhetorical purposes and therefore to the overall coherence of the speech.

Exercise 3.2

> Identify examples of reference in the Kennedy inaugural address (p. 74). Try to categorize these by deciding whether reference is exophoric or endophoric.
> Analyse deixis in the Kennedy inaugural speech.
> Discuss whether it relies primarily on person, place or time deixis.

3.3.3   Anaphoric reference

Anaphoric reference arises when a hearer understands a word by referring **back** to something previously said. The term originates from the Greek 'ana' meaning 'up', because a reader looks upwards to find the referent. We find that the majority of endophoric references are also anaphoric; for example:

> To those new states whom we welcome to the ranks of the free, we pledge our word that one form of colonial control shall not have passed away merely to be replaced by a far more iron tyranny (7.1). We shall not always expect to find them supporting our view (7.2).

'Them' in 7.2 refers anaphorically to 'those new states' in 7.1; we can only understand the meaning of 7.2 with reference to 7.1. 'We' in 7.1 refers back to 'we' in 5.1, and in 6.1–6.3 we assume that each use of 'we' refers to the same group of people of whom the speaker is one. But 'we' is deliberately imprecise in political rhetoric and it could also be interpreted in a critical analysis as referring to different entities – for example, the government, Americans and so on, in which case it would be analysed as exophoric reference. The speech continues:

> But we shall always hope to find them strongly supporting their own freedom – and to remember that, in the past, those who foolishly sought power by riding the back of the tiger ended up inside (7.3).

Here, 'them' refers back to a sub-section of 'those new states whom we welcome to the ranks of the free', so anaphora can stretch back over more than one sentence. Notice that there is a contrast between 'them' referring to *all* the newly independent nations towards which Kennedy is reaching out, and 'those who foolishly sought power by riding the back of the tiger'.

The audience may wonder if this is the same 'those' as in 'To those peoples in the huts and villages across the globe struggling to break the bonds of mass misery' (8.1). The answer is 'no' because 'those' in 7.3 refers to potential US allies who made the wrong choice by backing the Soviet Union.

Why is the encoding of meaning so potentially ambiguous? First, because the purpose of the speech was not to antagonize the Soviet Union – as already noted, no reference is made to the Soviet Union, only indirectly to the ideology of communism. This deliberate imprecision reflects also in expressions such as 'allies', 'countries to the south of our border' and so on. Indirectness in political rhetoric shows concern for the 'face needs' of the hearer – that is, showing respect so that they don't 'lose face': we do not insult potential allies outside our group, nor do we seek lifelong enemies. By allowing meaning to be inferred, rhetoric gains a more subtle influence than if everything that was intended was made explicit and evident from the surface of language.

3.3.4   Cataphoric reference

The other type of endophoric reference is cataphoric reference; this is when a word refers forward to something that will follow in the text. It originates from the Greek prefix 'cata' meaning 'downwards', because when reading the text the referent would be lower down the page. Consider, for example, 'This much we pledge – and more (5.1); 'and more' refers to the pledges in the subsequent six sentences and so is an example of cataphoric reference. It signals the start of a series of pledges and contributes strongly to the overall rhetorical purpose of the text. Cataphoric reference is much less common than anaphoric reference, but its scarcity can enhance its potential for creating rhetorical effect.

Endophoric references can be analysed as either anaphoric or cataphoric, as shown in Figure 3.3.

As well as distinguishing between 'backward' or 'forward' directions, we can refer to the grammatical function of reference, using parts of speech or other grammatical terms. We have already seen how 'those' can be

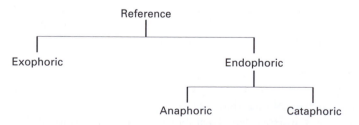

Figure 3.3   Categories of reference

described as a 'demonstrative' reference; perhaps the most frequent type of anaphoric reference is formed through the pronoun system:

> In the long history of the world, only a few generations have been granted the role of defending freedom in its hour of maximum danger (24.1). I do not shrink from this responsibility – I welcome it (24.2).

'It' in 24.2 is refers anaphorically to 'the role of defending freedom in its hour of maximum danger' in 24.1 and is a pronoun, so this could be described as 'anaphoric pronominal reference'. Though it is also endophoric, this does not need to be stated, because it may be assumed that if reference is anaphoric it is necessarily endophoric as well.

3.3.5   Other reference categories

The other three types of grammatical cohesion identified in Halliday and Hasan (1976) were: substitution; ellipsis; and conjunction, and I shall illustrate each of these briefly below.

Substitution
This is a relationship where one word takes the place of a phrase. So, for example, in 'If a free society cannot help the many who are poor, it cannot save the few who are rich' (8.2); 'the many' is a substitution for 'the many people'. In practice, this category does not occur very frequently and you will do well if you can find other examples in the speech.

Ellipsis
This is a cohesive relation in which a word or phrase is omitted, but would need to be supplied by the hearer in order to understand the text. It is sometimes known as 'substitution by zero'. Consider:

> All this will not be finished in the first 100 days. Nor will it be finished in the first 1,000 days, nor in the life of this administration, nor even perhaps in our lifetime on this planet. But let us begin (20).

'*Let us begin*' could be expanded to include the various aspirations referred to in previous sentences, such as: 'let us begin to explore what problems unite us', 'let us begin to explore the stars, conquer the deserts, etc.'; in these cases the verb phrases are omitted because they are taken for granted and so can be analysed as ellipsis.

Conjunction
Halliday and Hasan (1976) used an established grammatical term for words that connect various sentences. While conjunctions are usually found

Table 3.1   Categories of conjunction

Type	Logical relationship	Examples
additive	add/give an alternative	and; or; furthermore; in addition; likewise; in other words
adversative	opposition	however; but; yet; (even) though; on the contrary; on the one hand ... on the other hand
causal	one idea/event causes another	because; so; then; for this reason; consequently; it follows that; as a result
temporal	one event follows another in time	one day; then; finally; up to now; the next day
continuative	please continue to follow the text	well; now; of course; anyway; surely; after all

within sentences, they are only relevant for the analysis of cohesion when they join separate sentences:

> But neither can two great and powerful groups of nations take comfort from our present course – both sides overburdened by the cost of modern weapons, both rightly alarmed by the steady spread of the deadly atom, yet both racing to alter that uncertain balance of terror that stays the hand of mankind's final war (13.1).

Here 'but' is a conjunction that contrasts the preceding emphasis on strengthening the US nuclear deterrent in 12.2 with 13.1, which outlines the dangers of a nuclear arms race. Conjunctions contribute to cohesion through various forms of logical relationships between clauses; Table 3.1 summarizes these relationships.

There are a large number of conjunctions in English that express various types of logical relation between clauses: adding further information, expressing logical opposition by contradicting what was said previously, and expressing causal relationships – either by giving an effect followed by a cause, or a cause followed by an effect.

Exercise 3.3

➤ For each of the references you analysed as endophoric in the previous exercise decide whether it is anaphoric or cataphoric.
➤ Now analyse other types of grammatical cohesion (substitution, ellipsis, conjunction). What percentage of all the examples of grammatical cohesion did you classify as reference?

➜

> ➤ Can you think of certain types of text that may rely more on a particular type of grammatical cohesion?
> ➤ What groups of learners of English may encounter difficulty with grammatical cohesion?

3.4   Lexical cohesion

The type of cohesion that is created by the related senses of words is known as 'lexical cohesion', and is perhaps the primary means for creating cohesion. According to Halliday and Hasan (1976) there are only two main types of lexical cohesion: repetition and collocation. However, subsequent work has extended the number of categories of lexical cohesion; for example, Hoey (1991) developed four categories of lexical cohesion: simple and complex repetition, and simple and complex paraphrase.

Difficulties emerge in the analysis of lexical cohesion over the degree of lexical or semantic variation that is permitted between two words that it is claimed form a cohesive tie. For example, a word can be repeated exactly, or another part of speech (using the same root form) or a synonym could be used. 'Reiteration' is sometimes used for a word that is a closely related but not identical form. Semantic relations can arise from synonyms, antonyms, hyponyms or superordinates (these terms are described below). However, semantically based cohesion differs from the other type of lexical cohesion first identified by Halliday and Hasan (1976): collocation. The current understanding of this concept is that two words are related simply because they often occur together, not because they are related semantically. We see evidence of this in fixed phrases. For example, 'sex', 'drugs' and 'rock 'n' roll' are semantically unrelated, but because they are associated in experience they have become collocates. This means that when one of the words occurs (for example, 'sex'), there is a likelihood that another one of the group will also occur (for example, 'drugs'), though there is no explanation in the semantic system – having sex is different from drug-taking, but because people who take drugs sometimes do so to enhance sexual experience the two words have become associated in experience and therefore in meaning.

While Halliday and Hasan (1976) is considered to have provided a thorough analysis of grammatical cohesion, it is less successful in its account of lexical cohesion. In the following analysis I shall identify three main categories of lexical cohesion: repetition; semantic relations; and collocation. A summary of my analysis of lexical cohesion in the first half of the speech using these categories is presented at the end of this chapter. The full version of the speech is shown there for use in the exercises.

3.4.1   Repetition and reiteration

Perhaps the simplest and most frequent type of lexical cohesion is repetition – this is when exactly the same word is repeated in another sentence. In the analysis of the speech at the end of this chapter, repetitions are shown in bold; the first is 'forebears', which repeats a word first mentioned in (1.2). When the repetition has some morphological variation from a root form this is described as 'reiteration'; for example, 'revolution' in 3.1 reiterates 'revolutionary' in 2.3 – clearly the reference is very similar and contributes to cohesion. Another example occurs in 11.1, where 'anew' is cohesive with 'new' in 9.1, and both are cohesive with 'renewal' in 1.1. Hoey (1991) distinguishes between 'simple repetition' for repetition of an identical form, and 'complex repetition' where there is repetition of a word that shares the same root. I would like to illustrate how repetition organizes whole sections of the speech by considering 6.1:

> (6.1) To those old allies whose cultural and spiritual origins we share, we pledge the loyalty of faithful friends.

The word 'pledge' in 6.1 refers back to the same pledge in 5.1, so this is an example of lexical cohesion through repetition. But 'pledge' in 5.1 is also repeated in 7.1, 8.1, 9.1, 10.1 and 11.1; each time we come to one of these words, it refers back to both the previous occurrence and all the previous occurrences of 'pledge' to create a lexical chain. This increases the rhetorical effect, as the repetition of a word reinforces the speaker's conviction: the initial 'pledge' in 5.1 is not just a one-off pledge, but is part of a series of American commitments. While repetition is simple it is also very effective; in the same way that water dripping on a stone can eventually wear it away, it gains its effect through each successive reiteration and conveys determination and strength of purpose. These were important for a young leader, especially one uncertain about his health and physical stamina. Analysis of lexical chains is therefore important in identifying major themes in a speech.

3.4.2   Semantic relations: antonyms and synonyms

Words occurring in different sentences of a speech can be related according to their place in the semantic system of English. The most common type of semantic relation is synonymy – when words have similar senses. A simple test is to substitute one word with another to establish whether the meaning is changed; if it is not, then we have a pair of synonyms. The more the meaning stays the same, the more the words can be considered as synonyms; for example, if we substituted 'globe' in 2.3 with 'world' from 2.1 to produce 'And yet the same revolutionary beliefs for which our forebears fought are still at issue around the world' this would not change the meaning of the utterance. Sometimes the substitution will produce a form that is not quite as felicitous in terms of style as the original; for example, if in 3.1 we replace 'today' by 'now' to produce 'We dare not forget now that we are the heirs of that first revolution' the style is less acceptable but the meaning is hardly affected. Quite often a synonym is used to avoid repetition and enhance style; for example, at the end of 4.1, 'to assure the survival and the success of liberty' sounds better than 'to assure the survival and the success of freedom', because 'freedom' has already been used in 1.1. and occurs four other times in the speech, whereas this is the only example of 'liberty'. Such lexical variation enhances a speech: 'liberty' will have more impact when used only sparingly.

Antonyms are words that have an opposite sense; for example:

United, there is little we cannot do in a host of cooperative ventures (6.2). Divided, there is little we can do – for we dare not meet a powerful challenge at odds and split asunder (6.3).

'United' has the opposite sense to 'divided'. Bringing the two adjectives to the front of each sentence gives them more prominence and emphasizes the contrast between them. There are other instances of lexical cohesion between 6.2 and 6.1, including lexical repetition of 'there is little' and other words that contribute to semantic opposition: 'cannot do' contrasts with 'can do'; and 'cooperative ventures' contrast with 'split asunder'. The semantic relation here is more complex, because 'cooperative ventures' is a noun phrase whereas 'split asunder' is a verb phrase. But they have opposite senses that contribute to the lexical cohesiveness between the two sentences. We could test the semantic relation by replacing 'split asunder' with 'not co-operate'; this would not change the meaning but would be less stylistically attractive. Given their parallel structure – syntactically and lexically – we might expect to find these two sentences next to each other in the text and to be tightly bonded by lexical cohesion.

Sometimes the relations between antonyms may be more ones of contrast than opposition; for example, is 'heirs' really the opposite of 'forebears', or are they contrasted with each other? There is also a semantic distinction between gradable and non-gradable antonyms; gradable antonyms such as 'wet' and 'dry' can be put on a scale so there are degrees of wetness or dryness that can be contrasted with each other. Conversely, 'dead' and 'alive' cannot be positioned on a scale, they are *opposite* states, since you cannot be 'more' or 'less' dead (other than figuratively). In the speech we might consider 'united' and 'divided' as gradable, since there are degrees of unity and division, whereas 'turning on the light' and 'turning off the light' are non-gradable, because we cannot partially turn on a light. In Hoey (1991) antonyms are termed 'complex paraphrases'.

> **Exercise 3.4**
>
> ➢ Analyse the second half of the speech for examples of repetition and reiteration.
> ➢ Now analyse it for synonyms and antonyms.
> ➢ Which occurs more frequently – cohesive ties formed by repetition/reiteration, or ties formed by the semantic relations of synonymy and antonymy?

3.4.3   Collocation

Apart from lexical repetition, the other main type of lexical cohesion is 'collocation'; this is the frequency with which words are found together, or co-occur. Words related by collocation arise from patterns of language use; for example, there is a connection between 'pledge' is 5.1 and the verb phrases 'pay any price', 'bear any burden', and 'support any friend' in 4.1. This is a different type of lexical relationship from repetition because it is based on the idea of 'pledging'; there is a range of patterns of 'pledge' that link its meaning to *situations* when pledges are made – such as when friends need support or are short of money. We make pledges to protect us against the possibility of times being hard because of poverty, illness, loneliness and so on.

How might we go about proving this semantic relationship? It is possible to identify collocation by using a corpus (an electronically searchable database of language). Since this is an American speech it would be more reliable to search the Corpus of Contemporary American English (COCA). When searching the corpus it is possible to vary the range over which two words co-occur; for example, Table 3.2 shows collocations of 'pledge' and 'pay' within a space of three words.

It is evident that 'pledge' and 'pay' often occur together in American English. The corpus data show there is a phrase 'pledge to pay', though it can occur with other variations. These lines were from the 'newspaper', 'magazine' and 'spoken' sections of the corpus, and we could limit the search to a particular section of the corpus, such as spoken language. The claim made by Halliday and Hasan is that when these two words occur in different sentences they retain a link with each other *because they commonly occur together in the language*. What this means is that part of our understanding of speeches depends on how words are *normally* used – as well as their isolated meaning when taken out of context; these 'normal' meanings also contribute to the cohesion of the speech. Large corpora, such as the COCA, were not available until relatively recently, so Halliday and Hasan were not able to test the concept of collocation. We are now in a position where it is feasible to do so, and to find out how cohesion is formed by lexical patterns in general in language.

The corpus provides a useful resource for testing other cohesive ties that I have analysed as collocations; for example, I suggest that 'revolutionary'

Table 3.2   Collocations of 'pledge' and pay' in COCA (three-word range)

Now that the financial markets are beginning to stabilize and the big Wall Street players **pledge** to **pay** back their bailout billions, they are digging in against fundamental change.

[A]nd wonder why county prosecutors are rebelling at President Todd Stroger's reneging on his **pledge** for a **pay** raise.

[T]alk about money, but the difference between actually getting people to **pay** after they **pledge** is a big difference.

Eventually he withdrew his **pledge** to **pay** for the church's construction.

Medical students from Lesotho must **pledge** to **pay** back their education [costs] with years of service back home.

[S]eems perfect – until his niece is accepted at Harvard and reminds him of a **pledge** he made to **pay** her tuition.

The rankings can change on the hour as companies **pledge** to **pay**.

Here's how the new deal works: the Hawks have made an unsecured **pledge** to **pay** the $12.5 million in annual debt service if arena revenue falls short.

Such principles might include a **pledge** to **pay** the U.S. minimum wage at Mexican operations.

[S]ay they will not agree to take the necessary environmental actions unless the developed nations **pledge** in advance to **pay** for them.

[A]greed to undertake the project itself, and in August 1972 California rescinded its earlier **pledge** to **pay** for it.

Source: http://corpus.byu.edu/coca/

(2.3) collocates with 'renewal' (1.1). From COCA we find in the academic section:

> efforts to preserve their economic independence. The Choctaws took advantage of the American **Revolution** to **renew** the 'play off' system, this time vacillating between the American–French–Spanish

> do not have much interest in traditional cultures, even those in the throes of **revolutionary renewal**

Another collocation is between 'prey' in 9.2 and 'tiger' in 7.3; Table 3.3 shows collocations of these two words within a range of only two words in COCA.

There is evidence from the natural history and bioscience sections of the corpus that these words often occur together; therefore when we come across them in separate sentences of a speech they form a cohesive relation.

Table 3.3   Collocations of 'tiger' and 'prey' in COCA

... the trees in Amur tiger range. The pines' cones are critical food for **tiger prey** such as wild boar.

The delta still has enough healthy tugai to offer cover to good numbers of **tiger prey** such as wild boar.

'This delta still has enough healthy tugai to offer cover to good numbers of **tiger prey**,' Pereladova says. 'Without **prey**, there can be no tigers.'

[T]he Asian traditional medicine trade in big cat organs and bones and the decline of **tiger prey** species, and better protect habitat.

The tiger was found by field workers conducting a survey of **tiger prey** species. Aside from minor abrasions from the snare cable, the tiger was ...

Then, just as the stranger pounced on his unhappy **prey**, **Tiger** leaped out. The mouse darted away, but Tiger kept a firm grip ...

... for grazing their animals, thick forests for gathering firewood – enhanced the habitat for **tiger prey** such as deer and wild pigs. It wasn't until demographic pressures began ...

... of work. Unsanctioned traffic in animals and animal parts – birds of **prey**, **tiger** skins, tiger bones and bear gallbladders out of Russia; rhino horns and elephant ...

Source: http://corpus.byu.edu/coca/

The colourful metaphor in 7.1 warns those nations who are considering allying with a dangerous ally (by inference a communist one), and is extended into 9.2 by repeating this warning to 'our sister republics south of our border'. We saw when analysing cognitive circumstances that this refers to nations that were considering following Cuba by forming alliances with the Soviet Union. A corpus can be genuinely helpful in testing candidate collocations; for example, when I initially relied on intuition I assumed that 'writ' in 10.1 might be cohesive with 'government' in 9.1; but Table 3.4 shows that corpus provides evidence that they are collocates.

To give a final example of a collocation – consider 'destruction' in 11.1 and 'abolish' in 2.1; an initial search of the corpus did not produce any matches of these two words; however, Table 3.5 shows what happens when changing them both to the verb form.

The collocation of 'destruction' and 'abolish' seems quite important in creating cohesion because, while many cohesive ties are in sentences that are close together in the text, these are nine paragraphs apart; yet the idea introduced in 11 'before the dark powers of destruction unleashed by science engulf all humanity in planned or accidental self-destruction' seems to fit well with the rather menacing claim of nuclear danger at the very start of the speech: 'For man holds in his mortal hands the power to abolish all forms of human poverty and all forms of human life' (2.2). We

Table 3.4   Collocations of 'writ' and 'government' in COCA

President Hamid Karzai's government currently faces: extending the reach and **writ** of the **government** in Kabul across the full extent of Afghan territory and directing it toward effective governance.

[E]ventually, not only to ease US pressure but also to reestablish the **writ** of **government**. 'There is a mismatch between the Pakistani priorities and what the US would …

… and its prime minister, Ismail Haniya of Hamas, and named a new emergency **government** whose **writ** runs only in the West Bank. Mr. Abbas says he can no …

… headquarters, ceding control of much of the country-side to the Maoists. The **government's writ** hardly extends beyond the capital and other district centers. The Maoists control …

Source: http://corpus.byu.edu/coca/

Table 3.5   Collocations of 'abolish' and 'destroy' in COCA

Disgruntled students carry signs saying 'BAN Social Security!' Words like **abolish** and **destroy** are bandied about. Says one student, 'We're just trying to get …

… our position for the last 40 years has been to **abolish** and **destroy** both nuclear tests and nuclear weapons … we shall …

Source: http://corpus.byu.edu/coca/

could claim that the semantic relation between 'abolish' and 'destruction' is synonymy, but the reason we did not do so is because one is a verb and the other a noun, and it is therefore rather hard to substitute one for the other. However, there is scope for discussion over this type of lexical relation, and Hoey (1991) refers to it (along with antonymy) as 'complex paraphrase'.

Exercise 3.5

➢ Calculate the total number of instances of each type of lexical cohesion in paragraphs 1–13. What conclusions do you draw from this?
➢ Analyse the second half of the speech for examples of collocation: draw a table showing the two words that collocate with each other and their location in the speech.
➢ What do you notice about the distance over which cohesion operates?
➢ What is the value of identifying lexical cohesion?

3.5   Summary

Coherence depends on cognitive knowledge of what is normal in one's experience of the world. This varies according to considerations of experience and knowledge; for example, someone with historical knowledge of post-war international politics will bring more schematic knowledge to the Kennedy speech. This explains why readers *vary in their estimate of coherence*, whereas cohesion is objectively present in the text. This can be proved empirically as, if a model is applied consistently, *different* readers would come up with *the same number* of cohesive ties.

    Figure 3.4 summarizes the main cohesion categories from the Halliday and Hasan approach.

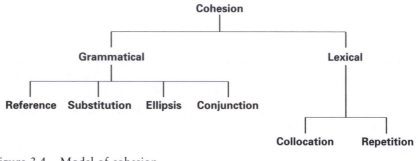

Figure 3.4   Model of cohesion
(Based on Halliday and Hasan (1976).)

Core Text: John F. Kennedy inaugural speech, 20 January 1961

Key: Bold – **repetition**
        Bold italics – ***synonyms and antonyms***
        Italics – *collocation*

Vice President Johnson, Mr. Speaker, Mr. Chief Justice, President Eisenhower, Vice President Nixon, President Truman, reverend clergy, fellow citizens, we observe today not a victory of party, but a celebration of freedom – symbolizing an end, as well as a beginning – signifying renewal, as well as change (1). For I have sworn before you and Almighty God the same solemn oath our forebears prescribed nearly a century and three-quarters ago (2).

1 Lexical choices in the first paragraph introduce themes that will be returned to through cohesive ties in the remainder of the speech; in particular 'renewal' and 'forebears'.

The world is very different *now* (1). For man holds in his mortal hands the power to abolish all forms of human poverty and all forms of human life (2). And yet the same *revolutionary* beliefs for which our **forebears** fought are still at issue around the *globe* – the belief that the rights of **man** come not from the generosity of the state, but from the **hand** of **God** (3).

2 *ANTONYM* 'ago' (1.2)

   COLLOCATION '*renewal*' (1.1)
REPETITION 'forebears (1.2)
SYNONYM 'world' (2.1)
REPETITION man (2.2)
REPETITION hand (2.2)
REPETITION God (1.2)

We dare not forget *today* that we are the *heirs* of that first **revolution** (1). Let the word go forth from this time and place, to friend and foe alike, that the torch has been passed to a new generation of Americans – born in this **century**, tempered by war, disciplined by a hard and bitter peace, proud of our ancient *heritage* – and unwilling to witness or permit the slow undoing of those human **rights** to which this Nation has always been committed, and to which we are committed today at home and around the **world** (2).

3 *SYNONYM* 'now' (2.1)
ANTONYM 'forebears' (2.3)
REPETITION 'revolutionary' (2.3)

   REPETITION 'century' (2.2)
COLLOCATION '*forebears*' (2.3)
REPETITION 'rights' (2.3)

   REPETITION 'world' (2.1)

Let every **nation** know, whether it wishes us well or ill, that we shall pay any price, bear any burden, meet any hardship, support any friend, oppose any foe, to assure the survival and the success of *liberty* (1).

4 **REPETITION** 'nation' (3.2)

   SYNONYM 'freedom' (1.1)

This much we *pledge* – and more (1).

5 *COLLOCATION* '*pay*' (4.1)

To those old *allies* whose cultural and spiritual origins we share, we **pledge** the loyalty of faithful **friends** (1). United, there is little we cannot do in a host of cooperative ventures (2). *Divided*, **there is little** we can do – for we dare not meet a powerful *challenge* at odds and *split asunder* (3).

6 *SYNONYM* 'friend' (3.2)
REPETITION 'pledge' (5.1)
REPETITION 'friend' (3.2)

   ANTONYM 'united' (6.2)
REPETITION 'there is little' (6.1)
COLLOCATION '*disciplined*' (3.2)
ANTONYM 'cooperative ventures' (6.2)

To those new *States* whom we welcome to the ranks of the **free**, we **pledge** our word that one form of colonial control shall not have passed away merely to be replaced by a far more iron tyranny (1). We shall not always expect to find them **supporting** our

7 *SYNONYM* 'nation' (4.1)
REPETITION 'freedom' (1.1)
REPETITION 'pledge' (5.1)

   REPETITION 'support' (4.1)

view (2). But we shall always hope to find them strongly **supporting** their own **freedom** – and to *remember* that, in the past, those who foolishly sought power by riding the back of the tiger ended up inside (3).

REPETITION 'supporting' (7.2)
REPETITION 'freedom' (1.1)
ANTONYM 'forget' (3.1)

To those *peoples* in the huts and villages across the **globe** struggling to break the bonds of mass misery, we **pledge** our best efforts to help them help themselves, for whatever period is required – not because the Communists may be doing it, not because we seek their votes, but because it is **right** (1). If a **free** society cannot help the many who are *poor*, it cannot save the few who are *rich* (2).

8 *COLLOCATION* 'allies',
   'friends' (6.1)
REPETITION 'globe' (2.3)
REPETITION 'pledge' (7.1)

REPETITION 'rights' (3.2)
REPETITION 'free' (7.1)
SYNONYM 'misery' (8.1)
ANTONYM 'misery' (8.1)

To our sister *republics* south of our border, we offer a special **pledge** – to convert our good **words** into *good* deeds – in a **new alliance** for progress – to *assist* **free** men and **free** governments in *casting off* the **chains of poverty** (1). But this **peaceful revolution** of **hope** cannot become the *prey* of *hostile* **powers** (2). **Let all our** *neighbors* **know** that we shall *join* with them to **oppose** aggression or subversion anywhere in the **Americas** (3). And **let every other power know** that this *Hemisphere* intends to remain the *master* of its own *house* (4).

9 *SYNONYM* 'States' (7.1)
REPETITION 'pledge' (8.1)
REPETITION 'word' (7.1)
COLLOCATION 'right' (8.1)
REPETITION 'new' (7.1)
REPETITION 'allies' (6.1)
SYNONYM 'support' (4.1)
REPETITION 'free' (8.2)
REPETITION 'man' (2.2)
COLLOCATION 'break' (8.1)
SYNONYM 'bonds of mass
   misery' (8.1)
REPETITION 'peace' (3.2)
REPETITION 'revolution' (3.1)
REPETITION 'hope' (7.3)
COLLOCATION 'tiger' (7.3)
COLLOCATION 'foe' (3.2)
REPETITION 'power' (7.3)
COLLOCATION 'friends' (6.1)
REPETITION 'let ... know' (4.1)
COLLOCATION 'allies' (6.1)
REPETITION 'oppose' (4.1)
COLLOCATION 'tiger' (7.3)
REPETITION 'Americans' (3.2)
REPETITION 'let ... know' (9.2)
COLLOCATION 'globe' (8.1)
REPETITION 'power' (2.2)
COLLOCATION 'power' (2.2)
COLLOCATION 'hut' (8.1)

To that **world** *assembly* of sovereign **states**, the **United Nations**, our last *best* **hope** in an age where the instruments of **war** have far outpaced the instruments of **peace**, we **renew** our **pledge** of **support** – to prevent it from becoming merely a forum for invective – to strengthen its shield of the **new** and the weak – and to enlarge the *area* in which its *writ* may run (1).	10	REPETITION 'world' (3.2) *SYNONYM* 'governments' (9.1) REPETITION 'states' (7.1) REPETITION 'united' (6.2) REPETITION 'nations' (4.1) *COLLOCATION* 'good' (9.1) REPETITION 'hope' (9.2) REPETITION 'war' (3.2) REPETITION 'peaceful' (9.2) REPETITION 'renewal' (1.1) REPETITION 'pledge' (9.1) REPETITION 'support' (4.1) REPETITION 'new' (9.1) *COLLOCATION* 'south of the border' (9.1) *COLLOCATION* 'governments' (9.1)
Finally, to those **nations** who would make themselves our *adversary*, we **offer** not a **pledge** but a request: that *both sides* begin **anew** the *quest* for **peace**, before the dark **powers** of *destruction* unleashed by science engulf all **humanity** in planned or accidental self-destruction (1).	11	REPETITION 'nations' (10.1) *SYNONYM* 'foe' (4.1) REPETITION 'offer' (9.1) REPETITION 'pledge' (10.1) *COLLOCATION* 'any friend ... any foe' (4.1) REPETITION 'new' (9.1) *COLLOCATION* 'seek' (8.1) REPETITION 'peace' (10.1) REPETITION 'power' (9.4) *COLLOCATION* 'abolish' (2.1) REPETITION 'human' (3.2)
We dare not tempt them with **weakness** (1). For only when our *arms* are sufficient beyond doubt can we be certain beyond doubt that they will never be employed (2).	12	REPETITION 'weak' (10.1) *COLLOCATION* 'shield' (10.1)
But neither can two great and **powerful** groups of **nations** take comfort from our present course – both **sides** overburdened by the cost of modern *weapons*, both rightly alarmed by the steady spread of the *deadly atom*, yet both racing to alter that uncertain balance of terror that stays the **hand** of **mankind's** final **war** (1).	13	REPETITION 'powers' (11.1) REPETITION 'nations' (11.1) REPETITION 'sides' (11.1) *SYNONYM* 'arms' (12.1) *SYNONYM* 'arms' (12.1) REPETITION 'hand' (2.3) REPETITION 'war' (10.1)
So let us begin anew – remembering on both sides that civility is not a sign of weakness, and sincerity is always subject to proof (1).	14	

Let us never negotiate out of fear. But let us never fear to negotiate (2).

Let both sides explore what problems unite 15 us instead of belaboring those problems which divide us (1).

Let both sides, for the first time, formulate 16 serious and precise proposals for the inspection and control of arms – and bring the absolute power to destroy other nations under the absolute control of all nations (1).

Let both sides seek to invoke the wonders of 17 science instead of its terrors (1). Together let us explore the stars, conquer the deserts, eradicate disease, tap the ocean depths, and encourage the arts and commerce (2).

Let both sides unite to heed in all corners of 18 the earth the command of Isaiah – to 'undo the heavy burdens ... and to let the oppressed go free' (1).

And if a beachhead of cooperation may push 19 back the jungle of suspicion, let both sides join in creating a new endeavor, not a new balance of power, but a new world of law, where the strong are just and the weak secure and the peace preserved (1).

All this will not be finished in the first 100 20 days (1). Nor will it be finished in the first 1,000 days, nor in the life of this Administration, nor even perhaps in our lifetime on this planet (2). But let us begin (3).

In your hands, my fellow citizens, more than 21 in mine, will rest the final success or failure of our course (1). Since this country was founded, each generation of Americans has been summoned to give testimony to its national loyalty (2). The graves of young Americans who answered the call to service surround the globe (3).

Now the trumpet summons us again – not as 22
a call to bear arms, though arms we need;
not as a call to battle, though embattled we
are – but a call to bear the burden of a long
twilight struggle, year in and year out,
'rejoicing in hope, patient in tribulation' –
a struggle against the common enemies
of man: tyranny, poverty, disease, and war
itself (1).

Can we forge against these enemies a grand 23
and global alliance, North and South, East
and West, that can assure a more fruitful life
for all mankind? Will you join in that
historic effort (1)?

In the long history of the world, only a few 24
generations have been granted the role of
defending freedom in its hour of maximum
danger (1). I do not shrink from this responsibility – I welcome it (2). I do not believe
that any of us would exchange places with
any other people or any other generation
(3). The energy, the faith, the devotion
which we bring to this endeavor will light
our country and all who serve it – and the
glow from that fire can truly light the
world (4).

And so, my fellow Americans: ask not what 25
your country can do for you – ask what you
can do for your country (1).

My fellow citizens of the world: ask not what 26
America will do for you, but what together
we can do for the freedom of man (1).

Finally, whether you are citizens of America 27
or citizens of the world, ask of us the same
high standards of strength and sacrifice
which we ask of you (1). With a good
conscience our only sure reward, with
history the final judge of our deeds, let us go
forth to lead the land we love, asking His
blessing and His help, but knowing that here
on earth God's work must truly be our own
(2).

Essential reading

Halliday, M. A. K. and Hasan, R. (1976) *Cohesion in English*. London: Longman.

Hoey, M. (1991) *Patterns of Lexis in Text*. Oxford: Oxford University Press, ch. 3.

Jones, R. H. (2012) Section B2: 'Cohesion and Coherence'. In R. H. Jones, *Discourse Analysis: A Resource Book for Students*. London/New York: Routledge.

Mullany, L. and Stockwell, P. (2010) *Introducing English Language: A Resource Book for Students*. London/New York: Routledge, pp. 20–3.

PART II

Critical Approaches to Discourse

Chapter 4

Critical Analysis: Context and Persuasion

4.1 What is power?

In this part of the book I first examine, in this chapter, two concepts that are central to all critical analysis of discourse: context and persuasion. I present a theory of persuasion and illustrate how this works with reference to a speech by a very young and possibly aspiring leader. In Chapter 5 I analyse the verbal processes of modality and transitivity that are employed in critical linguistics. I follow this in Chapter 6 with an account of one of the most well-known critical linguistic approaches – the discourse-historical approach associated with Ruth Wodak. I illustrate how naming choices reflect underlying value systems as well as integrating within this chapter a discussion of argument theory drawing on the work of Stephen Tolmin. In critical discourse approaches a concern with how arguments are constructed is a point of continuity with earlier classical approaches to rhetoric. I shall begin by considering a topic equally important to critical discourse: the question of power.

Critical discourse analysts believe that language is crucial in determining social power relationships. They identify how differences in power and knowledge are created by inequalities in access to linguistic resources – for example, by inequality of access to high-quality education – and how we can identify these imbalances of power by the analysis of language. Critical analysis is concerned in particular with the 'abuse of social power by a social group', so we should remember that:

◇ Relations of domination are studied from the perspective of, and in the interests of, the dominated group, on the assumption that the powerful do not need the help of linguists.
◇ It can be shown that the discursive actions of the dominant group are illegitimate; this means that they do not have the right to use language to enforce their power.
◇ There are also viable *alternatives* to the discourses of the dominant, and that the use of these alternatives could benefit the dominated group(s).

Critical linguists ask themselves why, of all possible language uses, *one* particular language feature is chosen from an almost unlimited range of options, and the effect of this feature on social relations. Language represents a state of affairs: 'in such a way that it either reflects, more or less closely, the social relations of the participants, or it projects – more or less plausible – versions of such a relation. The motivating dynamic for the choice of one form rather than another is a power-difference' (Kress, 1992, p. 89). This point of view assumes that power is not distributed equally in society and that language is central to how this power is enforced. Rogers (2011) provides an excellent theoretical introduction to critical discourse analysis – organized around the work of James Paul Gee, Norman Fairclough and Gunther Kress. Gee (2011) places especial importance on the influence of context which he analyses in terms of 'situated meanings', and 'figured worlds'.

Power is a central notion in critical discourse analysis and can be taken to mean the way that a particular social group is able to enforce its will over other social groups. Power is when a powerful social group (A) persuades another social group (B) to do things that are in A's best interests, and prevents B from doing the things that are in B's best interests. We should also distinguish between legitimate and illegitimate forms of control: that is, between power and the abuse of power, as van Dijk (2008a, p. 9) puts it: 'Traditionally control is defined as control over the actions of others. If such control is also in the interest of those who exercise such power and against the interest of those who are controlled we may speak of power abuse.' Critical discourse analysis is interested in the detailed analysis of social and political relations of power, dominance and inequality, and in the role of discourse in their reproduction in, and permeation through, society. Social variables such as gender, race, ethnicity, region, social class, sexual orientation or physical body/capability are all potentially of relevance in working out how power is distributed and exercised in a society.

However, all societies are formed around power relations – as good parents should have legitimate control over their children, and are criticized when they do not, so teachers have legitimate authority over their students, and in general society has legitimate forms of control over those who commit crimes. Some inequalities are normal or legitimate because without them society could not operate. In critical discourse analysis we are interested in the *abuse* of language and power: that is, when power is being used illegitimately. But how do we know when power is being used illegitimately, and who is to decide whether it is or not? Reisigl's (2008a) answer to these questions is that texts are illegitimate when they have *negative mental consequences* – that is, they contribute to disinformation, stereotypes and prejudices. However, decisions about when mental effects are negative will ultimately depend on the individual's ability *to demonstrate and to argue that they are.* So critical discourse analysis sees texts as a site of contestation or struggle – in only a few cases would all analysts agree that a text has a negative consequence. In the majority of cases it will be up to the analyst to demonstrate that a particular use of language is *illegitimate* and that there is a preferable alternative; even then, a case still needs to be argued as to the perspective from which this alternative is deemed preferable.

One major means by which discourse is controlled is through access to, and control over, particular types of text, or genres. It is not always easy to identify powerful groups, but they probably include politicians because they make laws; lawyers who interpret them; and the policemen who have the authority to enforce them should they so wish. But money symbolizes power as much as does the legal system, and so those who control money, such as chief executives of financial institutions and insurance companies, and traders in stocks and shares, are also powerful. Those who control access to information through technology, such as leaders in the computer industry, are also powerful. In reality it is often quite hard to gain access to forums of power, because restricted access to information is a key means of social control. Then there are other groups whose power is perhaps more *symbolic* than substantial, these include journalists who write news stories; makers of TV and radio programmes; those who write books, artists, directors – maybe even university professors: all these groups influence our values, beliefs and ideologies through their representations of social reality. Because these symbolic elites contribute to the making of public knowledge, their texts are often more readily accessible to analysts.

We should always be aware of *whose* voices we are hearing and *who* has access to the public mind – usually through some type of privileged access to the media. Politicians speak as representatives of political parties and so their speeches reflect the perspective of their party as much as themselves as individuals; they also contain a range of voices – usually those of the various audiences to whom they appeal. There is, of course, a wide range of sub-genres of speeches, and Reisigl (2008a, 2008b) provides a valuable overview of these. Political speeches constitute a highly accessible source of data because, once spoken, political speeches are in the public domain.

Exercise 4.1

➤ Write your own definition of 'power'.
➤ Write three examples of legitimate uses of power and three examples of illegitimate uses of power.

4.2   Critical discourse analysis, context and circumstances

One of the hallmarks of critical discourse analysis is close attention to social context: the identity and relative social positions of speaker and addressee, and the role of language in constructing these relationships. Critical analysis of public communication maps out correspondences between particular language and other semiotic choices, and the underlying purposes and intentions that provide an explanation of these choices. This mapping and explanation involves identifying the speaker's choices and relating these to the particular social context in which the speech was made, and the speech's impact, allowing us to infer the speaker's purposes – which may not be evident from an analysis that does not refer to a social context. We need to observe and record key event details around a speech, such as when, where and to whom it was made. Analysis of circumstances involves identifying the speaker's beliefs and his or her purposes in making a speech, as well as identifying the audience's beliefs, how these influenced the speech and how they were influenced by it. The defining characteristic, then, of discourse analysis is close attention to 'context'; however, this term seems to conceal the fact that in critical discourse analysis we need to analyse a range of 'contexts', which is why I prefer the more general term 'speech circumstances'. These are the situation in which a speech was given, the cognitive states of the speaker and audience, the processes through which a speech was generated, and those involved in its delivery. It is motivated by the idea

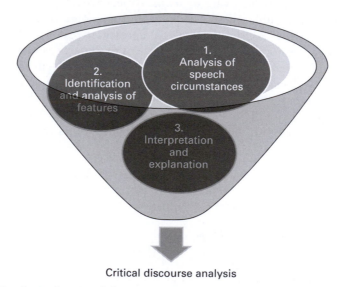

Critical discourse analysis

Figure 4.1   Stages in critical discourse analysis of public communications

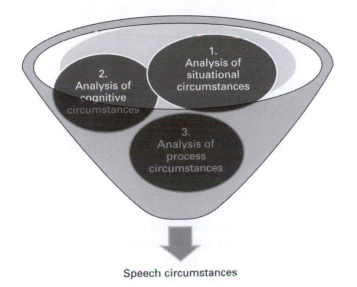

Speech circumstances

Figure 4.2   Stage 1: analysis of speech circumstances

that analysing the reasons behind language choices helps us to understand how the social world is created.

Figure 4.1 summarizes the stages involved in critical discourse analysis. The diagram shows three stages in analysing public communication: analysis of the speech circumstances; analysis of linguistic and performance features; and interpreting and explaining these with reference to the speech circumstances. Each of the three stages will be explained in more detail below, starting with the analysis of speech circumstances, as summarized in Figure 4.2.

Analysing speech circumstances involves the following stages: considering the situation in which a speech was given and the states of mind of both speaker and audience; and consideration of both the process through which a speech was produced and the processes involved in its delivery. These stages are summarized below.

4.2.1   Stage 1: analysis of speech 'circumstances'

◇ *Situational circumstances*
  • Speech setting – speaker, location, date, occasion and audience
◇ *Cognitive circumstances ('background knowledge')*
  • Speaker's beliefs, assumptions and purpose
  • Audience's beliefs, assumptions and purpose
  • Interaction between speaker and audience's beliefs, assumptions and purposes

◇ *Process circumstances*
  • Interaction between speaker and speech writer
  • Norms of interaction between speaker and audience

Each of these will be considered in more detail below.

Situational circumstances
In the first stage we analyse the circumstances in which the speech was given. Situational circumstances concern details of the speech setting, such as the social identity of the speaker, where, when, to whom and on what occasion the speech was given. Other information that could be recorded is the duration of the speech (measured in time or number of words), and situational information such as dominant current issues of concern that are part of general knowledge, including what has happened in the world in the days or hours leading up to the speech. For example, at the time I was writing this paragraph, the American presidential election had been suspended temporarily as a result of a large hurricane affecting areas of the east coast of the USA.

Cognitive circumstances
Cognitive circumstances concern details of the state of knowledge of the participants and interaction between their states of knowledge. While cognitive circumstances could be referred to as 'background knowledge', I have not used this term because it is not really clear whether the source of this knowledge is in the mind of the speaker, the audience or the person reading the analysis; it is also not clear in what sense it is in the 'background'. It is important to consider both the speaker's pre-existing beliefs, prejudices and knowledge frames, and how these interact with those of his/her audience and other parties. For example, an audience that listens to a speech by a far-right speaker will know that the speaker is likely to have a strong negative view of immigration, and the speaker will know that the audience may have experienced some negative effects from this (or believed themselves to have done so) – and a person reading a critical analysis of the language of the far right will know both angles. It is the interaction between the audience's and speaker's beliefs that determines the choice of words such as 'flood', and metaphors relating to pressure, stress and burdens.

We should be wary of simplification. For example, when analysing audience beliefs and assumptions we should remember that the audiences addressed by political orators are often not homogeneous – in Britain, they are typically multi-ethnic and socially mixed – so that we may expect to hear a range of different voices. Some of the knowledge necessary for the first stage is more readily available – situational information is more accessible than cognitive information that relies on sources such as biographies.

Process circumstances

Process circumstances concern the processes between the participants in the production and delivery of a speech. Often the speech writer may be unseen, because his or her presence would undermine the authenticity of the speech, and there is a tension between the speech writer, who is aware of the social context of the speech, and the politician, who is more concerned with issues such as image and persona. For this reason a political orator may give an extemporary speech – improvised in response to a sense of mood. Information about this process is only available retrospectively from biographical accounts of retired politicians and speech writers. Nevertheless it is an important consideration and is becoming more accessible as speech writers are gaining prominence in their own right.

Process circumstances also include a knowledge of speech forms, of political events. or the norms of interaction between an orator and an audience; for example, whether cheering is permitted.

Exercise 4.2

Undertake an analysis of the situational, cognitive and process circumstances of John F. Kennedy's inaugural address (see the end of Chapter 3).

4.2.2   Stage 2: identification and analysis of features

The second stage, summarized in Figure 4.3, involves the identification and analysis of language and performance features, which could be at a number of different levels (language itself is a set of interlinking systems). We could analyse any of the following:

◊ Smaller units, such as lexical choices.
◊ Larger units, such as the syntactic patterns of sentences.
◊ Stylistic features that permeate a whole speech; these can include lexis and syntax metaphor and tone of voice, and, as we see later in the next chapter, command of the modal system of English.

When analysing words, we might consider to which semantic fields these words belong (for example 'war' or 'the family'); what parts of speech they are; and whether their associations are usually negative or positive. When analysing syntax, we might consider whether language is dense or simple; the extent to which agency is concealed by the use of noun forms; and the passive voice in preference to verb forms and the active voice. Stylistic features also include how certain a speaker is about the claims being made – typically through the use of modality. Of necessity, these levels of analysis interact with each other: for example, if a speaker expresses certainty during

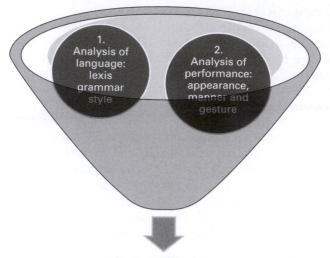

Analysis of features

Figure 4.3   Stage 2: identification and analysis of features

a speech by using forms such as 'must' or 'necessarily', this also affects the syntax of individual sentences. As well as the language that is used, equally, if not more important, are aspects of performance and delivery. When analysing performance and delivery we could examine any of the following:

◇ bodily appearance – hairstyle and eyes
◇ bodily performance – eye movements and hand gestures
◇ dress – formal or informal
◇ voice – prosodic features such as accent and voice quality
◇ use of notes, teleprompts or technology related to voice projection

Semiotic aspects, such as head position, eye contact or voice quality, may have a subliminal effect on a television audience. They have come increasingly to the fore with the introduction of adversarial style pre-election TV debates, in which audiences are influenced by each speaker's body position, gaze, smile, use of pointing and other hand gestures as well as by tone of voice and the emotional mood that is conveyed. For example, in the first of the 2012 TV presidential debates, Obama was considered to have lost ground to Mitt Romney because of his lack of sufficient interest and emotional energy – he appeared at times to be rather bored. These multi-modal features of communication are explored in Charteris-Black (2007).

This highlights an important practice in critical discourse analysis: while much purely textual material is available via the internet, so too are recordings of the speech delivery that allow us to match the non-verbal aspects with the linguistic ones. We should never forget that politics is a theatrical domain, and that the skills of the actor become more prominent in a media-driven culture.

Exercise 4.3

Watch a video of John F. Kennedy's inaugural address and analyse his performance and delivery.

4.2.3   Stage 3: interpretation and explanation

The third stage of Figure 4.1, summarized in Figure 4.4, aims to produce an understanding of the social world by interpreting the persuasive effect and social purpose of the speech; it explains how the situational and cognitive circumstances interact with the linguistic and performance features, and process circumstances to realize socially persuasive outcomes. These outcomes are described by van Dijk (2008a), using the concept of 'social cognition'. Stage 3 is an account of what motivates choices, and assumes that the language features observed in Stage 2 are not arbitrary, but motivated by the circumstances of the speech.

So, in the case above, views about immigration commonly arise through an act of social cognition, in which an orator says what he or she believes an audience wants to hear: discourse arises from an interaction between speaker and audience knowledge structures (for example, frames and

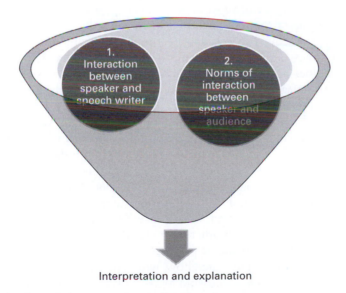

Interpretation and explanation

Figure 4.4   Stage 3: interpretation and explanation

schemata) and beliefs. For example, hearers will have a pre-existing template formed through stereotypical media representations of an immigrant whose primary purpose in travelling to a Western country is to obtain access to its welfare services without working. The Conservative Party sought to activate this schema in their 2005 campaign by using the poster slogan 'Are you thinking what we're thinking?' as it relied for its interpretation on a pre-existing schema for immigrants. The most powerful form of control over others is control over their minds – how people think as individuals is strongly influenced by the language employed to describe social relations, because language contributes to individual mental representations – beliefs, attitudes, ideologies and so on – that we have about the world. An example of the sorts of questions that arise when interpreting a speech is provided by the notion of 'recontextualization' (which Fairclough borrowed from Bernstein, 1990):

◇ Which elements of the event (or events in a chain of events) are present/ absent, prominent/backgrounded?
◇ What is the degree of abstraction/generalization from concrete events?
◇ How are events ordered?
◇ What is added in representing events – explanations/ legitimizations (reasons, causes, purposes), evaluations?

(Fairclough, 2003, p. 139)

Reactions to speeches do not necessarily *determine* how we think, as people also have their own attitudes and beliefs (based on their experiences) that influence how they critically evaluate texts as individuals. Explanation involves analysis of the interaction between the speaker and other parties involved in producing a speech, such as the speech writer and the audience. These can concern speech authorship – how far, in what ways and with what effect does an orator discuss his/her speech with the speech writer? How does the speaker interact with an audience? Typically, a speech exists in some form, usually written, prior to the time when it is delivered. It will usually be multi-authored, though individual politicians vary in how far they adapt the texts their speech writer(s) supply. Speech writers often have a clearer notion of the audience for the speech in mind; they make assumptions about the listeners' state of knowledge and this influences the choice of words, grammatical patterns and other language features, such as how complex or dense the speech is, the appropriateness of humour and so on. Individual politicians are often more concerned with projecting an image that differentiates them from other politicians, since the creation of style is crucial in developing their public persona.

In this section, I have illustrated how, while the classical rhetoric drew on the three appeals of ethos, pathos and logos, a discourse-based critical analysis requires attention to three phases: the analysis of speech circumstances, analysis of linguistic features, and finally interpretation and explanation. Within each of these phases are embedded phases; for example, the analysis of speech circumstances requires attention to three aspects of circumstance: situational, cognitive and process. But to understand discourse it is also necessary to consider the intentions that underlie a political speech – in this respect, then, we need to consider the notion of persuasion. I shall do this in the next section, before going on to illustrate how the interaction between circumstance and intention unfurls in actual language use. This will be done in the next chapter by considering how persuasive language relies on a command of modality.

Exercise 4.4

Undertake an interpretation and explanation of President Kennedy's inaugural address.

4.3   Persuasion

I have outlined in Charteris-Black (2011) an approach to persuasion which I shall summarize here. When we say that someone has been persuaded we usually mean that they have changed their point of view about a topic according to the influence of a persuasive agent, and that this changing of mind might be marked by an expression such as 'You are right'. In this sense there is no such thing as unsuccessful persuasion. Effectively 'being right' is central to persuasion and I suggest that there are five primary means by which an orator can get audiences to believe that he or she is right; these are by:

◇ having the right intentions
◇ thinking right
◇ sounding right
◇ telling the right story
◇ looking right

Not all are likely to occur when a particular speech is made, but in most cases a speaker will rely on more than one of these methods. The means of persuasion are summarized in Figure 4.5. It may be helpful to illustrate each in turn with reference to the speech given by Rory Weal, the 16-year-old orator referred to at the start of this book, to the Labour Party conference in September 2011. A video of the speech is readily available on YouTube.

When Weal said, 'I ask David Cameron: what does he advise when I can't afford to go to school any more?' he appeared to be sincere, and as

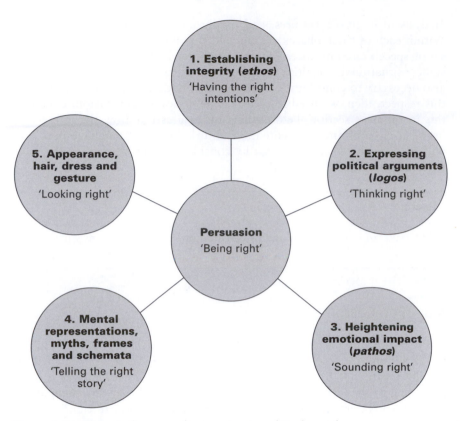

Figure 4.5   Rhetorical means of persuasion in political speeches
Source: Based on Figure 1.1 in Charteris-Black (2011, p. 14).

'having the right intentions' for a 16-year-old: to improve his situation by education. Classical rhetorical theory recognized the importance of the orator establishing his moral character or 'ethos'; in a sense an audience can only ever be persuaded by someone they respect, so this is a necessary prerequisite for the other so-called artistic proofs. Ethos expressed itself through demonstrating wisdom and expertise, through virtuous behaviour, and by demonstrating goodwill towards an audience. The measure of a speaker's ethos would be whether he or she prioritized his/her own interests or those of the public. Here the speaker seemed to be demonstrating intentions, expertise and a level of public concern that was appropriate for someone of his age.

'Thinking right' implies stating an argument and providing relevant evidence in support of it, as well as the necessary logical transitions. In this case Weal began his speech with a clear statement of his main argument: 'This government appears to have taken a bit of a dislike to young people', which was then supported with reference to unemployment statistics for young people, and changes in the funding of education, with the increase in tuition fees and removal of the educational maintenance allowance (EMA).

'Sounding right' requires the ability to evoke some emotional response from an audience; here, the young speaker clearly evoked feelings of protection and concern from the audience. Rhetorical competence contributes to 'sounding right' by demonstrating the ability to engage with an audience in a personal way by speaking fluently without long pauses, or over-reliance on a script prepared by others; it involves confidence and self-belief – all qualities that the young Rory Weal had on this occasion. Engagement with an audience can lead to laughter. After the speaker made his initial statement he paused and there was a little audible laughter around the arena – perhaps sparked off by the euphemism 'a bit of a dislike', but triggered by the pause. It also implies a command of traditional rhetorical figures – and as we have seen, he used a rhetorical question, and he followed this question with two further ones to produce a triple structural repetition: 'What does he advise when I can't buy the materials and textbooks I need to go to school?' and 'What does he think I should do when I can't afford to go on a school trip?' Finally 'sounding right' can also be expressed by phonological features such as accent, and here the young speaker has a strong 'estuary English' accent – the one that is growing fastest among young middle-class speakers throughout southern England.

The young orator then raised the empathetic appeal further by narrating a personal life-story event that led to his entry into politics:

> Two and a half years ago the home I had lived in since birth was repossessed; we had nothing, no money, no savings, I owe my entire well-being and that of my family to the welfare state, that is why I joined the Labour Party, that very same welfare state is being ruthlessly ripped apart by a vicious right-wing Tory-led government.

'Telling the right story' means providing a set of frames or schemata that fit with the audience's assumptions about how the world works. Here, the emotional impact is heightened by creating a contrast, or antithesis, between sources of protection – the Labour Party and the welfare state – and a source of danger – the Conservative Party. The welfare state is represented as protecting him at a time of when he was at his most vulnerable – a time of family break-up, and the social entity that threatens his well-being is 'the right-wing Tory-led government'. Vulnerability is conveyed by listing the hallmarks of poverty, and danger suggested by animal metaphors: the verb 'rip apart', the adjective 'vicious' and the adverb 'ruthlessly'. Word choices activate a script that the audience would be familiar with – the unsympathetic Thatcher-led government of the 1980s and its associations with social unrest and hardship for some sections of society. At the level of myth, 'telling the right story' often entails the creation of heroes – here the welfare state; villains – the Tory party; and victims – here, a defenceless young person.

Finally, equally important is 'looking right', and here the orator looked precisely that – young and innocent like a schoolboy, wearing a smart jacket, a white shirt and a tie, tied just off-centre as a schoolboy would. The fact that he is rather a good-looking young man with clean, straight hair and smooth skin no doubt contributed at an unconscious level to his over-all appeal. 'Looking right' can also include other visual semiotic modes such as gesture; emotional commitment is conveyed by hand movements – imme-diately after he said 'I ask David Cameron' he paused and raised open-palm hands from mid-level up to touch his shoulder to emphasize the emotional nature of his plea: he is a supplicant who is appealing to the prime minister rather than a tub-thumping socialist. Much depends on the initial rapport (or lack of it) that is created between orator and audience, which is why, in classical oratory, it was considered very important to establish a speaker's ethical credentials early in the speech – through, for example, displaying humility, just as Rory Weal does here.

How do we know when public communication is successful? The effect(s) of a speech can be judged in real time by audience reactions during a speech, such as applause. After the first rhetorical question, 'I ask David Cameron: what does he advise when I can't afford to go to school any more?' there was a full ten seconds of applause, and after the conclusion of this section of the speech with the statement 'This government is showing how completely out of touch it is with the lives of ordinary people in the UK' there were eight seconds of applause – implying that the case had been well argued. Following the statement that the 'welfare state is being ruth-lessly ripped apart by a vicious right-wing Tory-led government' there were 14 seconds of applause, implying that this had had a powerful emotional appeal to the audience. The oratorical success of the speech coda: 'It is up to us in the Labour Party to get a vision of what a better Britain looks like – let's get to work' was indicated by loud cheering as well as lengthy applause.

We also know how successful public communication is by media responses following a speech: has it shifted from being an exercise in oratory to one in public communication? In this case, most of the press ran stories the following day, though these were coloured by the political loyal-ties of the newspaper. However, the fact that the *Daily Mail* employed a reporter to investigate the boy's personal family history is indicative of the speech's impact. Impact can also be measured by straw polls, individuals' responses in focus groups or interviews, and increasingly, though with a tendency to hyperbole and abuse – blogs.

I decided to evaluate the theory of persuasion outlined in Figure 4.5 by seeing to what extent some comments made in *Daily Mail* blogs could be classified into each of its five elements. For each element I have selected a comment that supported the speaker and another that criticized him. The results are shown below.

Having the right intentions

For ?:
an inspired speech by an earnest young man who has had a very under-privileged upbringing, poor thing. Adjusting to life after no more private education. Poor thing … thank goodness for the welfare system

Against:
Like the rioters, he is a teenage subscriber to the 'something for nothing' culture, but far more insidious. Rather than just taking advantage of it, he actually promotes it. You can already see the next Blair in the making – the contrived 'gavel banging' hand gestures to emphasize the points. So indignant, such a sense of entitlement. You'd think he was talking about real injustice here. This nauseating, deluded little class warrior will surely be leading the socialists in the near future.

Thinking right

For:
the day you become, work with or have friends who end up bankrupt, homeless, jobless, unable to work through ill-health or experience the 'nanny state' I think your narrow-minded idealistic view may change. I was a Tory who believed it wasn't as bad as they made out, loads of people cheated and they just didn't try and find a solution. I WAS VERY VERY WRONG. Our social security system saves many from becoming impov-erished and helps people retrain to get a job. IT CREATES WEALTH!!

Against:
I don't know anybody who needs EMA. It was supposed to be for enabling people on low income to get an education but it went to people from fami-lies that were perfectly capable of buying textbooks, railcards, season tick-ets, bus fares – the lot. Everybody I knew who received EMA spent it on weed, clothes and petrol. I recognise that welfare is necessary and am glad that EMA is being replaced, not scrapped, but EMA was just lavish.

Sounding right

For:
Even a bit of estuary 'Cock-a-Ney' 'H'-dropping for good measure. Well rehearsed though and all credit to you lad. Makes the head boy look all grown up.

Telling the right story

For:
GO RORY!

Yours is the voice of young modern Labour speaking for all Britain young and old. LibDemTories, by contrast, are washed-out dinosaurs.

Against:
A number of comments attack the authenticity of his story that the welfare state saved him from poverty:

He's the son of a man who was a millionaire property developer, and he went to a private school until his dad's business went bust under the Gordon Brown Labour government. Now he goes to a selective grammar school, which Labour policy opposes. Although Labour politicians have a habit of using things that they wish to deprive the rest of us of. So Weal would make a typical Labour politician. Although it must be said that he's a better actor than that 6th form debater (and fake) Miliband.

Rory, if you can't afford to get to school, I suggest you ask your multi-millionaire property developer father Jonathan Weal, if it's that much of a problem for him, maybe he should have sent you to a state school and saved the £14,000 annual tuition charges at the grammar school he sent you to, you typical lying socialist scumbag.

Looking right

For:
Who looks like a leader and who looks like the 16-year-old?

Against:
A number of comments show awareness of some components of the persuasive model I have outlined that alerted the bloggers' cheat detectors:

Surely his Mum should have straightened his tie before he went on to the platform. Echoes of Tory Boy Hague's speech all those years ago (not in content obviously … !). Pauses for applause (after just 15 seconds!), hand gestures, eye contact with autocue … clearly coached and groomed by the Millbank machine.

16-year-olds in today's age, dressed in sharp suits is not a natural or good look. call me a cynic … but this speech is just depressing … the hand gestures, pacing, raising of the voice etc. … its all been ruthlessly pre-organized, and the kid knows it.

I mean he says he can't afford a school trip, but he's wearing an extremely expensive looking suit and tie. if it doesn't sit right, you know something's amiss.

Overall, the negative comments outweighed the positive ones, but this is typical of the genre of the blog, which makes this medium unreliable as a source of insight into long-term impact. Longer-term and more reliable effects on audience beliefs can be measured by public opinion polls and eventually, of course, by voting behaviour.

Exercise 4.5

➤ Select a speech of your choice and analyse it terms of the rhetorical means of persuasion summarized in Figure 4.5.
➤ Is there any evidence in blogs of the effectiveness of these rhetorical means for persuasion?

Now we have seen how persuasion works within a social context we need to consider in more detail a method for analysing the linguistic features of the language that occurs in speeches – and primary among these is exploitation of the modal resources of English.

4.4   Summary

In this chapter I began by defining 'power', I have demonstrated how critical discourse analysis requires the context of speeches to be analysed, and this in turn requires attention to speech circumstance by analysis of linguistic and performance features, followed by interpretation and explanation of these with reference to the speech circumstances. I then outlined a theory of persuasion and suggested that a crucial persuasive strategy in speeches is the expression of a high degree of self-conviction. Various linguistic means can contribute to how convincing, and how convinced, a speaker sounds through the presentation of opinions as 'fact'; this is done by, for example, the use of the simple present tense, the use of short sentences, and by drawing on other modal resources of English to produce 'Conviction Rhetoric' – a concept that will be discussed more fully in the following chapter.

Essential reading

Fairclough, N. (2003) *Analysing Discourse: Textual Analysis for Social Research.* London: Routledge, pp. 1–18.

Fairclough, N. (2006) 'Global Capitalism and Critical Awareness of Language'. In A. Jaworski and N. Coupland, *The Discourse Reader*, 2nd edn. London: Routledge.

Richardson, J. E. (2007) *Analysing Newspapers*. Basingstoke: Palgrave Macmillan, ch. 1.

Rogers, R. (2011) *Critical Discourse Analysis in Education*, 2nd edn. New York/Oxford: Routledge, ch. 1.

Thomas, L. (2004) *Language, Society and Power*, 2nd edn. London/New York: Routledge, ch. 1.

van Dijk, T. (2008a) *Discourse and Power*. New York: Palgrave Macmillan, ch. 1.

Chapter 5

Social Agency and Modality

5.1 Agency

5.1.1 What is agency?

In this chapter I consider how agency is communicated through the choice of nouns and names, and through the choice of verbs and verbal processes. I then go on to analyse the grammatical system of English, to evaluate how political agents express uncertainty or, more commonly, conviction, through using the system of modality. The chapter therefore shifts from the broader concepts of context and persuasion to a more detailed analysis of the actual language through which speakers become persuasive by finding the right words for a particular set of speech circumstances.

A major contribution of critical linguists (for example, Fairclough, 2003) has been to explore how language is used in the representation of social agents, so that the presence of an agent can either be 'foregrounded' – brought to the front of our attention; or 'backgrounded' – that is, pushed further from the attention of the reader. The term 'agent' refers to the person or entity that performs an action described by a verb, or a process. An agent will therefore typically be a person who is named individually, though it could also be a social category, such as 'investors', 'welfare claimants' or 'scroungers'. Both the presence and the identity of social agents can either be made very clear by using language that states plainly who is doing what to whom, or it can be obscured, so that the subject–object relations in a process are unclear. Typically, speakers will foreground their own role in relation to events that they think will be evaluated positively, and their opponents' role in relation to events that they anticipate will be evaluated negatively. For example, following their election in 2010, the Conservative Party sought to foreground the agency of the previous Labour government in relation to the cause of the financial crisis of 2008 and to background their own role in contributing to this through their policies of public spending reductions:

who busted our banks, who smothered our businesses ... who racked up our debts, who wrecked our economy ... who ruined our reputation,

who risked our future ... who did this? – Labour did this – and this country should never forget it. (David Cameron, September 2012)

Conversely, speakers will background their own role in events that may be
evaluated negatively, and their opponents' role in events that may be evaluated positively. For example, in the same speech, Cameron said:

> Though the challenge before us is daunting, I have confidence in our
> country. Why? Because Britain can deliver. We can do big things. We saw
> it this summer. The Jubilee, the Olympics, the Paralympics ...

Here the fact that much of the planning for the Olympics had been done by
the previous Labour government is not mentioned, because the speaker
hopes that the success of the event will be related to the Conservative
government that was in power when it took place.

There are a number of ways in which agency can be manipulated in
language to give such positive or negative representations of political
actors. I shall begin by summarizing two broad linguistic categories that
influence representation:

◊ *Nominal forms* (that is, involving nouns): methods of foregrounding or
  backgrounding social agency by referring to social actors. These include
  the use of pronouns, individual names and social or professional roles or
  collective nouns.
◊ *Verbal processes*: methods of foregrounding or backgrounding social
  agency by using verbs in the active or passive voice, or by using transitive
  and intransitive verbs.

Halliday (1994) identified the importance of such nouns and verbs in influencing how processes are represented. According to his functional grammar,
which was adopted later by critical linguists such as Norman Fairclough,
there is a primary distinction between participants and processes, as follows:

◊ The *participants* are the people who are involved in a process. We can
  distinguish between actors who are the 'doers' of actions, and 'patients' –
  the people who are affected by what is done. The participants will either
  be present in the form of nouns, or concealed when it does not fit an
  author's intentions to make their identity explicit.
◊ The *process* is what happens, and is indicated by the verb. What is
  brought to our attention also depends on how verbs are employed to
  represent participants as being present or absent; as active or passive.

To understand how participants are represented, I shall first consider nominal forms and names.

5.1.2 Nominal forms and names

Initially, a speaker has to choose between a noun and a pronoun, and if a pronoun is selected, which person it will reflect; typically, in political rhetoric, speakers use 'we' in a rather loose way that could refer either to the speaker alone, or to his or her party, or to *any* group who he seeks to represent himself as speaking for – such as the nation or even the whole of humanity. Therefore it is always crucial to work out to whom 'we' refers in each context that this pronoun is used. For example, in his 2012 party conference speech, David Cameron uses 'we' to refer to a number of different groups. First, to the government (rather than all members of the Conservative Party): 'We knew then that it was not just the ordinary duties of office that we were assuming.' Soon after this, 'we' refers to the British public: 'All of my adult life, whatever the difficulties, the British people have at least been confident about one thing: we have thought we can pay our way.' And later, 'we' refers to all members of the Conservative Party: 'Since we gathered here in Birmingham on Sunday, British aid money has vaccinated 130,000 children around the world.' While the party is the most common referent of 'we', Cameron later uses 'we' to refer to him and his father: 'When I was a boy I remember once going on a long walk with him in the village where we lived.' The use of pronouns typically has a vagueness that is valuable to politicians, who need to make appeals to different audiences according to the topic they are addressing.

When nouns are used to refer to the participants, the identity of agents can either be revealed explicitly by using their names, or concealed by using a collective noun that refers to their institutional role or profession (for example, 'lawyer') or nationality (for example, 'an Afghan soldier', 'a Kurdish asylum seeker' and so on). When individuals are named specifically it is either to foreground the positive actions of supporters or negative actions of opponents. For example, it has become a characteristic of public communication to introduce and name individuals who are known to be supporters of the party and who are physically present in an audience. On other occasions, agents are referred to collectively using a very general noun (in the example above, Cameron referred to 'the British public'). Sometimes individual identity is concealed by referring to a person by his or her role in representing an institution – for example, 'a spokesman for British Gas/Scottish Power' and so on.

I shall illustrate how naming contributes to ideology, and propose that they are closely interlinked because relationships of power between different social groups are often realized in language through the selection of names. Three questions arise in the creation of difference through the naming of groups of people:

◇ What values are attached to particular groups – are they positive or
negative?
◇ How do these names arise?
◇ Are they acceptable or not?

The analysis of naming involves identifying the system of values that
underlies the choice of a name and *how* such a choice creates, constitutes
and reinforces a particular perspective or point of view. This involves identifying the names themselves, the traits that are associated with them, and
the perspectives they imply. The naming of a social group entails some
form of social differentiation – that is, the creation of differences between
some people and others on the basis of social class, gender, ethnicity, religion or any other identifiable variable that contributes to social identity.
The notion of 'difference' depends on two things: what is being taken as
the base line for 'normality' or 'homogeneity'; and to what this is
compared.

For example, professional footballers often find they have more in
common with other professional players – even though they may be from
different racial and ethnic backgrounds – because they are doing the same
type of job. This identification may exceed what they have in common with
others who share the same ethnicity but have a different educational background or are from a different social class. Footballers may have more similarities when compared with other footballers than they do when compared
with people from the same ethnic origin who are not footballers. The search
for sameness and difference is crucial to how people create social meaning.
Inevitably, this is inter-discursive, because each time a name is used in a
positive (or more likely a negative) way, it relates to the other occasions on
which the name is used. It is through intertextual and interdiscursive relations over time that stereotypes are created by names.

The media play a vital role in arbitrating between various social agents
– mainstream or minority groups or institutions – by deciding *which* names
will be employed in news stories. Lexical decisions made by the media can
be organized into a quadrangular diagram that involves two scales: one for
emphasis and one for positive/negative characteristics. The values on the
emphasis scale are: '+ or – emphasis' and values on the characteristics scale
are 'good' or 'bad characteristic'. So both good and bad features can either
be highlighted or hidden, as summarized in Figure 5.1.

When a group in power is referred to as 'a regime' this de-emphasizes the
positive characteristic of legitimacy that is implied when it is referred to as
a 'government'. Conversely, when it is referred to as an 'elected government' this emphasizes the positive characteristic of being democratic. If it is
referred to as a 'fascist regime' this emphasizes its negative characteristics.
Use of the term 'regime' is often a type of a coded threat that 'military intervention' is being planned. Use of 'military intervention' de-emphasizes the

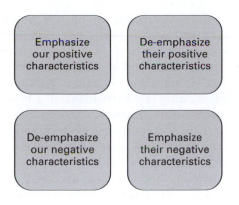

Figure 5.1   The ideological square
Source: van Dijk (1998, p. 267).

negative aspects of using armed force. Conversely, the term 'invasion' emphasizes the negative aspects of using force.

5.1.3   Verbal processes

Verbal processes are crucial in foregrounding or backgrounding actors, and in highlighting or concealing agency. Typically, agency can be present when the active voice of verbs is used or absent when the passive voice is used or when a material process is used, especially in the transitive form so that there is a clear distinction between a subject and an object. To clarify these terms, we need to go over some background grammar. There are four types of verbal process in English:

1 Verbal processes: for example, speaking, shouting, declaring.
2 Mental processes: for example, thinking, reminding, deciding.
3 Relational processes: for example, verbs such as 'have' and 'seem', which involve an agent and an attribute, for example, 'the nation is bankrupt'.
4 Material processes: these are physical actions and are divided into *transitive actions* which involve two or more participants – for example, 'Britain invaded Iraq'; and *intransitive actions* with only one participant – for example, 'Iraqi resistance collapsed'.

Transitivity refers to the relationship between participants and the roles they play in processes; it communicates the representation of actors, actions and those acted upon: what kinds of actions there are, who acts, and who is affected by their actions – so transitivity concerns the relationship between active agents and the entities they act upon. Transitivity choices also have an important effect in representing a situation from a particular perspective. An important distinction in English is between intransitive verbs – which *do not* take have an object, and transitive verbs – which *do* take an object. For example, the verb 'die' is intransitive because it only requires a subject (who died) and so highlights only *one* participant; whereas the verb 'kill' is transitive because it requires a subject *and* an object – therefore highlighting *two* participants in a process.

Table 5.1 is an extract from David Cameron's 2012 party conference speech; the verbs are shown in italics and their classification according to the verbal process and transitivity is in the right-hand column. The brief analysis in this table shows that mental verbs are used to indicate areas of shared knowledge between speaker and audience; for example, 'The Olympics reminded us how great it feels to be successful.' When Cameron wants to represent the attributes of countries, relational verbs are used – though these attributes can be positive or negative (and they are contrasted with reference to metaphors of health). When talking about those of countries that he admires, such as China, material verbs are used to represent actions as real and concrete. He also uses material verbs when giving prominence to his own active role in leading Britain: 'I am not going *to stand* here as Prime Minister and *allow* this country *to join* the slide.' He avoids the passive voice because he wants to give prominence to his own agency, and that of his party, in improving Britain's standing in the world. This use of material transitive verbs in the active voice occurs later in the speech, when emphasizing concrete achievements:

We're making things again.

In the last two years, Google, Intel, Cisco – the big tech firms – they've all set up new bases here.

And we are selling to the world again.

They saw the huge gap in the market– and they started a mobile banking firm.

I visited a business the other day that wanted to open a big factory just outside Liverpool.

In newspaper headlines, intransitive verbs can be used in place of transitive verbs to *conceal* who did what to whom, whereas, theoretically, transitive verbs could have been used in place of a relational verb to *reveal* who did what to whom. When analysing transitivity it is important to identify *all* the participants, processes and circumstances and then to evaluate the effect of this angle of viewing and what other linguistic means could have been employed to describe the same event.

Table 5.1   David Cameron's Conservative Party conference address, 2012

BRITAIN ON THE RISE

Big, Conservative things – *delivered*[1] by this government; *made*[2] possible by this party.	(1) Material transitive (2) Material transitive
We can *deliver.*[1] We can *do*[2] big things.	(1) Material transitive (2) Material transitive
The Olympics *reminded*[1] us how great it *feels*[2] to be successful.	(1) Mental (2) Mental
But we mustn't *let*[1] that warm glow *give*[2] us a false sense of security.	(1) Material transitive (2) Mental transitive
All around the world, countries *are*[1] on the rise.	(1) Relational
Yes, we've been *hearing*[1] about China and India for years …	(1) Mental
… but it's hard to *believe*[1] what's *happening*[2] in Brazil, in Indonesia; in Nigeria too.	(1) Mental (2) Material intransitive
Meanwhile, the old powers *are*[1] on the slide.	(1) Relational
What do the countries on the rise *have*[1] in common?	(1) Relational
They *are*[1] lean, fit, obsessed with enterprise, spending money on the future – on education, incredible infrastructure and technology.	(1) Relational
And what do the countries on the slide *have*[1] in common?	(1) Relational
They're[1] fat, sclerotic, over-regulated, spending money on unaffordable welfare systems, huge pension bills, unreformed public services.	(1) Relational
I *sit*[1] in those European Council meetings where we *talk*[2] endlessly about Greece …	(1) Material intransitive (2) Verbal
… while on the other side of the world, China *is moving*[1] so fast it's *creating*[2] a new economy the size of Greece every three months.	(1) Material intransitive (2) Material transitive
I am not going to *stand*[1] here as prime minister and *allow*[2] this country to *join*[3] the slide.	(1) Material intransitive (2) Material transitive (3) Relational
My job – our job – is to *make*[1] sure that in this twenty-first century, as in the centuries that came before, our country, Britain, *is*[2] on the rise.	(1) Material intransitive (2) Relational
And we here know how that *is done.*[1]	(1) Material transitive
It *is*[1] the collective result of individual effort and aspiration …	(1) Relational
… the ideas you *have,*[1] the businesses you *start,*[2] the hours you *put in.*[3]	(1) Relational (2) Material transitive (3) Material transitive
Aspiration *is*[1] the engine of progress.	(1) Relational

5.2   Modality

5.2.1   What is modality?

When we think of a politician we usually have an image of someone who is very convinced that what he or she is saying is true, perhaps with a finger raised to the heavens claiming divine authority! Politicians are rarely hesitant or doubtful for very long because, like astrologers, racing tipsters or surgeons, their role requires them to sound convincing and authoritative. One way to do this is by speaking with a high level of conviction to make what is possible appear certain. As with other types of persuasive speaker – estate agents, horoscope writers or purveyors of alternative medicines – they are unlikely to air serious doubts about the likelihood of their predictions coming true, and when they do so this will usually be for an ulterior rhetorical purpose – such as changing the mood. When orators are seeking to convince audiences in English they will inevitably be drawing on its complex system of modality characterized by modal verbs such as 'should' and 'might' as well as many other features that will be discussed below.

The projection of a powerful and convincing image when speaking is sometimes referred to as 'conviction rhetoric'; this is where a speaker conveys a strong sense of purpose and self-belief through a range of word choices, figures of speech and delivery features such as fluency, volume and intensity of expression. The combined effect of these rhetorical features is to convey certitude and authority. Conviction rhetoric appeals to ethos and pathos; the conviction originates in a sense of moral purpose and is emotionally intense because ethical beliefs require passionate commitment if they are to be realized. When speakers express strong emotions it is usually because they hope to evoke similar emotions in their audiences, but the first person they have to convince is him/herself.

Charteris-Black (2011) argues that Tony Blair drew on conviction rhetoric to reformulate his beliefs about 'good' and 'evil' into powerful myths of creation and destruction. It came readily to him because his Christianity provided a strong ideological basis for his views on international affairs, especially in relation to the weapons of mass destruction (WMD) that he claimed Iraq was concealing. His self-righteous wrath at Saddam Hussein's duplicity contributed to arguments as to why Saddam's 'regime' should be ended. Blair often talked about morality in terms of conflict, and conflict in terms of morality. For example, he used personifications to provide self-representations as a moral arbiter, and chose verbs that implied the use of force such as: *seize, strip away* and *expose*. But there are dangers in using conviction rhetoric to demonize political opponents, because when views are expressed with such force they become irreversible – ignoring actualities and evidence. The unswerving commitment to an unpopular war in Iraq eventually led to Blair's downfall. Other politicians, such as Margaret

Thatcher (whom he admired) showed a similar sense of self-assurance and moral certainty – and with a similar outcome.

Political language looks to remove doubt, because people expect their leaders to present a plan of well-defined future actions, rather than a set of hypothetical abstractions. Sounding convincing about the future means knowing what action to take now so that the future is represented as something within reach. The way that leaders communicate this state of knowledge, truth and conviction is by drawing on the modality system of English. I shall illustrate this with the rhetoric around a key political decision: whether to take military action against another state; this is likely to be recommended in language that emphasizes that this state presents a real material threat – not just a hypothetical one. Consider the following transcript of a speech by Margaret Thatcher (the style features in the extract will be cross-referred in the analysis that follows):

> We in Europe <u>have</u> unrivalled freedom. But *we must never take it for granted*. <u>The dangers to it are greater</u> now than they have ever been since 1945. <u>The threat</u> of the Soviet Union <u>is ever present</u>. It **is growing** continually. Their military spending <u>goes up</u> by 5 per cent a year. A Russian nuclear submarine is launched every six weeks. Every year the Russians <u>turn out</u> over 3,000 tanks and 1,500 combat aircraft. Their military research and development <u>is</u> enormous.
>
> The Soviet forces are organised and trained for attack. <u>The Russians</u> <u>do not tell us</u> why **they are making** this tremendous and costly effort to increase their military power. Heaven knows, <u>they have enough to do</u> on the consumer side. But <u>we cannot ignore</u> the fact that this power **is there and growing**. So far, the North Atlantic alliance has preserved our freedom. But in recent years the Soviet Union's growing strength has allowed it to pull ahead of the Alliance in many fields. We and our allies are resolved to make the effort that will restore the balance. *We must keep up all our defences*, whether nuclear or conventional. It <u>is</u> no good having first-class nuclear forces if we can be overwhelmed by an enemy's conventional forces. Deterring aggression cannot be piecemeal. If <u>it is,</u> our effort is wasted. (Speech to the Conservative Party, 12 October 1979)

Margaret Thatcher was arguing a strong case for increasing military expenditure, on the grounds that the Soviet Union presented a major threat; she does this in different ways, as follows:

◇ She emphasizes obligation through short, clear statements using phrases with the modal verb 'must' (in italics).
◇ She communicates the truth of what she is saying by using the simple present tense (underlined): for example, 'the dangers to it are greater',

'the threat ... is ever present' and so on); the present tense is often used with factive verbs to represent beliefs as objective facts.

◇ She provides evidence in the form of lists of weaponry, statistics and so on.

◇ She uses continuous or progressive forms (in bold) to describe processes that are ongoing; for example, 'growing' is repeated to emphasize that the Soviet threat is increasing.

◇ She uses closely related present participles ('deterring aggression') and the present perfect for actions continuing right up to the present ('have ever been'; 'has preserved').

◇ Some of the verbs are in the passive voice: 'is launched', which is often used when the subject of an action is unknown or not relevant. It does not matter particularly who launched the nuclear submarine: it is the actuality that is the focus.

The overall rhetorical effect of Thatcher's use of verbs is to express with certainty and conviction the point of view that the Soviet Union presents a serious threat, and something needs to be done about this. The fact that this is *a point of view* is concealed – it is presented as a state of affairs rather than as a leader's opinion.

The linguistic term that describes *how* certainty and conviction are expressed is 'modality'; this is the linguistic means for conveying *how sure someone is about what he or she is saying*. It assumes a basic distinction between (1) what is said; and (2) what the speaker thinks about what is said. So it describes how people communicate the relationship between *the things they are saying* and *their own mental state*: how they use language to give a perspective on their utterances. It indicates the speaker's stance, attitude or position towards what he or she is saying, and in particular the extent to which he or she believes it is:

◇ true;
◇ necessary or obligatory; or
◇ desirable or undesirable.

All of these convey how far the speaker is committed towards the truth of what he or she is saying. In the above example, Thatcher argues that the Soviet Union is truly a threat and therefore it is necessary, obligatory and desirable to do something about it.

Since critical text analysis is concerned with representations of states of knowledge and belief, the analysis of modality is essential. Commitment is an important part of how a speaker represents his or her thoughts to others. As Lyons (1977, p. 725) notes: 'when we communicate some proposition to another person, we do so, normally because we wish to influence in some way his beliefs, his attitudes or his behaviour'. In this respect, modality can be equated with a speaker taking a particular stance or position on what he or she is saying by providing an ongoing commentary about what is probable, or morally necessary. In the above example, Margaret Thatcher wanted to make as strong a case as possible for raising the level of military investment on the basis that (1) there was evidence of a real threat; and (2) this was the right thing to do, so she uses language to reduce the subjective element in her representation of the Soviet Union – so that it is no longer seen just as a representation of a state of affairs but as a reality; no longer subjective but objective. As Palmer (1986, p. 16) put it:

> Modality in language is concerned with subjective characteristics of an utterance, and it could even be further argued that subjectivity is an essential criterion for modality. Modality could, that is to say, be defined as the grammaticalisation of a speaker's (subjective) attitudes and opinions.

5.2.2   Levels of modality

In the discussion over whether to go to war with Iraq in 2003, the British government produced a lengthy 'dossier' investigating the evidence that Iraq had weapons of mass destruction; however, to strengthen the support for their claim that Iraq presented a serious threat to world peace, certain modifications were made to this dossier. Consider the effects of changing the modality in the following:

Original text:
Iraq **may be able to** deploy weapons of mass destruction to attack British bases within 45 minutes.

After editing:
Iraq **are able** to deploy weapons of mass destruction to attack British bases within 45 minutes.

In the original text a modal verb is used ('may') and in the edited version this is replaced by a verb in the simple present tense ('are'); 'may be able to' expresses a considerably lower level of commitment to the truth than 'are able to'. This, of course, heightened the threat posed by Iraq (as Mrs Thatcher's speech did for the Soviet Union) and therefore strengthened the grounds of the argument for military action.

A high degree of commitment to the truth of a claim implies that the speaker is authoritative *because* he/she has evidence for what he/she is claiming, and that subjective opinion is based on objective evidence. A lower degree of commitment to truth status implies a degree of uncertainly, perhaps because there is less evidence or because the outcome of an action

Table 5.2   Modality – degrees of commitment and certainty

Must, have to, will, ought to truth or obligation	Highest degree of commitment
May, could, should Might Should not	Low degree of commitment to truth or obligation,
Could not, must not	Negative degree of commitment to truth or obligation

is less sure. This means that modality can be used to represent events that are uncertain (when viewed objectively) as if they were certain, and events that are certain (objectively) as if they were uncertain. This is very important in influencing perceptions of the truthfulness or rightfulness of utterances, as degrees of certainty can be manipulated for rhetorical effect.

Modality can be conveyed to express ideas about truth and obligation using a range of modal forms that can be positioned on a scale according to the level of the commitment they express, as shown in Table 5.2. So, when Thatcher said 'We must keep up all our defences, whether nuclear or conventional', she was expressing the highest degree of commitment by emphasizing obligation. And when she said, 'we must never take it for granted' she was expressing a negative degree of commitment to obligation. As well as using modal verbs such as 'must', or 'should', the speaker may also vary the level of certainty or commitment to the truthfulness of an utterance through the lexical choice of the verb itself, as in the following list:

◊ 'I *think* that ...' or 'I *reckon* that' indicates that someone is speculating about a personal view.
◊ 'I *conclude* ...' or 'I *claim* that' indicates that the speaker has deduced something from objective or empirical evidence.
◊ 'X *has told me* that ...' or 'it *is said* that ...' indicates that the speaker has verbal evidence because he/she has heard something.
◊ 'It *seems* that ...', 'it *appears* that ...' indicates a personal view based on some evidence.

Modality can also be communicated by using phrases containing adverbs or abstract nouns, as follows:

Adverbs: *certainly, necessarily, possibly*
Abstract nouns: it is *necessary* to; it is a *possibility* that; *certainty*

The speaker makes choices according to the level of truth or obligation that he or she wishes to communicate. While there are many points on a scale

Table 5.3   Levels of modality

	Truth	Obligation	Modal verb
High	certainly	required to	must/have to
Medium	probably	supposed to	could/would/should
Low	possibly	allowed to	may/might

of conviction, these levels of modality might be simplified by summarizing them into three levels, as shown in Table 5.3.

Exercise 5.1

Read the following section from a speech given by David Cameron soon after he became prime minister. Identify where modality is used and what level of modality is expressed.

He was speaking at the Conservative Party conference on the topic of proposed reductions in government spending ('cuts') and I have inserted numbers for cross-reference purposes.

That's why it's right to deal with this problem now, and right to deal with it properly (1). And I promise you that (2) if we pull together to deal with these debts today, then just a few years down the line the rewards will be felt by everyone in our country. The big society spirit means facing up to this generation's debts, not shirking responsibility. ... And here I want to say something to the people who got us into this mess. The ones who racked up more debt in 13 years than previous governments did in three centuries (3) ... I tell you what: these Labour politicians, who nearly bankrupted our country, who left a legacy of debts and cuts, who are still in denial about the disaster they created (4). They must not be allowed anywhere near our economy, ever, ever again (5). Reducing spending will be difficult (6). There are programmes that will be cut (7). There are jobs that will be lost. There are things government does today that it will have to stop doing (8). (David Cameron, conference address, 6 October 2010)

5.2.3   Types of modality

There are two main types of modality, *epistemic* and *deontic*.

Epistemic modality
Epistemic modality refers to the level of commitment a speaker can express in relation to the truth, accuracy or certainty of what he or she is saying. So epistemic modality is concerned with how *possible* or how *probable* or *likely* it is that something has happened, is happening, or will happen. According to Coates (1983, p. 18) epistemic modality is not only

'concerned with the speaker's assumptions or assessment of possibilities' but also 'indicates the speaker's confidence (or lack of confidence) in the truth of the proposition expressed'.

Deontic modality

Deontic modality expresses a speaker's beliefs about the 'necessity or possibility of acts performed by morally responsible agents' (Lyons, 1977, p. 823). So deontic modality expresses the extent that the speaker is obliged to do something, or needs to do something, or has permission to do something. Ideas about *obligation, necessity* and *permission assume* that there are shared norms for evaluating behaviour as right and wrong without necessarily making these norms explicit. For this reason, deontic modality is also rhetorically influential.

I shall illustrate the difference between the two main types of modality and how they often interact with each other by analysing them in a crucial speech made by Tony Blair entitled 'We face a tough and stark choice'. The speech was given in the House of Commons on 18 March 2003, because Blair needed to obtain some political backing for his recommended strategy of supporting George W. Bush in an invasion of Iraq. There was a great deal of opposition to this, both in Britain and internationally, including the largest-ever demonstrations in London, so in this respect Blair was fighting for support for his policy from the elected representatives as well as for his own political survival as he had become personally associated with this policy. It was a long speech and I have edited it down to 1,380 words from the original 4,700 words. The edited speech is shown in Table 5.4.

It was a masterful and convincing speech, and Blair won the vote convincingly. What contributed to his persuasiveness was how he integrated claims made on the basis of epistemic modality with deontic modality. His use of epistemic modality shows in the evidence that the WMD have not been destroyed, though he lowers the level of modality when describing the reports of the weapons inspectors in line with what they actually reported. But he does not make explicit the difference in expression of levels of certainty between his views and those of the inspectors. Then there is the claim that the decision taken will influence international politics for a long time (something he was right about).

The shift to deontic modality comes in two forms: first, the evidence that Saddam is deliberately deceiving the inspectors. This introduces a frame of cheating, lying and immorality that places an obligation on Blair to do something because Saddam is not following the same ethical code. Then the linking together of Islamic terrorism and WMD; this was part of the so-called 'War on Terror' that had become official US policy after the events of 9/11: because these two are connected (though no evidence of this connection is given), it is morally necessary to act now.

Table 5.4 Tony Blair's Iraq War speech, House of Commons, March 2003

The speech	Analysis of modality
At the outset I say: it is right that this House debate this issue and pass judgement. That is the democracy that is our right but others struggle for in vain. And again I say: I do not disrespect the views of those in opposition to mine. This is a tough choice. But it is also a stark one: to stand British troops down and turn back; or to hold firm to the course we have set. I believe we must hold firm (1).	1 DEONTIC MODALITY It is necessary and morally right to have this debate.
So, why does it matter so much? Because the outcome of this issue will now determine more than the fate of the Iraqi regime and more than the future of the Iraqi people, for so long brutalised by Saddam. It will determine the way Britain and the world confront the central security threat of the twenty-first century; the development of the UN; the relationship between Europe and the US; the relations within the EU and the way the US engages with the rest of the world. It will determine the pattern of international politics for the next generation (2).	2 EPISTEMIC MODALITY It is certain (that is, true) that what happens now will determine international politics for a long time.
It became clear after the Gulf War that the WMD [weapons of mass destruction] ambitions of Iraq were far more extensive than hitherto thought. When the inspectors left in 1998, they left unaccounted for: 1 10,000 litres of anthrax 2 a far-reaching VX nerve agent [nerve gas] programme 3 up to 6,500 chemical munitions 4 at least 80 tonnes of mustard gas, and possibly more than ten times that amount 5 unquantifiable amounts of sarin, botulinum toxin and a host of other biological poisons 6 an entire Scud missile programme We are now seriously asked to accept that, in the last few years, contrary to all history, contrary to all intelligence, he decided unilaterally to destroy the weapons. Such a claim is palpably absurd (3).	3 EPISTEMIC MODALITY 'It became clear' implies that it is known beyond doubt. Notice the impersonal use of 'it' (rather than, say, 'I believe'). The truth of the claim is upheld by listing chemical and biological weapons. He is certain that the counter-claim that the weapons have been destroyed is false.
On 7 March, the inspectors published a remarkable document. It is 173 pages long, detailing all the unanswered questions about Iraq's WMD. It lists 29 different areas where they have been unable to obtain information. For example, on VX, it says: 'Documentation available to UNMOVIC [United Nations Monitoring, Verification and Inspection Commission] suggests that Iraq at least had had	4 EPISTEMIC MODALITY While its length is taken to be proof of its accuracy, when he quotes from the inspectors' report there is only mid-level

Table 5.4   *continued*

The speech	Analysis of modality
far-reaching plans to weaponize VX ... Based on unaccounted-for production of anthrax could have been in the range of about 15,000 to 25,000 litres ... Based on all the available evidence, the strong presumption is that about 10,000 litres of anthrax was not destroyed and may still exist' (4). On this basis, had we meant what we said in [the UN] Resolution 1441, the Security Council should have convened and condemned Iraq as in material breach (5). What is perfectly clear is that Saddam is playing the same old games in the same old way.	modality – 'suggests', 'may still exist' and 'could have been' imply that this is possible but by no means certain. However, the modality increases with 'strong presumption'.
	5 Blair is certain that there is an obligation (DEONTIC) on the Security Council to pass the second resolution because of Saddam's repeated deception.
From December 1998 to December 2002, no UN inspector was allowed to inspect anything in Iraq. For four years, not a thing. What changed his mind? The threat of force. From December to January, and then from January through to February, concessions were made. What changed his mind?	6 EPISTEMIC MODALITY It is certain that what forced Iraq to accept the weapons' inspectors was the threat of force. He repeats rhetorical questions (3 times) and gives the same answer.
The threat of force. And what makes him now issue invitations to the inspectors, discover documents he said he never had, produce evidence of weapons supposed to be non-existent, destroy missiles he said he would keep? The imminence of force (6). The only persuasive power to which he responds is 250,000 allied troops on his doorstep.	
It is dangerous if such regimes disbelieve us. Dangerous if they think they can use our weakness, our hesitation, even the natural urges of our democracy towards peace, against us. Dangerous because one day they will mistake our innate revulsion against war for permanent incapacity; when in fact, pushed to the limit, we will act. But then when we act, after years of pretence, the action will have to be harder, bigger, more total in its impact. Iraq is not the only regime with WMD. But back away now from this confrontation and future conflicts will be infinitely worse and more devastating (7).	7 EPISTEMIC + DEONTIC MODALITY It is certain that if we do not act now then future action will need to be greater. So we should act now and such action will be necessary.
Confidence is the key to prosperity.	
Insecurity spreads like contagion.	
So people crave stability and order.	

The threat is chaos.

And there are two begetters of chaos.

Tyrannical regimes with WMD and extreme terrorist groups who profess a perverted and false view of Islam (8).

Let me tell the House what I know.

I know that there are some countries or groups within countries that are proliferating and trading in WMD, especially nuclear weapons technology.

I know there are companies, individuals, some former scientists on nuclear weapons programmes, selling their equipment or expertise.

I know there are several countries – mostly dictatorships with highly repressive regimes – desperately trying to acquire chemical weapons, biological weapons or, in particular, nuclear weapons capability. Some of these countries are now a short time away from having a serviceable nuclear weapon. This activity is not diminishing. It is increasing.

We all know that there are terrorist cells now operating in most major countries (9). Just as in the last two years, around 20 different nations have suffered serious terrorist outrages. Thousands have died in them. And these two threats have different motives and different origins but they share one basic common view: they detest the freedom, democracy and tolerance that are the hallmarks of our way of life.

I have come to the conclusion after much reluctance that the greater danger to the UN is inaction: that to pass Resolution 1441 and then refuse to enforce it would do the most deadly damage to the UN's future strength, confirming it as an instrument of diplomacy but not of action, forcing nations down the very unilateralist path we wish to avoid (10).

But there will be, in any event, no sound future for the UN, no guarantee against the repetition of these events, unless we recognize the urgent need for a political agenda we can unite upon.

I have never put our justification for action as regime change. We have to act within the terms set out in Resolution 1441. That is our legal base.

But it is the reason, I say frankly, why if we do act we should do so with a clear conscience and strong heart (11).

8 EPISTEMIC MODALITY
He knows that Islamic terrorism and WMD are closely connected in that they both cause chaos. The phrase 'Tyrannical regimes with WMD' links to Iraq in 7.

9 Use of factive verb 'know' and pronoun shift from 'I know' to 'we know'; raises level of certainty by listing 'facts'.

There is then a shift to DEONTIC MODALITY on the obligation to resist terrorism as it threatens our way of life.

10 DEONTIC MODALITY
It is necessary and right to act now because not to so is more dangerous as it would undermine the status of the UN.

11 DEONTIC MODALITY
It is morally right to act now.

Table 5.4 *continued*

The speech	Analysis of modality
We must face the consequences of the actions we advocate. For me, that means all the dangers of war. But for others, opposed to this course, it means – let us be clear – that the Iraqi people, whose only true hope of liberation lies in the removal of Saddam, for them, the darkness will close back over them again; and he will be free to take his revenge upon those he must know wish him gone.	12 EPISTEMIC MODALITY + DEONTIC MODALITY It is certain that if we do not take military action it will improve Saddam's position and embolden both him and other terrorist states. This will be morally wrong.
And if this House now demands that at this moment, faced with this threat from this regime, that British troops are pulled back, that we turn away at the point of reckoning, and that is what it means – what then?	
What will Saddam feel? Strengthened beyond measure (12). What will the other states who tyrannize their people, the terrorists who threaten our existence, what will they take from that? That the will confronting them is decaying and feeble.	
Who will celebrate and who will weep?	
This House wanted this decision. Well it has it. Those are the choices. And in this dilemma, no choice is perfect, no cause ideal.	13 EPISTEMIC MODALITY It is certain that what happens now will determine international politics for a long time.
But on this decision hangs the fate of many things (13).	
Of whether we summon the strength to recognize this global challenge of the twenty-first century and meet it.	
Of the Iraqi people, groaning under years of dictatorship.	
Of our armed forces – brave men and women of whom we can feel proud, whose morale is high and whose purpose is clear.	
Of the institutions and alliances that will shape our world for years to come.	

There are other deontic arguments developed from this: that there is a moral necessity for the allies to act now in order to prevent both a worse international situation developing (the fact that Blair generalizes from a particular situation, Iraq, to the global situation is concealed) and to prevent greater action being necessary later. It was the subtle interplay between claims made on the basis of truth and evidence (for example, the listing of weapons, detailing past infringements of the inspection regime) with those made on the basis of obligation (if we don't do something things will only get worse) that proved to be so convincing. His audience would find it difficult to unpack the rhetorical use of modality and were also strongly influenced by the level of commitment in his impassioned and fluent delivery. There is little doubt that Blair believed himself – even if not many others did – and this was sufficient to embark on a war that caused an immense amount of suffering. As with all history, we never know what might have happened, but it is hard to imagine it being any worse than the events that did happen.

Exercise 5.2

Weapons of Mass Distraction
In an early morning broadcast of the *BBC's Today* programme on 29 May 2003, the journalist Andrew Gilligan made the controversial claim that the government 'ordered [the September Dossier, a British Government dossier on WMD] to be sexed up, to be made more exciting, and ordered more facts to be ... discovered'. The broadcast was not repeated.

Table 5.5 shows the changes that were made between the original Joint Intelligence Committee (JIC) assessment of the threat posed by Iraq to the eventual published dossier which formed the textual basis for the decision by the British government to go to war with Iraq in March 2003. Critically analyse these changes by:

> Identifying the differences between the drafts.
> Deciding how you could describe these differences through an analysis of modality (distinguishing between epistemic and deontic modality).
> Then discuss their rhetorical effect on a political audience.

The USA abandoned its search for WMDs in Iraq on 12 January 2005.

Table 5.5 The September Dossier, September 2002

	JIC assessment	Draft dossier	Published dossier
1	Title: Iraqi use of Chemical and Biological Weapons – possible scenarios	Title: Iraq's programme for Weapons of Mass Destruction	Title: Iraq's Weapons of Mass Destruction
2	We … know little about Iraq's CBW [chemical and biological weapons] work since late 1998	This section sets out what we now know of Saddam's chemical, biological, nuclear and ballistic missile programmes, drawing on all the available evidence.	This chapter [Chapter 3 of the dossier] sets out what we know of Saddam's chemical, biological, nuclear and ballistic missile programmes, drawing on all the available evidence.
3	Intelligence remains limited … much of this paper is necessarily based on judgement and assessment.		The intelligence picture … is extensive detailed and authoritative. (Blair in House of Commons)
4	We continue to judge that Iraq has an offensive chemical warfare programme, though there is very little intelligence relating to it.	Intelligence confirms that Iraq has covert chemical and biological weapons programmes, in breach of UN Security Council Resolution 687.	Intelligence shows that Iraq has covert chemical and biological weapons programmes, in breach of UN Security Council Resolution 687.
5	Recent intelligence indicates that Qusai Saddam Hussain has directed the Military Industrialisation Commission to ensure that all sensitive weapons and chemical technology was well hidden in case of further UN inspections.	Recent intelligence indicates that Iraq has begun dispersing its most sensitive weapons, equipment and material, because Saddam is … preparing plans to conceal evidence of its weapons of mass destruction from any renewed inspection.	Intelligence also shows that Iraq is preparing plans to conceal evidence of these weapons, including incriminating documents, from renewed inspections.

6	Intelligence suggests that Saddam has already taken the decision that all resources, including CBW, be used to defend the regime from attack.		... intelligence indicates that as part of Iraq's military planning Saddam is willing to use chemical and biological weapons.
7	Recent intelligence indicates that Iraq has developed for the military, fermentation systems which are being capable of being mounted on road trailers or rail cars.	Recent intelligence indicates that Iraq has acquired mobile laboratories for military use, corroborating earlier reports [sic] about the mobile production of biological warfare agents.	We judge that Iraq has developed mobile laboratories for military use, corroborating earlier reports about the mobile production of biological warfare agents.
8	Intelligence also indicates that chemical and biological munitions could be with military units ready for firing within 20–45 minutes.	The Iraqi military may be able to deploy chemical and biological weapons within 45 minutes of a decision to do so.	... the Iraqi military are able to deploy chemical or biological weapons within 45 minutes of an order to do so.
9	We judge but cannot confirm that Iraq is conducting nuclear related research and development into enrichment of uranium and could have longer-terms plans to produce enriched uranium for a weapon.	Main conclusion: Iraq continues to work on developing nuclear weapons.	What I believe the assessed intelligence has established beyond doubt is that Saddam continues in his efforts to develop nuclear weapons.

5.3   Summary

In this chapter we have explored the resources within English grammar for expressing either how agency is revealed and emphasized, or concealed. We have done this by considering ideas related to participants and processes. Participants are represented by the choice of nouns, pronouns and names, or may be concealed by the use of either the passive voice or intransitive verbs that require no subject.

We have also seen how a speaker can communicate his or her level of commitment or conviction by drawing on the system of modality to express his/her own stance regarding the claims being made. There are different levels of modality that can be used to convey the extent to which the speaker holds his or her claims to be true, necessary or desirable. Various linguistic means are used to convey these shades of conviction, including verb forms such as 'think', 'appear' and 'seem', but also the system of modal verbs that is unique to English. These provide a rich yet subtle resource for expressing possibility, probability, obligation and necessity, using forms such as 'may', 'might', 'can', 'could' and 'should'. Modality can be analysed according to level (high, medium and low) and by distinguishing between epistemic and deontic modality.

Epistemic modality is concerned with expressing states of belief as to how true or false a claim is, while deontic modality is concerned with expressing states of belief concerning the rightness or wrongness of claims. We have explored how changes in level of modality in the various drafting stages of political documents can have a profound effect on their meaning, with serious consequences that have the potential to affect many lives. Now that we have established what is meant by a 'critical' approach, the next chapter considers perhaps the earliest of the 'critical' approaches – the discourse-historical approach.

Essential reading

Coates, J. (1983) *The Semantics of the Modal Auxiliaries*. London: Croom Helm.
Chilton, P. (2004) *Analysing Political Discourse*. London/New York: Routledge, ch. 4.
Fairclough, N. (2003) *Analysing Discourse: Textual Analysis for Social Research*. London: Routledge, pp. 105–20, and 164–90.
Lyons, J. (1977) *Semantics*. Cambridge: Cambridge University Press.
Palmer, F. R. (1986) *Mood and Modality*. Cambridge: Cambridge University Press.

Chapter 6

The Discourse-Historical Approach

6.1 Introduction

The discourse-historical approach (from now on 'DHA') is associated primarily with the work of Ruth Wodak and originates in a focus on political power differences and the historical context in which they have emerged. Drawing on a range of authors, Wodak and Meyer (2009) and Wodak (2011) have developed it more broadly into offering a methodology for analysing discriminatory language in fields of action that are related to the distribution of power in society. Discourse is believed to be essential in establishing power relationships and can only be fully understood by paying attention to the historical context and the social and political setting. It is by understanding how language contributes to the formation of social relations that we understand how power is realized in and through discourse. In the context of this book, DHA is a politico-linguistic approach to the analysis of speeches. Critical approaches, rather than treating language as a separate cognitive domain, explore the relationships between linguistic choices and social contexts. The DHA explains how power relationships are constituted by the use of language that have political implications – whether they actually occur in the field of politics or not.

DHA claims that prevalent ideologies accounting for injustices and relations of domination can be changed by an understanding of their rhetorical basis. Since power relations have a historical origin, they can also be challenged, because there is a dynamic interaction between social relationships and discursive practice. Just as existing power relations influence how talking *is currently done*, so changes in our understanding of the relationship between language, social relations and power can influence how talking will be done in the future. Therefore, it is claimed, DHA can contribute to social change. DHA brings together areas of knowledge that are often considered to be separate: Linguistics and English Language; Sociology and Social Psychology; Political Science and History. As its authors summarize:

> The discourse-historical approach attempts to integrate a large quantity of available knowledge about the historical sources and background of the social and political fields in which discursive 'events' are embedded ... it analyses the historical dimension of discursive actions by exploring

the ways in which particular genres of discourses are subject to
diachronic change ... we integrate social theories to be able to explain
the so-called context. (Wodak and Meyer 2001, p. 65)

Evidently, DHA is ambitious, because its scope is so broad and students
may feel they lack the relevant 'background knowledge' to fully understand
the social, political and historical context of discourse. The approach
entails a broad analysis of what I referred to in Chapter 1 as the 'speech
circumstances'. Chilton *et al.* (2009, p. 93) analyse context at four different
levels, as follows:

1 The other language in the text, or co-text of the practice.
2 The evocation of other texts leading to intertextual and interdiscursive
   relationships, as it is often similarity between utterances in different texts
   that creates genres and discourses.
3 The particular extralinguistic context of situation (such as the institution
   where this discursive practice occurs).
4 The broader sociopolitical and historical context of the practice.

Additionally, analysis of context encourages analysis of 'recontextualization', which is when a text is taken out of one context and placed in another
– for example, when a politician's 'tweet' is reported in a debate in the
House of Commons.

In terms of its methods, DHA first requires the identification of a 'field
of action' – either an institutional setting for language such as the House of
Commons, or an area of language use such as political marketing, where
the media project a persuasive self-representation. The principles of data
collection emphasize the need for triangulation (the use of diverse sources
of data regarding the same phenomenon), including participants' own interpretations of texts, to provide multiple perspectives on the same topic of
enquiry. Theory and method interact in DHA by identifying discursive
strategies for making an argument (known as 'topoi'); this may lead to
further theories, which are explored using an additional set of data. This
interaction between theory and data is sometimes known as *abduction*. A
better understanding of the linguistic means through which relations of
power and dominance are executed is seen by its proponents as an empowering form of knowledge. This should serve as motivation to acquire both
contextual and rhetorical knowledge of how arguments are constructed. In
Figure 6.1 I have sought to explain my own understanding of DHA.

In Figure 6.1 the broad arrows represent influences and show an interactive relationship between societal power relations and discursive practice,
or ways of using language in institutional and other settings: how, over
time, social relations influence discursive practices which, in turn, influence
social relations, and so on. The solid lines represent interdependencies

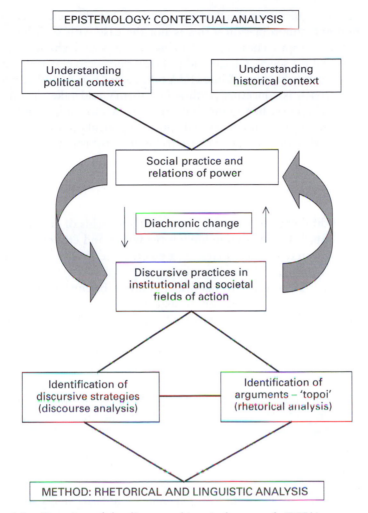

EPISTEMOLOGY: CONTEXTUAL ANALYSIS

Understanding political context

Understanding historical context

Social practice and relations of power

Diachronic change

Discursive practices in institutional and societal fields of action

Identification of discursive strategies (discourse analysis)

Identification of arguments – 'topoi' (rhetorical analysis)

METHOD: RHETORICAL AND LINGUISTIC ANALYSIS

Figure 6.1   Overview of the discourse-historical approach (DHA)

between particular epistemologies and methodologies. The figure shows a distinction between society (social knowledge and practice), analysed as 'Context' in its upper part, and language practice (discursive strategies and arguments), shown in the lower part as rhetorical and linguistic analysis.

It is worth pointing out the difference between DHA and sociolinguistics – since relations between language and sociable variables such as age, gender, social class and ethnicity are conventionally explored in sociolinguistics. However, there are at least two features that distinguish DHA from sociolinguistics. The first is describing power relations, so that DHA and other critical linguistic approaches are concerned with social relations of domination and subordination – this is not the case with sociolinguistics. Second, critical approaches seek to bring about social change, so their explanations take a social, ethical and political perspective, with the aim of influencing social behaviour. While DHA takes a *politico*-linguistic perspective, the approach is concerned with social theory and takes a utilitarian methodological approach, arguing that utility is the most important consideration for the selection of conceptual tools. Exponents draw on whatever discursive and rhetorical theories prove to be the most revealing of discriminatory uses of language.

Summary of the approach

◊ A range of different genres and types of text and fields of action are studied in an empirical approach involving fieldwork and ethnography.
◊ A range of different disciplinary frameworks are drawn on (including sociology, history, politics and psychology).
◊ A particular focus is given to historical context, because many discriminatory practices have their origin in history.
◊ The approach is oriented towards solving social problems – hence its concern with injustice, corruption and discrimination.
◊ There is constant interaction between investigations of data, theory and further hypotheses that emerge from the interaction between data and theory.
◊ Central to the method of analysing language is the identification of topics or 'topoi' that constitute the basis of how arguments are constructed.

Exercise 6.1

Reisigl (2008a, pp. 98–9) provides the following list of fields of action:

1 Law-making procedure.
2 Formation of public attitudes, opinions and will.
3 Party-internal formation of attitudes and opinions and will.
4 Inter-party formation of attitudes, opinion and will.
5 Organization of international and interstate relations.
6 Political advertising.
7 Political administration.
8 Political control.

Think of the types of speeches that might occur in each of these fields of action; for example, a party political broadcast would be considered as 'political advertising'.

→

We have seen that the analysis of 'Context' is crucial to DHA; however, we also found from Chapter 4 (pp. 86ff) that the term 'context' is very broad and can be interpreted in a number of different ways.

> Write a list of all the different types of context that might be relevant in identifying discriminatory discourses.
> Which of these do you think might be especially relevant for the analysis of public communication?

Discussion point
Proponents of DHA claim that greater awareness of how language is used in society can perpetuate, challenge, transform or destroy the status quo. Do you agree with this?

6.2 Discursive strategies and intention

As Reisigl (2008a, p. 100) notes: 'The starting point of the research is the awareness of a social or political problem that possesses linguistic aspects.' There is perhaps a risk of tautology, because if a problem arises from language that is then defined as problematic, how do we know that the problem exists outside of language? Inevitably, some form of extra-linguistic knowledge is necessary. For example, it may be generally accepted that *any* form of genocide is highly problematic – but this is, of course, an extreme case so, for example, interpretation of 'human rights' varies according to historical and cultural circumstance. Initially DHA considers the general question: Is there any evidence that a particular speech shows evidence of discrimination? This is not necessarily easy to answer with reference to purely linguistic considerations. Much work in DHA focuses on right-wing politicians and their negative attitudes towards social groups such as asylum seekers, immigrants, Muslims and so on. It could potentially be applied to other social groups who are believed to be discriminated against, such as those receiving welfare payments, or single or young unmarried mothers.

As we can see from the lower left-hand box in Figure 6.1, at the core of DHA is the identification of a range of linguistic features that characterize how relationships of dominance and subordination arise. These 'discursive strategies' are analysed subsequently in terms of 'topoi' or arguments (which are treated as one of the discursive strategies). A 'strategy' is a plan of practice consciously adopted to achieve a certain political, social or psychological aim. The term 'strategy' has a military origin, from the Greek *strategia* 'generalship', and we still speak of strategy in relation to armed conflict and sport. An examination of the concordances of 'strategy' in the British National Corpus indicates that these military contexts have largely been replaced by the use of 'strategy' in management and business contexts; common collocates include: 'economic', 'marketing', 'corporate' 'industrial', 'global' and so on. 'Strategy' also collocates with 'tactics', and this takes us back to the original military sense in which there is a distinction between an overall aim and the specific means ('tactics') through which it is realized.

Wodak and Meyer (2001) is a little ambiguous as to how far linguistic strategies identified by DHA are intentional. It seems to me that the notion of 'strategy' – along with related notions such as 'plan' and 'aim' – implies that linguistic behaviour is intentional when it is based on conscious reflection. However, this is not the same as saying that some types of discriminatory language used do not have unconscious motivation. For example, it was unlikely that Diane Abbot (Tweet, 6 January 2012) was being intentionally racist when she said 'White people love playing divide and rule' – since much of her political position is based on resistance to racism – however, there may have been some unconscious motivation behind the use of an ethnic stereotype such as 'white people'. The remark provoked some public debate leading to accusations of racism; for example, a newspaper columnist wrote that it was 'An extraordinary statement for someone who has built her entire political career on fomenting, exacerbating and inculcating racial differences' (Abhijit Pandya, *Daily Mail*, 8 January 2012). Since Diane Abbot apologized, this implies that she recognized that her remark – when taken out of context – could be interpreted as having an unconsciously racist motivation, although this was apparently not her intention. Intentionality is, then, problematic and we should be conscious that when we use 'strategy' we are implying an intentional language use.

Sometimes there is the potential for tension between intentions and unintended outcomes; for example, when in the UK people are invited to categorize themselves ethnically. When applying for a membership card at my local swimming pool I was invited to identify myself as one of 19 different ethnic categories, including 'White British', 'Black African', 'Black Caribbean', 'Black other', 'Black British' and 'Black Somali' (in that order); the form indicated that this would assist the Council 'to ensure that the facilities are accessible to everybody' (without any indication of how they might do this). While the intention behind ethnic categorization is to ensure equal opportunities it may also, unintentionally, contribute to seeing the world through an ethnic lens. Typically, the focus of discriminatory language is where a minority group – often ethnically identified – is perceived as being vulnerable to negative representation by a dominant group. There is perhaps an unstated assumption that 'minority' refers to a demographically small number, while 'majority' refers to a demographically large number – but we also need to consider the area over which the number is being counted, since 'whites' form a minority in some inner-city areas but not in Britain as a whole; this also needs the consideration of national context because, for example, in Syria, an ethnic Shia Alouite minority dominates a Sunni majority.

When we consider the upper part of Figure 6.1, we may note that some form of understanding of political and historical issues is a preliminary for the identification of discursive strategies. In the case of the comment by Diane Abbot, knowledge of processes of colonization and decolonization is essential to interpretation; she claimed de-contextualization in her defence: 'Tweet taken out of context. Refers to nature of 19th century European colonialism. Bit much to get into 140 characters' – it is worth noting that the tweet to which she was responding related to a debate over the judicial decision on the Stephen Lawrence case – a racially motivated fatal attack. She was recontextualizing a particular judicial decision about a racist event into the whole history of colonialism.

Evidently, then, the political and historical context determines the nature of the problems that DHA addresses, and offers a way out of tautology. Topics such as immigration, asylum seeking and benefit fraud which are often positioned by the media as being issues of public concern, form the basis of DHA topics because they are defined by the media as 'problems'. However, it is worth noting that a common strategy by those opposed to immigration is to associate it with a list of other issues to which it is only marginally related, such as asylum seeking. One of the risks of defining a particular social phenomenon as 'problematic' is that it unconsciously *links it with all the other social issues that are categorized in this way*. I shall first examine the more general notion of discriminatory discursive strategies and then explore in more detail the specific topoi or argument schemes which form one of these discursive strategies.

6.3   Discursive strategies and discrimination

In identifying discriminatory discourses there are a number of research questions that can be used by proponents of DHA, as follows:

1 How are people named linguistically? (Nomination)
2 Which traits, characteristics, qualities and features are attributed to them? (Predication)
3 From which point of view are these nominations and attributions expressed? (Perspective)
4 Are the respective discriminatory utterances articulated overtly or are they softened? (Intensification and Mitigation)
5 By means of which arguments and argumentation schemes do specific persons or social groups try to justify and legitimate exclusion, discrimination and exploitation of others?

This list of questions could be integrated into a single question: 'How is the system of language employed to enforce, and constitute, the ideology of a particular group?' I shall examine this by considering how ethnicity is used in naming practices. With the increased geographical mobility arising from colonialism, decolonization and globalization, ethnicity has become one of a range of social variables contributing to the formation of a social identity. The term 'ethnic' itself originates in the Greek ethnos or 'nation' – a community that shares a common history, cultural tradition and language – and the desire for things 'ethnic' may reflect a nostalgia for a time when history, culture and language converged, creating less complex social patterns and an assumed homogeneity among members of a particular ethnic group. Unlike other variables that might contribute to the creation of a personal identity – such as supporting a football team, having a religious belief, or a particular sexual orientation – ethnicity is highly visible and arises from the perceptions and reactions of others; this often involves the positioning of a minority ethnic group in terms of how it diverges from the mainstream or majority ethnic group (bearing in mind the constraints on simply comparing percentages, as discussed above).

The naming practices for ethnicity are often compound adjectives that combine aspects of race and ethnicity such as Afro-Caribbean; sometimes these may be combined with religion as, for example, in White Anglo-Saxon Protestant (motivated mainly by the derogatory acronym WASP that this term creates). The name that is used to refer to a particular social group often does not correspond with the ideological outlook held by the group to which the name is applied. In line with other critical approaches, DHA seeks to raise awareness of what the use of a name may imply for the named group and how it contributes to 'us' and 'them' relations. For example, in Germany, Turkish immigrant workers who arrived from the 1950s onwards have been referred to as 'Gastarbeiters' or 'guest workers'; this term denied them the status of being full German citizens, since it implied they would return to Turkey and that they might outstay the welcome of their German 'hosts'. However, the identification of this name as problematic would probably never have occurred without some background knowledge of Nazism and how the identification of a group of people as not fully German had disastrous consequences in modern European history. In this respect there is an interdiscursive aspect to the use of 'Gastarbeiter'– evoking at some level German nationalism.

DHA assumes that language is an area of contestation in which social groups compete for power, and that the situation is likely to be unstable as names shift through the exertion of political power. As we saw in Figure 6.1, there is a circular and interactive process between discursive practice and social practice. This linguistic and discursive struggle is often where social groups arm themselves with strategies such as humour and irony. Groups that experience pejorative naming can turn this around by using a derogatory names to refer to each other ironically – thereby taking owner-ship of their opponents' linguistic weapons to create a group identity.

For example, the racially-based term 'nigger' was used in the USA as a derogatory expression in the 1960s and 1970s; however, in ghetto and street culture in the 1980s African-Americans began to use 'nigger' ironi-cally to refer to other African-Americans. Though 'African-American' remained the standard high status term and implied acceptance of a citizen-ship defined in terms of both ethnicity and nationality, 'nigger' continued as an alternative in-group marker. This shows how groups employ naming practices – interdiscursively – as a way of embracing particular identities. The analyst needs to identify the naming practices, and examine *who* uses them and *with what intention*. The intention behind naming practices can often only be established by qualitative methods such as interviewing.

There is an ongoing interaction between a mainstream culture that devel-ops negative names for a minority group on the basis of whatever it is that marks it out as different, and how the group responds to such negative naming. This is an example at the lexical level of an angle of telling – a way of representing a particular group to reinforce a particular perception of that group. The mainstream culture creates one set of perceptions through naming, while the named group retaliates either by creating an alternative set of names, or by shifting the perspective implied by these names through irony, and so reversing the values attached to them. In this way intertextual references – how the use of a name on one occasion relates to its use on another – contributes to interdiscursive relations – the evolving and shifting social perception of a group.

An example of this process is the name 'pikey' which is a derogatory name originally used for 'travellers' or gypsies, but there is some uncer-tainty about its exact denotation, as indicated in the following from a conversation about cooking in the BNC:

> Do you want me to go and get something from cos it's cheaper. What's cheaper? Ah you, you can't. Bloody lucky though. You *pikey*! Typical! *Pikey? Pikey*! What's *pikey*? What does *pikey* mean? I dunno. Crusty. I've heard of crusty but not … Don't you know what *pikey* means? *Pikey*? You don't know what *pikey* means. I'll get us there, there for half past.

'Pikey' – along with 'crusty' – has broadened its meaning to refer to anyone from a very low social class. Its productivity is shown in its extension to different parts of speech; for example, it can be an adjective, as in 'pikey estate', or a verb, as in 'someone has piked my bike'. As a discursive strat-egy 'pikey' is a name that marks someone as an out-group member and is associated with negative traits associated with low social class, such as lack of money, dirty clothes and so on. 'Pikey' could also be analysed as a form of intensification. However, 'pikey' also provides an example of how groups reverse the negative connotation of a word by using it ironically. Fans of Gillingham football club refer to themselves as the 'Pikey Army' – in the same way as other fans use 'Red Army' and 'Blue Army'. As an inter-discursive strategy this reframes, or recontextualizes, the name as a marker of in-group solidarity.

The key issue to establish is *who controls the process* and *whose perspective* a name reflects: when the majority group imposes a name this is from an external perspective, but when a minority groups deliberately self-selects a name as an identity marker it becomes an internal perspective. Taking ownership of names by re-labelling is a form of empowerment because it reinforces group solidarity. We should also consider the role of official bodies and institutions in the selection and choice of names – for example, in legal and official documents. Think again of the Equal Opportunities forms mentioned above, where people self-select an ethnic identity as part of an administrative process, though this might have the unintended consequence of creating a world view where ethnic categorization is regarded as normal. Table 6.1 shows some discriminatory naming practices classified by variable:

Table 6.1   Discriminatory names in English

Ethnicity	Social class	Sexuality	Other
Nigger	Chav	Queer	Boffin (intelligence)
Yid	Toff	Gay	Yob (behaviour)
Paki	Pikey/crusty	Pillow eater	Nerd (obsession)

Exercise 6.2

> Look at Table 6.1 and add any further name from your own discourse community that could be interpreted as discriminating against a particular social group. Consider for each one whether discrimination is on the grounds of ethnicity, social class, gender, religion or some other variable. Use the table to discuss the discursive strategies that are at work in relation to the name 'chav'.

> Think of a minority social group that has both a negative and a positive name. Consider the origins of these names (perhaps using a corpus for evidence of their productivity). Discuss the contrast between positive and negative names in terms of the discursive strategies of nomination, predication and framing.

> Think of a name that was originally intended pejoratively, but whose meaning has since changed because those to whom it referred have adopted it as a form of identity marker. Try to identify the stages through which this process has occurred and discuss in terms of the interdiscursive strategies of framing and reframing.

6.4   Topoi, warrants and arguments

The term 'topos' (plural 'topoi') literally means 'place' or 'location' (as in topography); however it is used rather differently in the discourse historical approach from how it is used in classical rhetoric. In classical rhetoric it referred to commonplace arguments such as 'everything comes to an end' or 'tis an ill wind that blows no good' and this sense is retained in the notion of 'place' in 'commonplace'. In the DHA, 'topos' refers to an argument scheme that allows a conclusion to be derived from certain premises, as indicated in the following definition:

> *topoi* can be described as parts of argumentation which belong to the required premise. They are the formal or content-related warrants or 'conclusion rules' which connect the argument(s) with the conclusion, the claim. As such, they justify the transition from the argument(s) to the conclusion. (Kienpointner, 1992, p. 194; Chilton *et al.*, 2009, p. 110)

We can see from the quotation that 'topoi' are treated as being equivalent to 'formal or content-related warrants'. This treatment of 'topos' has been criticized as unclear because it treats 'formal' rules as being identical to 'content-related' rules (Žagar, 2010). 'Warrant' is a term introduced by Toulmin (2003) for that part of an argument structure that enables a transition to be made from evidence or data to a conclusion or claim. As Toulmin argues, we need facts to back up a statement, and they answer the question 'What have we got to go on?' So a claim such as 'traffic congestion is a problem' might offer as evidence some of its negative consequences such as delays in arriving at a destination, air pollution etc. However, as well as data that shows 'what we have to go on' a warrant should also answer the question 'How do you get there?' It may be conceptualized as a 'step' that allows a transition from the evidence or data, to the claim. In the case of traffic congestion a warrant might be a general hypothetical statement such as 'there are so many cars on the road' – as with a commonplace, it is a sort of truism that is difficult to challenge, since it draws on the everyday experience of space on the roads being limited.

In this section I shall use Toulmin's (2003) term 'warrant' when identifying the *argument's form* or structure (the formal stage in an argument) – here the insertion of a 'commonplace' about cars – and Wodak and Meyer's term 'topoi', to refer to the *content* of an argument. The aim is to create a distinction between Toulmin's use of 'warrant' and Wodak's use of 'topos'. It seems that the idea of 'general 'conclusion rule' applies equally to Toulmin's warrants as it does to Wodak's topoi. Formal warrants are likely to be more limited in number: since topoi are influenced by the context of an argument, they are likely to proliferate according to the range of specific rhetorical situations for which arguments are necessary.

Table 6.2   Discourse-historical topoi

Content-related topoi	Explanation/definition	Example
Usefulness	Indicating an advantage – if there are positive consequences of a decision, the decision should be accepted.	Immigration will help serve the needs of an ageing population because most immigrants are young.
Uselessness	Indicating a disadvantage – if there are negative consequences of a decision, the decision has to be rejected.	Immigration increases welfare payments, such as for unemployment and housing benefit.
Definition/naming	If an action, a thing or a person is named/designated as X, the person or group so named carries the qualities, attributes or traits contained in the literal meaning of X.	Naming someone as a 'failed asylum seeker' implies that they are a failure.
Danger and threat	If a political action or decision bears specific dangerous or threatening consequences, one should not perform it.	Immigrants and terrorists come from similar backgrounds, so immigrant communities may conceal terrorists.
Humanitarianism	If a political action does not conform with human rights and humanitarian values it should not be performed.	Those who are persecuted for their political beliefs should be allowed to seek asylum.
Justice	Ideas of equal rights for all.	All people are born equal.
Responsibility	Because a state is responsible for the emergence of problems it should act to find solutions.	The government is responsible for controlling immigration therefore it should do something about it.

Burdening, weighting	If X is burdened by a problem one should act to diminish the burden.	If immigration contributes to a rise in house prices, this creates a burden for the native population.
Finances	If something costs too much or causes a loss of revenue, one should perform actions that diminish the costs or avoid the losses.	It costs too much to provide for the social and welfare needs of immigrants (for example, housing), so there should be a priority system in housing allocation.
Reality	Because reality is like X, then Y should be done.	There are too many people in the UK, therefore we need controls.
Numbers	If the numbers prove a specific topos, a specific action should be performed.	Because the population of the UK now exceeds 60 million the country is overcrowded.
Law and right	If a law allows X, then Y can be done.	European law permits migration within the European Union, so once a person has citizenship of country A he can move from there to country B.
History	Because history teaches that specific actions have specific consequences, one should allow or forbid a specific action in a comparable situation.	History shows that after a time immigrants become well integrated so one should allow controlled immigration.
Culture	Because the culture of a specific group of people is as it is, specific advantages or disadvantages arise.	The Poles share our culture but Muslims do not, so Polish immigration is preferable to Muslim immigration.
Abuse	If a right or an offer of help is abused, the right should be changed or the help be withdrawn.	If immigrants abuse their host by committing crimes they should lose their rights.

Table 6.2, based on Wodak's categories of topoi (Wodak and Meyer 2009), provides a brief definition and explanation of topoi, along with invented examples taken from the context of arguments in favour of and against immigration, since much of the work on DHA concerns immigration.

In passing we might notice from the examples some overlaps between the content-related topoi of uselessness, finance and burdening in discussions of immigration since all these seem potentially relevant when analysing arguments based on the effect that immigration has on demand for housing: it means the housing system does not work (i.e. is 'useless'); that it is expensive to operate ('finance') and places a burden on limited resources ('burden').

As discussed above, because DHA describes 'topoi' as equivalent to Toulmin's 'warrants', there is a debate over whether topoi should be a term reserved for formal logical relationships (Žagar) rather than given a looser interpretation that equates it with 'warrants' (Wodak); I shall discuss this further in the last section of this chapter. As a warrant provides the grounds or premises of an argument, *it is more likely to be signalled by a discourse marker* rather than a fully stated 'conclusion rule' that relies on inferencing for its comprehension. I shall illustrate warrants in Example 1 below, with reference to the discussion about urban traffic congestion introduced above.

6.4.1   Example 1: traffic congestion

Consider a statement that might be made in a debate to support the claim (in bold) that there is traffic congestion:

> The problem of congestion is experienced by many of us on a daily basis: *it takes a long time to get anywhere in a city; there are traffic jams and it is difficult to find parking.*

This could be analysed using the DHA topos of 'uselessness', as the argument is based on stating negatively evaluated and socially disadvantageous results of congestion. The data (in italics) are the effects of traffic congestion. To strengthen the argument we might wish to insert a bridging statement, or 'warrant' (in bold italics) that connects the data with the claim:

> **The problem of congestion** is experienced by many of us on a daily basis: it takes a long time to get anywhere by car, there are traffic jams and it is difficult to park **as there are so many cars on the road**, since there is a the problem traffic congestion.

Drawing on Toulmin's approach, the specific warrant is the statement (underlined) that allows the move from the evidence to the claim, which might be referred to as 'causation' because it is the volume of traffic that

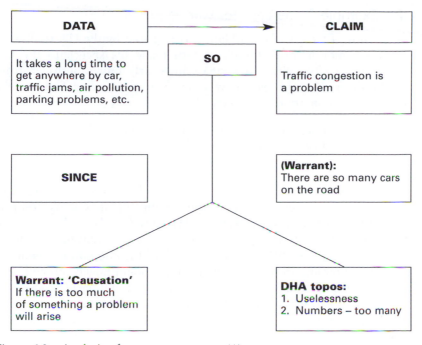

Figure 6.2   Analysis of argument structure (1)

causes congestion. The reference to quantity (so many) is an argument that could be described using DHA as 'the topos of numbers'. The connection between the causes of traffic congestion and the number of cars can be shown using an abstract representation as in Figure 6.2.

Using Wodak's terminology the 'topos' is the actual *content* of the argument – references to 'numbers' and the negative social outcomes arising from congestion ('uselessness'). However, since the topos of 'numbers' (so many) and 'uselessness' are logically related in terms of cause and effect, a formal relation of causality could be captured by a warrant such as 'Causation'. This would be a more formal use of 'warrant' to refer to *the formal statement of an argument*: here **too much of something causes a negative effect**. This would seem to provide an effective conclusion rule as it addresses the underlying cause of congestion: an excess of traffic. Differentiating between warrants (abstract argument schemes) and topoi (the content-related realizations of an abstract scheme) allows us to differentiate between the form and content of arguments. It may be helpful to provide a further illustration of this in Example 2, which is from a 'high-stakes' oratorical setting: Tony Blair's speech to the House of Commons arguing the case for the invasion of Iraq to remove Saddam Hussein.

6.4.2   Example 2: the case for war

We are now 12 years after Saddam was first told by the UN to disarm; nearly six months after President Bush made his speech to the UN accepting the UN route to disarmament; nearly four months on from Resolution 1441; and even now today we are offering Saddam the prospect of voluntary disarmament through the UN.

I detest his regime. But even now he can save it by complying with the UN's demand. Even now, we are prepared to go the extra step to achieve disarmament peacefully.

I do not want war. I do not believe anyone in this House wants war. But disarmament peacefully can only happen with Saddam's active co-operation. Twelve years of bitter experience teaches that. And if he refuses to co-operate – as he is refusing now, and we fail to act, what then? Saddam in charge of Iraq, his WMD intact, the will of the international community set at nothing, the UN tricked again, Saddam hugely strengthened and emboldened – does anyone truly believe that will mean peace? And when we turn to deal with other threats, where will our authority be? And when we make a demand next time, what will our credibility be? This is not a road to peace but folly and weakness that will only mean the conflict when it comes is more bloody, less certain and greater in its devastation.

There are at least four argument schemes or topoi in this extract:

1 The danger of *inaction*.
2 Numbers that emphasize the duration of the period when Saddam has been a threat by failing to disarm.
3 The uselessness of the UN policy of voluntary disarmament.
4 Responsibility: it would be irresponsible for the international community not to act, as this in itself would embolden Saddam.

These topoi are reinforced by repetition and rhetorical questions. Figure 6.3 shows the argument scheme using Toulmin's 'warrant'.

Using Wodak's approach, the topoi are danger and threat might be interpreted as being indicated lexically: 'And when we turn to deal with other threats' can be interpreted as a topos of 'danger and threat'. The topos of numbers is indicated lexically by 12 years (repeated), six months, four months and so on; the uselessness of disarmament is implied by the long duration of peaceful pressure, and 'Saddam hugely strengthened and emboldened' implies that it would be irresponsible to do nothing. Using Toulmin's approach, the warrant can be identified by formally paraphrasing Blair's argument that Iraq should be invaded because of the outcome of

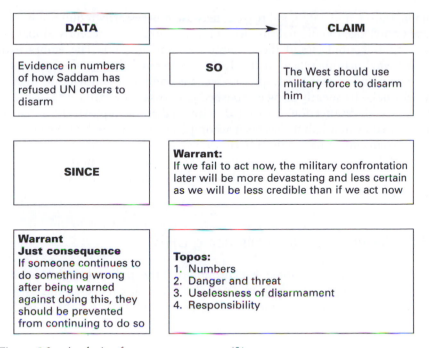

Figure 6.3   Analysis of argument structure (2)

not acting now – a type of 'slippery slope' argument (though Blair avoids this metaphor). The warrant of not acting now leading to a bad result can be reformulated as a generalization – that if someone does something bad then there is an obligation *not* to allow him or her to continue. I suggest that we could describe this warrant more formally as 'just consequences'.

We might notice from these examples that actual words in the text may correspond directly with the naming of a topos (in the second example, the word 'threat' is actually used) but need not necessarily do so – for example, 'numbers' is a superordinate terms for 12, six, four and so on, but the word itself does not occur. The topos of responsibility arises from a series of rhetorical questions about hypothetical future scenarios from which we can infer that action is necessary. Similarly, Blair does not state that disarmament is in effective, but implies this. So words may correspond with a warrant (as in Example 1) but need not necessarily do so when the formal structure of an argument is paraphrased (as in Example 2) rather than stated explicitly. The overlaps noted in Table 6.2 between topoi, such as 'uselessness', 'disadvantage' and 'burdening' might be removed by naming them using formal logical terms such as 'causation' (Example 1) or 'just consequence' (Example 2).

While DHA has been used to explore other problematic issues, such as climate change (Wodak and Meyer, 2009), there has been a strong focus on immigration, and with good reason, because it necessarily requires a historical knowledge of colonialism, decolonization and more recently globalization to fully understand the dynamics of immigration. The embrace of 'third way' neo-liberalism in the 1990s accelerated the speed of immigration as many sought to escape low-wage economies by moving to higher-wage ones – frequently using established patterns of migration to assist with this. Social disaffection associated with higher unemployment in areas populated by immigrants has been accompanied by a growth of the far right and expansion of nationalism across Europe. For this reason I shall illustrate DHA in the next section using an example from a significant agenda-setting speech given by Michael Howard, the leader of the Conservative Party in 2005.

6.5   Sample text analysis using DHA

I begin by providing some background on the political and historical context, then continue with an analysis of the discursive strategies and topoi in this speech (using the list of topoi given in Table 6.2, pp. 134–5).

Speech circumstances
During the period leading up to the 2005 General Election in the United Kingdom, immigration shifted from being a topic of marginal interest to a central issue for right and centre-right parties. The growth of immigration as a policy issue for the British political right can be related to an absence of an alternative political agenda to respond to their electoral failure in the 1997 and 2001 elections. Poor performance by the Conservative Party in the previous two elections meant that it could no longer rely on traditional Conservative policies, such as support for the family. A number of centralist policies initiated by the Conservative Party in the previous two elections had already been adopted by New Labour.[1] There was, therefore, a need for an innovatory policy area that was historically associated with the right and would be difficult for New Labour to adopt as its own: immigration provided just such a policy area.

In addition, an increase in the number of immigrants arriving in the United Kingdom received extensive attention from right-wing newspapers such as the *Daily Mail* and the *Daily Telegraph*, making the topic highly newsworthy. This increase had occurred for a number of reasons, of which

---

[1]   These policies include free market, neo-liberal economic policies; the reduction of the welfare budget through welfare to work; conceptualizing the user of public sector services as a consumer and thus encouraging 'choice' in schools and hospitals; a focus on crime and dealing with young offenders, in addition to support for the family through policies supporting 'hard working families'.

the British public was made increasingly aware. These included the War on Terror, with some (mainly Muslim) immigrant groups being represented by the media as a fifth column allied to terrorist networks. Equally important was the growth of political and economic instability in the countries surrounding Europe (for example, Algeria, Iraq, Iran and Kurdish parts of Turkey), which led to the emergence of 'people smuggling' as a lucrative activity. Economic migration was stimulated by the relative buoyancy of the British economy, which grew faster in the period 2000–7 than nearly all the other European countries. A major political factor was the enlargement of the European Union in 2004, from 15 to 27 countries – leading to over half a million immigrants from Poland – the largest ever migration to Britain. All these factors created a degree of uncertainty that could readily be exploited in a discourse elaborating the political, economic, social and cultural uncertainties arising from globalization.

Prior to 2003, the topic of 'immigration' was restricted largely to right-wing parties such as the British National Party – though 'asylum' had become a topic for the Conservative Party in 2001; but by 2003, both 'immigration' and 'asylum' had become central to Conservative discourse. The Australian campaign manager – Lynton Crosby – who had organized four successful campaigns for the Australian prime minister, John Howard – became a political adviser to the party in 2004. The Conservative Party leader, Michael Howard – ironically, the son of a Jewish immigrant – supported the new strategy. Both had identified the absence of an alternative political agenda and sought to exploit the topicality of immigration and asylum in the media. Table 6.3 shows an analysis of the *topoi* in the first half of the speech.

Core text: Michael Howard, immigration speech, 22 September 2004

Analysis of topoi shows that several of these arguments are recycled in the speech; first, the argument that it is the responsibility of the government to deal with what is defined as 'a problem' is explained in paragraphs 2, 3, 5 and 11; second, the reality of immigration and the need to control immigration is found in 4, 8 and 12; and, third, numbers are introduced in 8, 10 and 14. These three topoi work together to frame immigration as a problem; this is subtly introduced in 4 with the phrase 'cause for concern' – we don't know why it is a cause for concern other than it is claimed to be a 'problem' in other countries. This is known as a presupposition: once it is assumed that immigration is a problem, a whole set of arguments follow (including 'solutions' to the 'problem'). The problem–solution pattern argues that something needs to be done about it. In terms of discursive strategy, these topoi are ways of framing the argument from a particular point of view because they adopt the perspective that immigration is a problem.

Table 6.3   Analysis of topoi in the first part of Michael Howard's immigration speech, September 2004

Speech		Analysis of topoi
Today I want to address asylum and immigration, issues I first raised in Burnley last February. Immigration is not an easy subject for politicians to debate. It raises strong emotions.	1	Introduction of topic.
When I was Home Secretary and took action to get to grips with immigration, I was condemned by some commentators as being a traitor to my immigrant roots. They seemed to believe that British people from immigrant families could have no possible interest in wanting to see immigration controlled.	2	Responsibility: the speaker has been responsible for controlling immigration.
I've lost count of the times I have been told by British people from ethnic community backgrounds that firm immigration controls are essential for good race relations. Doubtless I will be condemned again tomorrow. And doubtless my opponents will claim that my speech today is a 'lurch to the right'.	3	Responsibility of government for imposing immigration controls is generally accepted.
But immigration and asylum are not side issues. They are a cause for concern across the world. Australia, Ireland, Denmark, America, India and Canada have all taken steps to address the problem. And it is a cause for concern right across Britain – irrespective of people's background, skin colour or religion.	4	Reality of the problematic nature of immigration globally.
People know that Britain's immigration and asylum system has broken down. They know that it is chaotic, unfair and out of control. They want politicians to be honest about the problem. And they want clear, fair and practical action to tackle it	5	Uselessness of present system. Responsibility of politicians to sort it out.
For centuries Britain has welcomed people from around the world with open arms. We have a proud tradition of giving refuge to those fleeing persecution. And we have always offered a home to families who want to come here, work hard and make a positive contribution to our society. My father was one of them …	6	Humanitarian instincts of 'Britain' based on its sense of justice for the oppressed.
Britain has an enviable record of racial integration. Over the years hundreds of immigrant communities have successfully integrated into British society. They have rightly held on to their traditions and culture, while also embracing Britain's and playing their full role in our national life.	7	Usefulness of immigrants who embrace the British way of life. Culture: integration.
But any system of immigration must be properly controlled. Firm but fair immigration controls are essential for good race relations, the maintenance of national security and the management of public services. Britain is a densely populated and prosperous country. There are, literally, millions of people in other, poorer, countries who would like to settle here if they could. Britain cannot take them all. So the scale of immigration is important.	8	Reality of Britain as a densely populated country that needs to impose controls because of the scale of potential immigration.

Sadly, Britain's immigration controls today are neither firm nor fair. They are chaotic and they are out of control. Consider these facts.

Only one out of every five failed asylum seekers is ever removed from the United Kingdom. Government officials have given work permits to people when they knew that their applications were fraudulent. David Blunkett has said that he sees 'no obvious upper limit to legal immigration'. Net immigration to Britain has averaged 158,000 people a year for the last five years. According to the Government's own predictions, Britain's population will grow by 5.6 million people over the next 30 years – equivalent to five times the population of Birmingham. Immigration will account for 85 per cent of that increase.

Population increases of this kind do have important public policy implications, which no responsible political party could – or should – ignore. Take housing, for example. The majority of immigrants settle in London and the South East, where pressures on housing are most pronounced ... On that basis we will need an additional 4.85 million homes – a million more than the Government is planning for.

David Blunkett may believe that there is 'no obvious upper limit to legal immigration'. I do not agree. While migration in both directions is part of a competitive and dynamic modern economy, immigration to Britain cannot continue at its present, uncontrolled levels. Britain has reached a turning point. As a country we need a totally new approach to immigration and asylum.

We need a system that helps genuine refugees and gives priority to those who want to come to Britain, work hard and make a positive contribution. We will start by cracking down hard on illegal immigration. It is quite wrong that hundreds of thousands of illegal immigrants are living in Britain. Some arrive undetected. Others come here legally as students, visitors or on a work permit but stay on illegally.

Many are failed asylum seekers who have not been deported. There are now over 250,000 failed asylum seekers living in Britain who have no right to be here.

Illegal immigration can be very dangerous. It often involves a long journey, concealed in a truck with little food, water or ventilation. People die in the process. But sadly for many it seems to be a risk worth taking.

When illegal immigrants arrive in Britain, they often end up living in very poor conditions, working in dangerous situations on very low earnings well below the minimum wage. The tragedy at Morecambe Bay earlier this year was a stark reminder of just how bad and how dangerous illegal immigrants' working conditions can be.

9 Uselessness of the present system of immigration control.

10 Numbers of immigrants, overall population and number of 'failed' asylum seekers who are returned.

11 Responsibility of government to deal with results of population increase. Burdening and weighting; burden on the housing stock.

12 Reality can no longer be ignored because of the lack of immigration control.

13 Usefulness of some immigrants contrasted with the threat of others.

14 Definition of asylum seekers as 'failed'. Numbers of them.

15 Danger of illegal immigration to the immigrants themselves.

16 Definition that does not distinguish between 'illegal immigrants' and other immigrants. Danger of type of work taken by 'illegal immigrants'.

Table 6.4   Second part of Howard's immigration speech, September 2004

If immigration officials don't check people as they come into and out of the country (as they do in America, Australia and Canada), then they can't do anything about those who fail to leave after their work permit or student visa has expired. According to a National Audit Office report into UK visas, a tracking exercise carried out in Accra found that 37 per cent of a sample of students issued with a visa could not subsequently be traced.	17
What is more, the administration of the work permits system is a shambles – as James Cameron, the British Consul in Bucharest revealed earlier this year.	18
A Conservative Government would re-introduce embarkation controls, as the first step in a package of measures to clamp down on illegal immigration. And we will take tough action against companies who employ people illegally. In the last three years there have been just 17 prosecutions and six convictions for employing illegal immigrants.	19
… Large-scale increases in immigration are not going to solve Britain's productivity problems. But if left unchecked and uncontrolled it will place growing demands on our public services and on housing – demands which we may not be able to meet. It also risks undermining community relations in the UK … I believe that each year Parliament should set a maximum limit on the number of people coming to Britain, just as they do in Australia.	20
That limit should be determined by Britain's economic needs, the demands of family reunion and our moral obligation to give refuge to those fleeing persecution. And within each category of immigration we need root and branch reform to ensure not just that Parliament's limit can be met, but also to create a fairer system, which is less open to abuse.	21
That will enable us to make a substantial reduction in the number of people coming into the UK. Labour have quadrupled the number of work permits issued each year from 40,000 to 175,000. The work permit system has become a major source of immigration. Once here, permit holders are usually able to stay indefinitely. After four years, permit holders can apply for settlement: a significant number do and 95 per cent of applications are granted.	22

23 Conservatives will restore strict control over work permits ... We will introduce a points-based system on the Australian model for the evaluation of applications. And we will reverse the assumption that a work permit will, almost automatically, lead to long-term settlement.

24 The asylum system is another area of chaos.

25 Many of those claiming asylum are not genuine refugees. The Home Office concedes that up to three-quarters of the people seeking asylum in Europe do not meet the criteria of full refugees ... Only one in five failed asylum seekers are deported. Failing to deport rejected asylum applicants encourages more people to claim asylum falsely. People who are not genuine asylum seekers know that even if their claim is rejected, they are overwhelmingly likely to be able to stay in the UK.

26 Claiming asylum is being used as a means of getting round Britain's immigration controls ... To get here most asylum seekers must undertake a long, dangerous and expensive journey, often at the hands of people smugglers. Genuine refugees who cannot afford the cost – or are not strong enough to make that journey – cannot apply ...

28 A Conservative government will tackle these problems at their roots ... We will also enter reservations against the relevant parts of the European Convention on Human Rights ... Genuine refugees will be welcomed, but those who are not will be swiftly removed. This will immediately deter people from falsely claiming asylum in Britain – significantly reducing the numbers ...

30 Everything I have I owe to this country. My family came here with very little and made a life for themselves. I want others to benefit from the opportunities I had.

31 Immigration is good for Britain – we are a stronger and more successful country because of the immigrant communities that have settled here. But we cannot continue to allow unlimited immigration into the United Kingdom indefinitely.

32 Immigration needs to be controlled and it needs to be fair. Parliament needs to set an annual maximum limit on the number of people coming to Britain in the light of our country's needs. We need to get a grip on illegal immigration, re-introduce strict controls on work permits and take action to reduce the number of people falsely claiming asylum in this country.

Then there is a theme related to the uselessness of the present system of immigration and asylum management (paragraph 9), this is a discursive strategy representing the present government as both impotent and irresponsible. A very good example of framing an argument through nomination occurs in paragraphs 14 and 16 in relation to the topos of definition because of how 'immigrant', 'refugee' and 'asylum seeker' are used in close proximity, implying that they are related conceptually.

Exercise 6.3

> ➤ Analyse the second part of the speech in Table 6.4 on pp. 144–5 and identity the topoi that are used.
> ➤ Examine how 'asylum seeker' and 'immigrant' are used through the whole speech. What does this show about the discursive strategies of predication and perspective?

6.6   Fallacious arguments

The proximity in the speech of two very different issues – immigration and asylum – implies that they are related without explaining the basis for the relation. The only element that both groups have in common is that they are based on a categorization as 'non-native' and 'native'. In cases such as 'asylum seeker', a category definition is deliberately obscured to heighten the perception of danger, and this becomes the basis for fallacious arguments. When the topos of danger is introduced in paragraphs 15 and 27 it is not the immigrants *themselves* that are represented as being dangerous to the native inhabitants (in the way that Enoch Powell represented them), it is the dangers posed to immigrants themselves (rather than the natives) by human trafficking. Why does he do this? Because he wants to distance himself from the far right (at that time, represented by the British National Party – BNP) by deliberately avoiding any accusation of racism. He does this by representing himself as a supporter of humanitarian values, since he is concerned about the welfare of illegal immigrants. This humanitarian self-representation reinforces the topoi in paragraph 6 and again in paragraph 21. This pre-empts his political opponents from framing him as racist.

In other speeches Howard gave in the election campaign, the threat of immigrants to the native population is part of an argument that, if immigrants can arrive illegally so can terrorists:

It is only through a combination of tough anti-terror laws and strict border controls that we will defeat the terrorist threat. (Michael Howard, 11 March 2005)

Firm border controls are essential if we are to:

◇ Limit immigration;
◇ Fight crime; and
◇ Protect Britain from terrorism. (Michael Howard, 29 March 2005)

This is an example of what is known in DHA as fallacious argument; an argument can be fallacious because it treats separate categories as being equivalent without stating the premises of the argument. Here, the linking of 'immigration' with 'terrorism' uses a topos of threat and danger. The unstated premises of the argument are that since *some* immigrants are illegal immigrants and *some* illegal immigrants are terrorists it follows that *all* immigrants are potential terrorists. It is a category error based on the premise that terrorists and illegal immigrants belong to the same category of 'criminal' because they have both broken the law. This relationship of equivalence creates semantic contagion between the categories of 'immigrant' and 'terrorist'. Adjacent textual positioning contributes to this fallacious inference and to a perspective of immigrants as being dangerous. This suggests that, if we are identifying the warrant of a logical argument rather than a content-driven topos, this might be described a 'category error' where things of one kind are presented as if they were another.

Reisigl and Wodak (2001) describe common fallacies characteristic of right-wing rhetoric using some terms deriving from Roman rhetoric:

◇ *argumentum ad baculum* – 'threatening with the stick', trying to intimidate;
◇ *argumentum ad hominem* – a verbal attack on an antagonist's personality and character;
◇ the fallacy of hasty generalization; and
◇ *argumentum ad populum* – an appeal to popular sentiments rather than rational arguments.

In the case analysed here Howard is using the third of these characteristics: the fallacy of hasty generalization, since there are many illegal immigrants who have are no ideological interests and therefore could not be terrorists, and there are also legal immigrants who incite religious hatred and are ideologically motivated opponents of the British state. I prefer to describe this using Toulmin's terminology as a category error.

6.7   A critique of DHA

DHA needs to respond to some of the criticisms that have been made in general about critical discourse analysis, such as:

> The producers and consumers of texts are never consulted, thus no attempt is ever made to establish empirically what writers might have intended by their texts. Their intentions are vicariously inferred from the analysis itself, by reference to what the analyst assumes in advance to be the writer's ideological position. Nor is there any consultation with the readers for whom texts are designed. Their understanding is assigned to them by proxy, which in effect means that the analysts use the linguistic features of the text selectively to confirm their own prejudice. (Widdowson, 1998, p. 143)

An example of this is that the fields of action of DHA are selected by the analyst as being areas that are 'problematic', and that could be from their own political perspective rather than from any independent standpoint. It could be argued that DHA begins with an assumption that some discourse is discriminatory and then looks for evidence in the form of strategies to support this point of view. Often the basis for this assumption is in values and attitudes that are evident in social labels – for example, in the names that are used to refer to these groups – so the evidence for 'attitude' and discriminatory practice is in language use or discourse. This risks tautology or circular argumentation – if discrimination arises from language use which in turn arises from discrimination, how can we know which causes which? One way to overcome this is by considering intention. It is for this reason that an analyst using DHA has to be explicit about his or her own intentions:

> It follows from our understanding of critique that DHA should make the object under investigation and the analyst's own position transparent and justify theoretically why certain interpretation and reading of discursive events seem more valid than others. (Wodak and Meyer, 2009, p. 88)

This means that authors should be frank about their own perception of power relations, and define how they understand concepts such as ideology and power. It also implies that textual evidence needs to be provided of textual readings; this can be done in the way illustrated above by analysing discursive strategies and topoi. For example, it was noted that Howard himself used the word 'problem' and the phrase 'cause for concern' in relation to immigration, and I have also shown how warrants based on logical arguments could be used as evidence. It could also be done by using corpus methods to identify particular collocations, so that a naming practice could be demonstrated as conveying a negative semantic prosody of a naming practice; I have illustrated this in the analysis of 'pikey' as compared with 'traveller'. Another possibility is to use receiver oriented methodologies to gain insight into ideology. Hearers' or readers' judgements in focus groups could include estimates of the ideological motivation of speeches.

As discussed above, the interpretation of 'topos' has been criticized as unclear because it confuses 'formal' argument rules with 'content-related' rules (Žagar, 2010). The difference is in the level of abstraction: the form of an argument is rather like a computer operating system – it is an abstract set of rules; however, the content of an argument refers to *rhetorical situations where these rules are applied* – following this analogy, the software that a computer runs. Žagar argues that, for Aristotle, topos referred to the *form* of an argument rather than its *content*:

> The Aristotelian *topos* (literally: 'place', 'location') is an argumentative scheme, which enables a dialectician or rhetorician to structure an argument for a given conclusion. The majority of Artistotle's interpreters see topoi as the (basic) elements for enthymemes, the rhetorical syllogism. (Žagar, 2010, p. 14)

Žagar goes on to illustrate the topos concerning opposites as:

> If action Y is desirable in relation to object X, the contrary action Y' should be disapproved of in relation to the same object X.

This is an abstract formulation of a general argument scheme that – as with any statement of rules – could be applied in *any number of different rhetorical situations*. We can derive from it an enthymeme for a situation advising how to behave with one's friends: 'If it is desirable to act in favour of one's friends, it should be disapproved of to act against one's friends.' Using an approach based on the verbal content of the argument, this is a topos of 'usefulness' since it is advantageous to behave consistently. The advantage of the more abstract formulation of opposites (following Žagar) is that it allows arguments to be *evaluated* by identifying their structure, whereas the content-based topos of 'usefulness' is descriptive and does not identify logical structure.

A further problem is that use of the phrase 'topos or fallacy' does not in itself differentiate between an argument that is reasonable and another that is fallacious. This is an admission made by the authors of the approach: 'However, we must admit, it is not always easy to distinguish precisely without context knowledge whether an argumentation scheme has been employed as reasonable topos or as fallacy' (Chilton *et al.*, 2009, p. 110). It would seem to be beneficial – perhaps using the model above in which warrants are identified – to have a systematic method for differentiating between rational and fallacious arguments. One such method might be to identify inconsistencies through analysis so that the data could be demonstrated as being partial or incomplete, or as not leading to a claim that is made. I have tried to demonstrate how this might be done by identifying arguments relating to logical structure in Examples 1 and 2 above and naming these as 'warrants' rather than as 'topoi'; reserving 'topoi' for the content of an argument.

A further criticism is that it is not clear how general or specific a 'field of action' should be; it is defined as 'a segment of social reality which constitutes a (partial) frame of a discourse. Different fields of action are defined by different functions of discursive practice' (Chilton et al., 2009, p. 90). They are illustrated with reference to various political (sub-)genres such as lawmaking procedure and political control, each of which requires different types of speeches. However, many of these speech types are classified as falling into different fields of action; for example, the inaugural speech is listed under four different fields of action: formation of public attitudes; formation of inter-party attitudes; formation of international relations; and political and executive administration. The State of the Union speech is also listed under four different fields of action: lawmaking procedure; formation of public attitudes; political advertising; and political and executive administration. A multiple classification occurs with other types of speech, leading to the question of whether there is any limit to the number of specific 'fields of action'. A similar multiple listing occurs in relation to topoi – for example, in the sample test analysis in Wodak and Meyer (2009) we have a number of topoi that did not occur in the first edition of this work (see Exercise 6.4). This raises a question regarding the limit to the number of topoi. The risk is that we end up with an endless list – rather as classical rhetoricians did when each school sought to identify new tropes and schemes.

Exercise 6.4

➤ Compare the lists of topoi used in the first and second editions of *Methods of Critical Discourse Analysis* (Wodak and Meyer, 2001 and 2009). What differences do you note? (You may consider some topoi as being completely new in the second edition, while others are re-named).
➤ Identify an argument made by Michael Howard in the speech above; analyse the argument structure of section (20) by identifying the claim it makes, the evidence for this claim and the warrant that related the claim to the evidence.
➤ Analyse the logical structure of section (20). Lay out your analysis in the way demonstrated by Examples 1 and 2 above. Can you name the warrant?
➤ Evaluate the different insights gained by identifying the warrant and identifying the topos.

6.8 Summary

◇ DHA examines a range of genres and fields of action.
◇ It draws on a range of different disciplinary frameworks (politics, psychology and so on), but with a special emphasis on history.
◇ It has an ethical purpose of addressing social problems arising from injustice and discrimination.
◇ The primary concepts are discursive strategies (see Table 6.5) and the identification of 'topoi' that constitute the basis for how arguments are constructed.
◇ The DHA uses 'topoi' to refer to both formal and content-related warrants. However, I have suggested restricting its use to content-related warrants, thereby allowing 'warrants' to refer only to formal warrants.

I have made some modifications to the original table used in Wodak and Meyer (2001); for example, I have not inserted a separate column for 'devices' because I consider there is too wide a range of potential devices. I have also moved 'argumentation' to the last position in the table because it appears to be of an epistemologically different status from the other strategies.

Table 6.5   Summary of discursive strategies

Strategy	Objectives
1 Nomination	Construction of social actors as in-groups or out-groups and of objects, events, processes and actions
2 Predication	Labelling of social actors, objects, events, processes and actions as having more or less negative or positive traits
3 'Perspectivization', framing and representation	Positioning of the speaker's point of view from a particular perspective such as being involved or distant, favourable or unfavourable
4 Intensification and mitigation	Modifying the epistemic or deontic status of a proposition by, for example, the use of hyperbole or euphemism
5 Argumentation	Justification of truth claims by the use of topoi

Source: Based on Wodak and Meyer (2001, p. 73).

Essential reading

Chilton, P. (2004) *Analysing Political Discourse*. London/New York: Routledge, ch. 7.

Chilton, P., Reisigl, M. and Wodak, R. (2009) 'The Discourse-Historical Approach'. In R. Wodak and M. Meyer (eds), *Methods of Critical Discourse Analysis*, 2nd edn. London: Sage, pp. 87–121.

Widdowson, H. G. (1998) 'The Theory and Practice of Critical Discourse Analysis', *Applied Linguistics* 19(1), 136–51.

Wodak, R. (2006) 'Review Focus: Boundaries in Discourse Analysis'. *Language in Society* 35(4), 595–611.

Wodak, R. and Meyer, M. (eds) (2009) *Methods of Critical Discourse Analysis*, 2nd edn. London: Sage.

Žagar, I. Ž. (2010) 'Topoi in Critical Discourse Analysis', *Lodz Papers in Pragmatics* 6(1), 3–27.

PART III

Critical Metaphor Analysis

Chapter 7

Researching Metaphor in Public Communication

7.1 Introduction: Blair and the 'beacon' metaphor

In this part of the book I shall consider how systematic analysis of political speeches can help us to understand the way that discourse processes are driven by underlying metaphors, beginning by illustrating the conceptual approach to analysis of metaphors that originated with the work of George Lakoff. I then go on to explore some of the general methodological issues in analysing metaphor in political discourse, such as how metaphors are identified. In Chapter 8 I propose a method for metaphor identification that is designed especially for *critical* metaphor analysis because it shows how a corpus of language can be used to provide insight into psycholinguistic considerations in metaphor identification, and how a similar approach can also be used when formulating conceptual metaphors. In Chapter 9 I demonstrate how such a critical approach provides the basis for explanation of why metaphors are used in political speeches by comparing van Dijk's notion of social cognition (van Dijk, 2008b) with a new concept of 'purposeful metaphor' (Charteris-Black, 2012). I suggest that conceptual metaphors can be related to social cognition, and that a corpus provides evidence of the individual processing of metaphor.

On 30 September 1997 a fresh-faced Tony Blair (the third-youngest prime minister in British history) mounted the podium at the Labour Party conference soon after New Labour had won an astonishing landslide victory and come into power for the first time since 1979. It was a time of hope and expectation, as established Conservative politicians had been defeated by generally younger, largely unknown, and in many cases female, politicians. Blair needed to give a speech that responded to the sense of expectation and hope for a real change in values that would sustain the momentum of this success. He chose for this purpose the image of Britain as: 'A beacon to the world' and used this metaphor at various intervals in the speech:

> Today I want to set an ambitious course for this country. To be nothing less than the model twenty-first-century nation, a beacon to the world.

Nearly 2,000 words further into the speech he repeated this image:

> We are free to build that model twenty-first-century nation, to become that beacon to the world.

And again used the same metaphor to give a positive representation of New Labour policies:

> We will lift the cap on student numbers and set a target for an extra 500,000 people into higher and further education by 2002. Our education system – a beacon to the world.

And a negative representation of Old Labour policies:

> We will not be that beacon to the world in the year 2005 with a welfare state built for the very different world of 1945. Our tax system should reward hard work.

The speech ended with an exhortation:

> Help us make Britain that beacon shining throughout the world. Unite behind our mission to modernize our country.

Evidently the metaphoric use of 'beacon' contributes to the coherence of the speech by introducing a theme early on, developing it throughout the speech and reiterating it in its conclusion. Of course, Blair is not alone in using this metaphor; in his 2013 State of the Union address, Barack Obama used the same metaphor:

> You see, America must remain a beacon to all who seek freedom during this period of historic change. I saw the power of hope last year in Rangoon, in Burma, when Aung San Suu Kyi welcomed an American President into the home where she had been imprisoned for years; when thousands of Burmese lined the streets, waving American flags, including a man who said, 'There is justice and law in the United States. I want our country to be like that.'

But why did Blair and Obama choose the metaphor of Britain or America as 'a beacon' rather than as, say, a constellation or a sun? A beacon is a fire or light set up in a high or prominent position either to warn or to celebrate; Blair was using the image as a symbol of social aspiration – a British equivalent of the 'American Dream'. He had studied closely the successful rhetoric on which Clinton had been re-elected and he had used the same metaphor in his 1997 State of the Union speech:

We should challenge all Americans in the arts and humanities to join with their fellow citizens to make the year 2000 a national celebration of the American spirit in every community, a celebration of our common culture in the century that is past and in the new one to come in a new millennium so that we can *remain the world's beacon* not only of liberty but of creativity long after the fireworks have faded.

But how does 'beacon' work as a symbol? To answer this we need to identify its conceptual elements. General knowledge tells us that a beacon provides light by shining; it is in a high location so that it can be seen from afar; and it is made of fire. Clinton re-activates this idea when he extends the metaphor with the expression 'long after the fireworks have faded'. The 'beacon' metaphor frames his political success by activating and integrating a set of cognitive schemata that are summarized in Figure 7.1.

It is by activating a rich range of associations, or 'entailments', that we can account for how 'beacon' works as a metaphor for both hope and

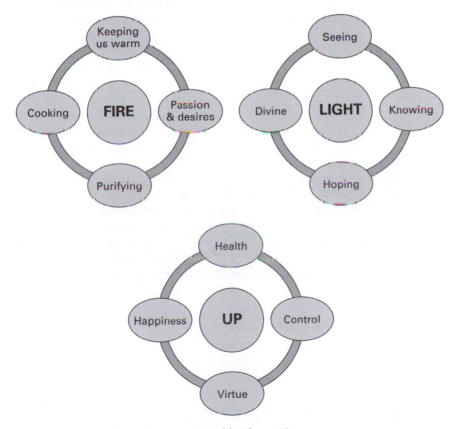

Figure 7.1   Cognitive schema activated by 'beacon'

emotional enthusiasm. The image of light is widespread in religious imagery – it is associated with seeing (it enables us to see at night), and seeing is conceptually linked to knowing and understanding; fire is associated symbolically with the divine but also with powerful emotions such as hope and enthusiasm (for example, 'to be fired up'), desire ('to burn with passion') as well as moral cleansing, as we use fire to sterilize and purify – as well as its everyday purposes such as cooking and keeping ourselves warm. Fire can be dangerous, of course, and those familiar with classical myths will know that Prometheus was punished for stealing it from the Gods. Its ambiguity is captured in speeches using metaphors, such as:

> Our brave men and women in uniform, *tempered by the flames of battle*, are unmatched in skill and courage. Our citizens, *seared by the memory* of those we have lost, know too well *the price that is paid for liberty*. (Barack Obama, second inaugural speech, January 2013)

Here, the destructive potential of fire is a precondition for its purifying moral benefits. High positions have universally positive associations with happiness (for example, 'on a high'), virtue (for example, 'upstanding citizen'), control (for example, 'on top of the situation'), and health (for example, 'feeling on top of the world'). Blair and Clinton and their supporters probably felt many of these things and realized the need to represent themselves as virtuous, happy, healthy and on top of things (though many of the New Labour MPs may have been exhausted, anxious and unsure of what to do next). A beacon is valuable because of its functions – but more important, at the level of unconscious appeal the image has a powerful positive symbolism.

One of the advantages of conceptual metaphor theory (Lakoff and Johnson, 1980) is that it offers a set of mid-level conceptual categories that are broad enough to provide an account of what motivates metaphors by identifying their systemic use. In the case of the 'beacon' metaphor we can identify what are known as the 'source domains' – or primary senses – of a beacon; these are an entity characterized by 'UP', 'LIGHT' and 'FIRE'; this then allows us to explain why the image of the beacon has the potential to symbolize hope and aspiration, by evoking any or all of the concepts listed below that arise from the cognitive schema activated by these source domains:

HEALTHY IS UP
CONTROL IS UP
GOOD IS UP
HAPPINESS IS UP
SUCCESS IS UP
VIRTUE IS UP

GOD IS LIGHT
EMOTION IS LIGHT
KNOWLEDGE IS LIGHT

ENTHUSIASM IS FIRE
HOPE IS FIRE
PASSION IS FIRE
DESTRUCTION IS FIRE
PURIFICATION IS FIRE

The metaphor of Britain as a beacon therefore worked for Blair rhetorically at a number of levels:

◇ contributing to its coherence by providing a theme for his speech;
◇ introducing positive and negative evaluations of actual policies (analogous to the celebratory and warning functions of the beacon);
◇ evoking a range of largely positive emotions associated with health and ethical beliefs, the divine and with knowledge (the emotional and the ethical are not divorced, so that believers in the ethical principles of New Labour were passionate about them in a way that was captured by the image of the beacon); and
◇ providing an image that affiliated Blair with American orators who often used this image; as well as Clinton and Obama, the metaphor has a long tradition in American political rhetoric, as in the extracts shown below.

It came as a *great beacon light of hope* to millions of disinherited people throughout the world who had dared only to dream of freedom. (Martin Luther King, 17 May 1957)

We will again be the exemplar of freedom and *a beacon of hope* for those who do not now have freedom. (Ronald Reagan, 20 January 1981)

The Statue of Liberty depicts the figure of a woman embodying freedom who is holding a beacon, and so for American politicians it is a form of exophoric reference to a symbol of national identity. Analysis of the 'beacon' metaphor reveals how Blair was establishing an identity of optimistic idealism that was more typical of empathetic and ethical appeals characteristic of American culture. His oratorical style can be interpreted as evidence of the growing influence of American political rhetoric.

7.2   Metaphor: definition and appeal

Aristotle proposed that 'Metaphor consists in giving the thing a name that belongs to something else' (Aristotle 1952, Poetics). While this assumed that a name 'belongs' to a particular thing, whereas we know that words have the potential to 'belong' to different things, it identifies a first core idea about metaphor: it connects two things that are not normally related. Further definitions of metaphor provide additional insight; Samuel Johnson proposed that metaphor 'gives you two ideas for one', and I. A. Richards noted, in his *Philosophy of Rhetoric*: 'The mind is a connecting organ, it works only by connecting and it can connect any two things in an indefinitely large number of different ways' (Richards, 1936, p. 125). This brings us to a crucial feature of metaphor: as well as requiring two elements *it stimulates some exchange or interaction between them*: metaphor therefore entails thought, or ideas, as well as language, and enables us to explore limitless different ways of thinking.

Metaphor is effective in public communication because it draws on the unconscious emotional associations of words and assumed values that are rooted in cultural and historical knowledge. For this reason it has potentially as a highly persuasive force and activates unconscious, often mythic, knowledge to influence our intellectual and emotional responses by evaluating actions, actors and issues. It can either do this directly, through novel, poetic or creative metaphors that provide a theme for a particular speech, one that may be active in the short-term memory, or it can do this indirectly through conventional or familiar metaphors such as 'beacons'. These are intertextual because they refer to concepts that have been established in political discourse by constant use. They are no longer processed actively but have become systemically present in long-term memory.

Since classical times, metaphor has been considered essential in oratory because it is by definition a multifunctional phenomenon; this means that it does not do just one thing at a time, but many things simultaneously. Metaphors arouse emotions that can be used as the basis for evaluating political actors and actions by offering persuasive representations of social groups and social issues. They are also creative – not just in an aesthetic sense (though that is important) but also in the manner in which they frame ways of thinking about the social world that actually construct power relations and become political realities. Consider how, in the post-Second World War period, the relationship between the Soviet Union and the USA was shaped by metaphors that originated in the language of politicians, which were then taken up by the media and in public discourse to become the 'normal' way of talking about these issues: 'the Cold War', 'the Iron Curtain' and 'the Evil Empire' were metaphors that highlighted *only* negative aspects of these relationships – coldness, hardness, immorality. They constructed relations between the USA and the Soviet Union with a set of unarticulated assumptions that constrained these relations.

Other metaphors described the strategies that emerged out of this framework of hostility; 'the domino theory' turned opposition to communism into a game, and the notion of an 'arms race' implied that there would be a winner and a loser if each 'side' did not expand their stock of nuclear weapons. From the source domain of physics, the notion of 'a power vacuum' implied that it was necessary for one of these 'powers' to involve itself in the affairs of other nation states, as if this were predetermined by the laws of nature. Such metaphors were limiting in so far as they blocked other positive ways of thinking about international relations between the superpowers, and other nations were only 'pawns' in the 'brokerage' of the superpowers (to use two other metaphors).

Metaphors can also be constructive; more recently, the phrase 'the Arab Spring' has highlighted the naturalness of the energy and enthusiasm for change that has swept across many Arabic nations. It is a positive evaluation of these actions because it implies that a summer will inevitably follow the spring. Rather like the metaphors of the 'beacon' and the 'torch', it draws on experiential knowledge from nature of what is good and life-giving. But, of course, it still does so from a particular perspective, as other metaphors were used by those leaders who lost power in the Arab Spring – for example, Libyan leader Muammar Gaddafi described his opponents as 'rats'. So how a metaphor *frames* an issue is not predetermined by metaphor but by the orator's skill in finding a metaphor that constructs reality in a way that is plausible, resonates with the popular view and complies with his or her own political objectives and world view.

There are also expectations that public figures will display a command of language, and metaphors that are memorable and persuasive contribute to a style of public communication that enhances the speaker's reputation as a skilled orator rather than merely a speaker. A command of metaphor associates the speaker with a classical pedigree, and with a literary canon that includes the Bible and Shakespeare – and in doing so makes a speaker sound like an orator. Take away the metaphors from the speeches of Winston Churchill, Margaret Thatcher or Tony Blair and they would lose the unique appeal that defined them as passionate, articulate and able to resolve the political problems of their time. In short, without metaphor (whatever its dangers – and critical analysts rightly draw our attention to these) these leaders would no longer sound like orators.

In my own research (Charteris-Black, 2009) I compared the use of metaphor in speeches by male and female British politicians and found that inexperienced female politicians had a tendency to avoid metaphor, whereas more experienced ones showed a pattern of metaphor use that was more in keeping with that of male politicians who were familiar with the genre. Female politicians either accommodated to the rhetorical norms of the House of Commons or avoided metaphor completely because of its association with the emotional appeals associated with stereotypical femininity. Successful politicians generally use metaphor, and this explains why it is of such interest to political scientists as well as linguists. Evidence for this is provided in two important edited volumes by political scientists that offer a range of theoretical and applied approaches to researching metaphor: Beer and De Landtsheer (2004) and Carver and Pikalo (2008).

In the remainder of this chapter I describe some research into metaphor that uses political speeches as a source of data, and then outline a set of methods that provide a framework for critical metaphor analysis (CMA); this is based on an approach to critical discourse analysis originally outlined in Fairclough (1995): identification and description, interpretation and explanation. In various places I shall refer to a speech that was given by Michael Foot at the Labour Party Conference in 1976 and at the end of the chapter is a case study where I apply the CMA method by identifying metaphors in Obama's first inaugural address. Throughout this chapter I emphasize the importance of ensuring that the methods for analysis of metaphor correspond with the aims of the research; when these are translated into research questions they provide the map for metaphor research.

Exercise 7.1

Read the speech by Michael Foot, 'The Red Flame of Socialist Courage' in MacArthur (ed.) *The Penguin Book of Twentieth Century Speeches*, p. 418). See what you can find out about the speech circumstances. Identify any candidate metaphors while you are reading.

> ➤ How might you group these metaphors?
> ➤ Why does Foot use these metaphors?
> ➤ How rhetorically effective do you think they are?

7.3 Research design for metaphor in political discourse: an overview

There is inevitably a range of approaches available when designing research into political metaphor, and which are used will depend on the research aims and epistemology of the particular disciplines. Since metaphor and public communication are of interest to linguists, rhetoricians, political scientists and those working in media studies and science communication, they will each have different theoretical perspectives on metaphor. In this section I shall describe research into metaphor with reference to a set of ten questions that a survey of the literature shows are implied by their research design. By making these questions *explicit*, I hope to assist researchers in locating their own research with other methodologically related research. The ten questions are as follows:

1 What counts as a metaphor?
2 How are metaphors classified?
3 Over what time period are metaphors looked for?
4 In what settings are metaphors looked for?
5 Which metaphor(s) are examined?
6 Which political issues are metaphors used to describe?
7 Which political actors use metaphor?
8 How and why are metaphors used?
9 What other discursive features occur in conjunction with metaphor?
10 How many data sources are used for metaphor research?

Some research is insufficient because it moves too swiftly to question 8; however, to provide an adequate answer to question 8 requires attention to the earlier questions.

Question 1, *What counts as a metaphor?*, is a question often overlooked by humanities researchers and is one that can lead to methodological weaknesses. Too often it is taken for granted that metaphor is self-explanatory and unproblematic. When making decisions about what counts as a metaphor, researchers usually assume that there was an alternative non-metaphoric or literal way of stating the same thing, but that a metaphor was chosen for some rhetorical reason. Identifying metaphors is also closely related to the question of how to classify them. One approach to classification is according to whether metaphors are novel – that is, rare and original – or conventional – that is, common and widespread. This may vary according to a particular genre as compared with language in general. Having broad categories of metaphor in the early phases allows us to include a wider range of candidate metaphors and then refine decisions later as to exactly their type, as this is also part of the interpretation stage.

In deciding what counts as a metaphor, studies vary in how far they systematically apply a definition of 'metaphor'. Some linguistically based approaches start with a working definition but many studies rely on intuition alone. They also vary as to whether informants are consulted when identifying metaphor, and how decisions are made when there is lack of agreement. There are also inter-disciplinary variations, as researchers from a language and linguistics background are more concerned with providing an explanation of how they set about identifying metaphor (at least by raising this as an issue; see Pragglejaz Group, 2007). By contrast, political scientists have a tendency to treat 'metaphor' as a 'natural' or self-explanatory category requiring no further definition; for example, in the two collections of papers on metaphor by political scientists referred to above (Beer and De Landtsheer (2004), and Carver and Pikalo (2008)), while many examples of metaphor are provided, there appear to be none that supply a clear definition of a metaphor or an account of the procedure through which metaphors were identified. The problem is that sometimes 'metaphor' is used in a very general sense for anything not explicitly literal. This is less of a problem in qualitative approaches to metaphor than it is in quantitative ones. When the researcher is actually counting metaphors it is necessary to define, as well as to illustrate, what counts as a metaphor. I shall explain my own approach later in the chapter.

Regarding Question 2, a common approach to classification is by 'source' or 'target' domain; for example, in a study of metaphor in British parliamentary debates, I found that New Labour politicians frequently used metaphors linked to words whose primary meaning referred to journeys, plants, health, and light and dark (Charteris-Black, 2009); these would be known by exponents of conceptual metaphor theory as 'source domains'. Classification by source domain may be integrated with judgements made at the identification stage; for example, metaphoric uses of words such as 'shadow', 'light' and 'dark' are conventional ways of making positive or negative evaluations in political rhetoric, whereas this may be less so in other genres. Politicians quite often discuss social issues in terms of illness and health – 'blights' and 'remedies', and their own actions in terms of 'healing' or 'restoring'. The domain of health and disease is more common in speeches than in other spoken genres such as conversation. I shall go into more detail in Chapter 8 about using categories from conceptual metaphor theory. The issue of how to classify metaphor is one that I shall discuss in more detail in section 7.4, where I shall introduce the method of using a corpus to test intuitive judgements as to the novelty or otherwise of a particular phrase analysed as a metaphor.

The next group of questions relate to the design of a dataset that corresponds with the aims of the research. For example, Question 3 concerns the time period over which metaphors should be examined; for example, Gregg (2004) and Shimko (2004) examine metaphors used during the Cold War, whereas L'Hôte (2010) looks at metaphor in the period of New Labour. Other studies look for more generally historical patterns, such as metaphor in times of international crisis (De Landtsheer and De Vrij, 2004), and during election periods (for example, Vertessen and De Landtsheer 2008). A large number of studies concern the use of metaphor in the period leading up to war, on the assumption that metaphor was influential in framing war so that it became acceptable to public opinion. These include Lakoff (1991), Jansen and Sabo (1994), Semino and Masci (1996), Herbeck (2004) and Ferrari (2007). Other studies relate to question 4, which concerns the setting for metaphor use; for example, van Hulst (2008) looks at the use of metaphor in local planning meetings, and Drulák (2008) looks at speeches given in the European Parliament because of a particular interest in these arenas of power.

When deciding on a dataset for metaphor there is also the possibility of a more dynamic (diachronic) approach by exploring the evolution of a particular metaphor over time and identifying change and continuity in its use.

This raises Question 5: which metaphor(s) to analyse. I gave a brief illustration of this at the start of this chapter, where I chose to analyse a particular metaphor – 'beacon' – and it would be possible to explore the evolution of the 'beacon' metaphor in Western political culture and perhaps expand this more generally to an investigation of LIGHT metaphors. A particular metaphor may be pre-selected because it is seen as offering an overarching historical or cultural symbol. Musolff (2010) examines the origins in Western thought of the 'body politic' metaphor that was used in Nazi propaganda. Billig and MacMillan (2005) examines the phrase 'smoking gun' that was used in relation to the controversy over the search for weapons of mass destruction in Iraq, tracing it back to the Watergate controversy. Stenvoll (2008) examines the metaphor of the 'slippery slope' in debates in the Norwegian parliament on sexuality, abortion and reproductive technologies. In such studies, research has been motivated by contextual awareness of the frequency of a particular metaphor in public discourse and its possible role in framing policy; and tracking it back in time helps in the understanding of how ideologies are formed. Such studies are valuable in tracing intertextual allusions, and an interaction between rhetorical traditions.

Perhaps more common than the study of the evolution of a single metaphor over time is the investigation of speeches on problematic or controversial topics of contemporary political and ideological importance. This raises Question 6 – also relating to dataset design: Which political issues are metaphors used to describe? Studies of speeches have examined the following topics, for which I give illustrative citations:

◊ globalization – L'Hôte (2010), Flowerdew (2002);
◊ immigration – Charteris-Black (2006), Hart (2011), Santa Anna (1999);
◊ security issues – Chilton (1996);
◊ patriotism – Flowerdew and Leong (2007);
◊ unemployment – Straehle et al. (1999);
◊ biotechnology – Holmgreen (2008);
◊ reform of the European Union – Drulák (2008); and
◊ international relations – Mio and Lovrich (1998).

Researchers may also be interested in the metaphors that characterize a particular genre of public communication – in this respect 'genre' could either be defined broadly – for example, in terms of deliberative, forensic or epideictic speeches, or more narrowly by considering sub-genres such as the political eulogy, inaugural speeches, declarations of candidacy, parliamentary debates or party election broadcasts (see Reisigl, 2008a, 2008b for an overview of types of political speeches). However, such studies are relatively rare for reasons I shall explain later.

Question 7 relates to a different type of research aim concerned with which political actors use metaphor. Broadly speaking, there is the option of examining metaphors used by *individual* politicians or by *groups* of politicians on the basis of their shared political role (for example, as policy formers) or their shared political orientation. Studies of single politicians are designed to investigate how metaphors contribute to the creation of a unique rhetorical style and political identity. Again, I offer a few examples:

◊ McEntee-Atalianis (2011) – speeches by the Secretary-General of the United Nations,
◊ Charteris-Black (2011) – speeches of ten different British and American politicians
◊ Semino and Masci (1996) – former Italian prime minister Silvio Berlusconi.
◊ Rosati and Campbell (2004) – a group of politicians in the years of US president, Jimmy Carter.
◊ Drulák (2008) the political leaders of EU member and EU candidate countries.

Some studies undertake a detailed study of a single speech (Flowerdew, 2002). As with the discussion of different genres of discourse, there is the possibility of comparing different individuals or groups of politicians; for example, Lakoff (2002) compares metaphors used by the Republicans and Democrats, while Charteris-Black (2004) compares metaphors used by British prime ministers and American presidents, and Charteris-Black (2006) compares the metaphors used by politicians from the centre and far political right. Some studies compare speeches with language in general; for example, Anderson (2004) compares metaphors in public addresses by Soviet political leaders with a representative sample of diverse Russian texts. For research into rhetorical style it is often effective to compile a reference corpus of politicians' language in a particular genre; for example, political speeches. Charteris-Black (2013) has put together a corpus of around 400,000 words called the *British Politicians' Corpus* to identify the style of David Cameron (see Chapter 10 for an application of this corpus). The sample of speeches should be selected according to a number of criteria: that the politicians are well known, experienced (and therefore familiar with the genre), that there is a gender balance, and that all major parties are represented. The number of words for each politician may vary according to their individual status and length of time in politics. The reference corpus can be added to and developed over time.

Whichever approach is taken in relation to research aims and dataset design, most researchers are likely to address Question 8 regarding *how* and *why* a metaphor was used. Typically, this will involve some linguistic and conceptual analysis of the discourse in which metaphors occur and some judgement on the content of these metaphors with regard to what they foreground and what they play down, what they reveal and conceal. This may be with reference either to ethical views on whether these metaphors were acceptable or otherwise (usually on the basis of an ideology that the reader is left to infer) or an evaluation of how far they were successful in achieving their persuasive purpose (even from a Machiavellian ethical perspective). In political science this often involves establishing a method for evaluating the rhetorical 'power' of metaphors that may predict their effect on an audience (for example, De Landtsheer and De Vrij, 2004).

Judgements as to the purpose or motive for metaphors are likely to be influenced by analysis of both the verbal and non-verbal contexts of metaphor; the verbal context (apart from considerations of the source and topic domains of metaphor) will also require analysis of *what other discursive features* occur in conjunction with metaphor. This is Question 9 and it could also be formalized as a specific research aim. Non-verbal evidence for metaphor effect may include changes in voting patterns as a result of metaphor use, and evaluation of the spread and influence of a particular metaphor by looking at its use in other related measures of public opinion such as the media (press, broadcast or digital). An approach to the explanation of metaphor will be developed more thoroughly in Chapter 8.

Metaphor is also relevant to researchers in areas such as media studies, political science and discourse analysis precisely because of how it pervades a range of discourses. This raises the final question, Question 10, which asks how many data sources are used for metaphor research. For example, a particular metaphor that originated in a speech may be reported in a TV broadcast, then in the press and subsequently taken up in parliamentary debates – consider metaphors such as 'the Iron Lady', 'the Big Society', 'Rogue State' or 'Smoking Gun'. For this reason many researchers into metaphor draw on more than one genre as a source of data; newspapers and other forms of print media are attractive to researchers both because they provide evidence of the potential influence of metaphors on public opinion and because of the relative ease of access to them.

Semino (2008) explores how the 'Road Map' metaphor was used both in speeches by George W. Bush and in an official document produced by the Quartet Group. Vertessen and De Landtsheer (2008) use a range of data sources to examine the influence of metaphor at election time: politicians' speeches in TV news broadcasts from two different channels, and the front pages of both broadsheet and tabloid newspapers. Increasingly, texts of political speeches are available on websites, making them equally accessible, and Charteris-Black (2006) explores immigration metaphors using political speeches, websites and online press associated with the political right. Ultimately, the rhetorical influence of a metaphor that may have originated in a speech can be gauged its 'viral' spread across a range of genres. So it can be important in metaphor analysis to identify the rhetorical range of a metaphor as this may assist in explaining why it became widespread.

Table 7.1 Comparison of published research on metaphors

Authors	Lu and Ahrens (2008)	L'Hôte (2010)	Drulák (2008)
Title and journal	'Ideological Influences on BUILDING Metaphors in Taiwanese Presidential Speeches', *Discourse & Society* 19(3): 383–408	'New Labour and Globalization', *Discourse & Society* 21(4): 355–376	'Identifying and Assessing Metaphors'. In Carver and Pikalo
CONTEXTUAL ANALYSIS AND SELECTION OF DATA			
When	New Year's days and 'Double Tenth' days, 1954–2006	1994–2007	Unspecified
Where	Taiwan	Unspecified	Unspecified
Who	Presidents of China (n = 4)	Unspecified representatives of New Labour	Members of an EU speech community
Genre and topic	95 Nationally televised 'State of the Nation' Speeches (235,757 characters)	3 manifestos 49 speeches (234,387 words)	74 Speeches on the debate on the future of the EU as evidence of EU institutional identity
METAPHOR IDENTIFICATION			
Identification	Intuition and use of an online Chinese general corpus to establish literal meanings	Use of software Wmatrix Qualitative analysis Use of keywords and key concepts	No stated target using concepts from theories of European integration

METAPHOR INTEPRETATION

Classification: linguistic	By source domain: buildings and reconstruction	By target domain: globalization	None
Classification: conceptual	By conceptual metaphors, e.g.: A COUNTRY IS A BUILDING; FORERUNNERS ARE BUILDERS; COMMUNISTS ARE DESTROYERS	By conceptual metaphors: GLOBALIZATION IS AN INDEPENDENT ENTITY; GLOBALIZATION IS A FORCE/ MOVING ENTITY	By conceptual source domains: MOTION; CONTAINER; EQUILIBRIUM COMPANY

METAPHOR EXPLANATION

Topic of findings	Contrast between retrospective and forward-looking metaphors that are oriented to recent historical events (i.e. damage of Communism). Cultural and individual variation	Globalization presented as being inevitable. New Labour reacts to it as if it were a threat to create a politics without an adversary	Business as usual – fitting in with the established style of discourse about the EU

The range of genres selected for a dataset should also correspond with a particular research aim.

Exercise 7.2

Select some published papers on metaphor in political speeches (see the Essential reading section at the end of this chapter). Use a framework as in Table 7.1 to analyse your research.

Table 7.1 provides an overview of three published studies that use political speeches as a source of data (either exclusively or in conjunction with other data sources).

7.4   Metaphor identification and classification

In current metaphor theory, a metaphor is a word or phrase that has a more basic meaning than the one that it has in the context where it is used. The very concept of metaphor relies on the idea of words having more than one sense; when Aristotle wrote 'Metaphor consists in giving the thing a name that belongs to something else', the use of 'belong' assumes that words have a primary or basic sense – but how is this 'belonging' established? The answer of a group of current theorists is that a more basic meaning is one that is more concrete, one that is related to bodily action, one that is more precise, or one that is historically earlier (Pragglejaz Group, 2007). They explain that the more basic meanings are not necessarily the most frequent ones. This immediately brings in two resources that are likely to be essential in identifying metaphors: a dictionary that will assist with identifying basic meanings, and a corpus for identifying how words are used. The *Oxford English Dictionary* is the most reliable source for identifying historically earlier meanings (which are usually also those that are more concrete and more related to bodily action). However, it is also possible to use a corpus-based dictionary that incorporates a broad and representative sample of contemporary language use. An effective compromise is to use both types of dictionary so that there is detailed evidence of both word etymologies and of current word use.

Counting metaphors
If one were to ask ten metaphor scholars to count the metaphors in a text, they would probably arrive at ten different answers. Similarly, experience shows that even as individuals we can easily produce quite different counts of metaphors on different days. Why is this, and what can be done about it? Well, it arises because of different views regarding:

1 where exactly a metaphor starts and ends; and
2 what exactly counts as 'a metaphor', which necessarily takes into account the cognitive processing and psycholinguistic aspects of metaphor.

The first point relates to whether to count all the words in a phrase containing a metaphor separately or whether to treat them as a single unit – for example, is the phrase 'the Iron Curtain' *two* metaphors, because 'iron' and 'curtain' are distinct lexical units, or *one* metaphor because they have been used together so frequently that they have produced a fixed phrase?

In Chapter 8 I shall describe the procedure I use in critical metaphor analysis.

Historically earlier meanings

From the point of view of metaphor identification, historically earlier meanings require special attention in relation to language change, since if what was originally a metaphor replaces a historically earlier meaning, then what was a non-basic meaning becomes a basic or literal one. For example, it may be the case that in 50 years from now, when all memories of the potato blight that caused the famine in Ireland have passed, the original meaning of 'blight' might have become even more restricted to its current sense as a technical term for horticulturalists (there were only three literal meanings in the corpus). What was originally a metaphoric sense 'something that spoils or damages' might have become the basic sense.

Cognitive processing of metaphors

There is some psycholinguistic evidence that when metaphors are first introduced they are processed by means of comparison, because there are two separate domains, but as they become increasingly conventionalized over time, an abstract category emerges to encompass the two separate ones so that they become processed in a different way – that is by categorization (Gentner and Bowdle, 2001; Bowdle and Gentner, 2005). In the case of 'blight', when processed by comparison, there would be the two domains of 'illness' and 'social problems', but over time, if processed by categorization 'blight' would represent just 'potentially harmful things'. Glucksberg and Keysar (1993) claim that metaphor works by establishing a general (that is, superordinate) category to which both parts related by a metaphor belong; they illustrate this with the example 'cigarettes are time bombs': as both cigarettes and time bombs are deadly, putting them together establishes a general category of 'deadly objects' to which they both belong. So 'blight' may simply activate a general category of illness rather than *comparing* a social problem with an illness.

Similarly, when Michael Foot used phrases such as 'the scourge of unemployment', if the more basic meaning of 'scourge' – 'whip' – is active, there may be a comparison between 'being whipped' and 'experiencing unemployment'. However, since 'scourge' is often used in a more general sense to refer to *any* cause of social suffering, then it could be that 'scourge' activates the general category 'cause of suffering' so that when someone hears 'scourge of unemployment' it is processed by categorization as 'unemployment' *is just one of a number of unpleasant social experiences*. The same may happen with 'war' when it is used metaphorically in expressions such as 'war on crime', 'war on drugs' or 'war on poverty' – there is no comparison, just a category of 'taking action against bad social experiences' of which war is the archetype. If these archetypal senses of words such as 'blight', 'scourge' or 'war' become established as the norm for talking about social ills then we may speak of 'entrenched metaphors' that are processed by categorization.

Exercise 7.3

Consider the following metaphors used in a Labour Party Conference speech by Michael Foot in 1976 and discuss whether you think they are likely to be processed by comparison or by categorization:

1 It is a recipe for the destruction of any Labour Government
2 the heart and soul of our Labour movement
3 we can face an economic typhoon of unparalleled ferocity
4 readiness to re-forge the alliance
5 the red flames of Socialist courage

7.5   Summary

It is recommended that researchers indicate clearly what counts as a metaphor; closely related to this is the need to explain how metaphors will be organized and categorized (this is explored in Chapter 8). Research aims will determine the time periods, settings and other factors relating to the sources of metaphors, such as whether they are about a particular topic or by particular political actors, or whether a comparative approach is adopted. All studies will need to provide an account of how and why metaphors are used. It is strongly recommended that researchers examine what other discursive features occur in conjunction with metaphors as well as considering the possibility of using more than a single data source for metaphor research – where possible, formalizing these considerations into specific research aims.

The counting of metaphors needs to ensure that a set of criteria are applied systematically, preferably using a clear definition of metaphor, a dictionary to access earlier meanings of words, and a corpus to establish norms in current use. These resources can also assist in identifying the likelihood of a metaphor being processed by categorization (where there is a general concept that integrates both the metaphor and the entity referred to) or by comparison (where the two entities related by metaphor are still cognitively separate).

Essential reading

Beer, A. and De Landtsheer, C. (eds) (2004) *Metaphorical World Politics*. East Lansing, MI: Michigan State University Press.

Bowdle, B. F. and Gentner, D. (2005) 'The Career of Metaphor', *Pyschological Review* 112(1), 193–206.

Carver, T. and Pikalo, J. (eds) (2008) *Political Language and Metaphor: Interpreting and Changing the World*. London: Routledge.

Charteris-Black, J. (2011) *Politicians and Rhetoric: The Persuasive Power of Metaphor*, 2nd edn. Basingstoke/New York: Palgrave Macmillan.

Mio, J. S. (1997) 'Metaphor and Politics', *Metaphor and Symbol* 12(2), 113–33.

Semino, E. (2008) *Metaphor in Discourse*. Cambridge: Cambridge University Press, ch. 3.

Chapter 8

Critical Metaphor Methodology

8.1 Introduction

Critical metaphor analysis (Charteris-Black, 2004) aims to identify *which* metaphors are chosen in persuasive genres such as political speeches, party political manifestos or press reports, and attempts to explain *why* these metaphors are chosen, with reference to the interaction between an orator's purposes and a specific set of speech circumstances. As well as general prag- matic motives for the use of metaphor – such as gaining attention, facilitat- ing understanding and framing issues in a way to encourage acceptance of the speaker's point of view – in a political context this explanation involves demonstrating *how* metaphors are used systematically to create political myths and discourses of legitimization and delegitimization that give rise to ideologies and world views.

Critical analysis of metaphor in public communication demonstrates how this aspect of vocabulary choice influences an audience by providing a favourable representation of speakers and their policies, or an unfavourable representation of opponents and their policies. Figure 8.1 provides a brief overview of the four principal stages of critical metaphor analysis.

Stage 1: Contextual analysis
The first stage is to develop research questions about metaphor that should emerge from an awareness of its potential for rhetorical impact in social and political contexts. Critical metaphor analysis identifies and investigates metaphors that are employed systematically to represent vulnerable social groups in a negative way, or to represent policies – such as war – as being in the interests of all. Questions might be, for example, 'What metaphors are used by British politicians to motivate followers in election campaigns?' Or 'How do these metaphors change once these politicians are in power?' These questions will influence the collection of the texts to be analysed. Decisions will be taken regarding the speaker(s), the time period, the number of speeches and so on – all of which determine the dataset to be examined.

Stage 2: Metaphor identification
Identification of metaphors entails deciding through analysis of words and phrases *what to count as a metaphor* in the context of the speech. At the

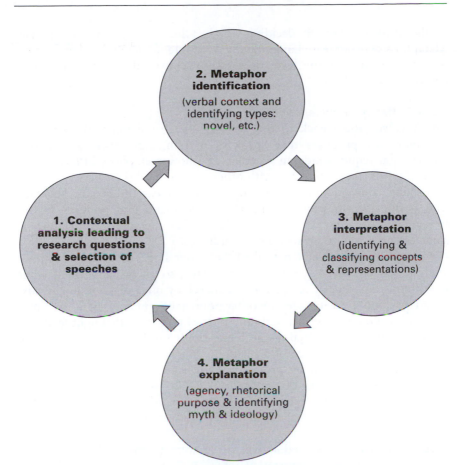

Figure 8.1   Principle stages of critical metaphor analysis

identification stage, metaphors can be grouped into preliminary categories such as 'novel' and 'conventional', as we saw in Chapter 7, and a dictionary and a corpus of electronically stored language can assist with this.

Stage 3: Metaphor interpretation

This is deciding *how metaphors are to be classified, organized and arranged* – for example, whether they are classified on the basis of shared lexical characteristics – such as words from the semantic field of 'sports' or 'light' – or arranged on the basis of to what they refer – for example, 'war' or 'hope'. Classification of metaphors on the basis of the literal meaning of words is known as organizing by source domain, whereas classification on the basis of what metaphors refer to in context is called organizing by target domain.

A subsequent stage in interpreting patterns of metaphor involves working out the particular meanings, representations and evaluations conveyed by the speaker – typically deciding whether these are positive or negative. Metaphors may be treated individually or as interacting with other features in the text, such as the level of certainty conveyed by other language choices.

Stage 4: Metaphor explanation

This involves going back to the broader social and political context to determine the purposes that speakers had in using these metaphors. Explanation requires judging whether and how metaphors *influenced* an audience, how they interacted with other features and their persuasive role in forming, consolidating or changing opinions, ideas and beliefs. This may lead to the identification of underlying ideologies and political myths. Researchers usually take little convincing that metaphor contributes in some essential way to persuading an audience.

In practice, while I have described these four stages of critical metaphor analysis sequentially, I see them as recursive, so an insight gained while interpreting a particular metaphor in a speech by one politician might raise questions about how it is used by other politicians and may spark off a new phase of metaphor identification (and part of a pilot study might lead to a reformulation of an original research question). Similarly, an insight gained while explaining the choice of a metaphor might start off a fresh cycle of metaphor interpretation by providing evidence of a positive or negative representation that can be incorporated into identifying patterns of metaphor use. Similarly, judging the function of metaphors may be influenced by the broader social context that motivated the original research questions.

All of the issues discussed above will at some point require a theory of metaphor and a clear statement of research purposes and research questions. What is identified and classified as metaphor, and how metaphors are organized, interpreted and explained depends on the researchers' theory of metaphor and the evidence of its role in persuasion. The more clearly these issues are defined, the more robust the methodology for critical research of metaphor. Building on the discussion of general considerations in metaphor identification and classification in Chapter 7, I shall now consider the question of identifying and categorizing metaphor from the perspective of critical metaphor analysis.

8.2   Metaphor identification in critical metaphor analysis

Counting metaphors

Metaphors in political rhetoric typically occur in phrases, or collocations, rather than as separate words, and for this reason the unit of measurement should be the phrase rather than the word. For example, in the speech by

Tony Blair given at the start of Chapter 7, 'beacon' occurs in the phrase 'beacon to the world', though it sometimes occurs as 'beacon of hope'; 'torch' occurs in the phrase 'torch of freedom'; since it is easy to search for these collocations in an electronic corpus of language they should be treated as *single* examples of metaphor.

This is where my procedure varies from that described in Pragglejaz (2007), who analysed the phrase 'wear the mantle' in the context 'Sonia Gandhi has struggled to convince Indians that she is fit to wear the mantle of the political dynasty into which she married' as two separate metaphors, because both 'wear' and 'mantle' occur as separate headwords in a dictionary source. When applied to political rhetoric this procedure would in my view lead to a considerable over-count of metaphor, because ideologically interesting metaphors are those that have become conventional collocations through recurrent use and so should be analysed as phrases. A corpus of political language readily shows evidence of these recurrent patterns; for example, a search of a corpus of Tony Blair shows that when he uses the word 'journey' it is most commonly in the phrase 'journey of change', though he has also used 'journey of renewal' and 'journey of conviction' and so on. For this reason, whenever there is a pattern JOURNEY + OF + ABSTRACT NOUN these should each be treated as single metaphors. We may then find that a general pattern such as CONCRETE ENTITY + OF + ABSTRACT NOUN accounts for a whole range of metaphors such as 'scourge of unemployment', 'torch of liberty' and so on. In language study, a repeated grammatical pattern such as this is known as *colligation*; concepts such as collocation and colligation are relevant in deciding how many metaphors there are in a text.

Which phrases to count?

After selecting the fixed phrase as the unit to count, we then need to decide *which* of these phrases counts as a metaphor. Because metaphors arise from transferred meanings, whatever sense a word or phrase originally had, a metaphor is formed when this word or phrase is used in a new context with a different sense that creates some type of semantic tension or incongruity. However, knowledge of historically earlier senses and how language is processed varies between individuals; for example, someone who is aware of the primary sense of 'beacon' as a fire in a prominent position will count it as a metaphor in the phrase 'Britain is a beacon' and experience some awareness of meaning shift. Conversely, someone who has only come across 'beacon' with an abstract sense – as in political rhetoric – will not do so, because they do not experience any resemblance relation. This is one reason why people vary in their estimates of metaphors in texts. Metaphor originates in an awareness of a resemblance relationship (usually known as the 'grounds') between the two entities it associates. The problem is that the perception of two entities as being separate (a precondition for any resemblance) varies between individuals, because there is individual psycholinguistic variation in the images and associations aroused by metaphor, depending on personal experience. The relationship between the two entities connected by metaphor is not one that *pre-dates* the metaphor, it is a relationship that is *created by it*. Awareness of incongruity is an act of interpretation and therefore depends on the viewer. Metaphors are not inherent in words, but arise from *how* words are used and understood, especially to the extent to which their contexts are understood as familiar or novel.

Use of a corpus to confirm categories
Evidence on use is available in a general corpus of language, which provides a robust method for critical metaphor analysis. For example, a search of the British National Corpus shows that in the first 100 examples of 'blight' only three refer to the disease of a plant (the original meaning); however, 94 of the first 100 examples of 'beacon' have the literal sense of a light that can be seen from afar. We can infer that while they are both metaphors, 'beacon' is more likely to be processed as a metaphor because *it is normally used literally* – this does not tell us how an individual will understand it in a particular context, however, nor does it show the psycholinguistic processes that an individual goes through when encountering a metaphor (as, say, in the empirical research by Gentner and Bowdle (2001)) but it shows a general social pattern arising from evidence of verbal context. This is confirmed by looking at the OED, where we find only the literal meaning of 'beacon', whereas for 'blight' there is an inclusive second meaning: 'a thing that damages or spoils something'. This is not to say that 'beacon' is any more persuasive than 'blight', or that it is an especially novel metaphor, but it is helpful in establishing the different types of metaphor we may wish to count, especially when building on the psycholinguistic approach discussed in Chapter 7.

Metaphor categorization: types of metaphor
An initial approach to categorization, as practised in Chapter 7, is on the basis of psycholinguistic criteria, as follows:

1 Novel metaphors (usually processed by comparison).
2 Entrenched metaphors (usually processed by categorization).
3 Conventional metaphors (processing shifts between comparison and categorization, depending on context).

Goatly (2008, pp. 31ff.) distinguishes between 'Tired' and 'Sleeping' metaphors, which correspond to 'conventional' and 'entrenched' metaphors, and refers to novel metaphors as 'Active' metaphors. I have shown corpus and dictionary evidence to support the classification of 'blight' and 'scourge' as entrenched metaphors and 'beacon' as a conventional metaphor. To be more specific, if using a corpus and a metaphor occurs fewer than five times in a sample of 100 corpus entries it is a candidate for being a novel metaphor; when more than half of the entries have a metaphoric sense it is an entrenched metaphor. Conventional metaphors are likely to be those that occur somewhere between 5 and 50 times in a sample of 100 corpus entries. In reality there is a continuum over time for novel metaphors to become conventionalized and then entrenched, so the researcher will need to note the period of time over which a corpus has been collected, since the more recent the sample of language, the more potential there is for metaphors to become established and fall into either the conventional or entrenched categories. In political speeches, the majority of metaphors are conventional and entrenched, with only a few likely to be novel – the opposite of the situation in literature or other more creative genres. As metaphor is a source of language change, its inherent instability leads to a situation where most metaphors are not processed by comparison because they are conventional or entrenched. Steen (2008) refers to this as 'the paradox of metaphor'.

We have seen in the analysis of 'Cold War' metaphors how conventional metaphors became so entrenched that they were accepted as the normal way of describing international relationships. Phrases such as 'The Iron Curtain', 'The Evil Empire', 'The Arms Race' and so on became the *only* way of framing certain international relations. But we cannot be sure *which* mode of processing any individual will use. There are two empirical approaches to dealing with this problem: a researcher can collect data from a sample of informants to gain insight into the psycholinguistic processing of words that are potentially metaphoric, or can search a representative corpus of language to identify the normal uses of a word – this can, as I have illustrated, assist in making distinctions between novel, conventional and entrenched metaphors. Though most of my own work uses the second, corpus-based approach, I think it can be integrated with an empirical psycholinguistic method.

As mentioned earlier, an analyst will come up with different metaphor counts on different days. Identification and classification of metaphors is necessarily a slow and at times laborious process, preferably undertaken by more than one analyst to ensure the reliability of the findings. A robust method is to analyse speeches in five phases, preferably on different days, as summarized in Figure 8.2.

1 Identify all potential metaphors by working through a text with a marker pen; initially, all candidate metaphors can be identified.
2 Confirm or reject initial decisions – drawing on dictionaries to establish whether there is a more basic sense of a word, and corpora to identify whether the word is usually metaphorical; and decisions taken with regard to the type of metaphor.

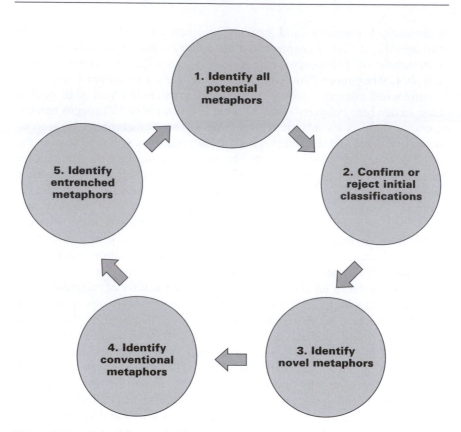

Figure 8.2   Method for critical metaphor analysis

3 From the list in stage two, identify novel 'metaphors' – that is, words and phrases that are likely to be processed by comparison. These may be indicated in the title of a speech. They are likely to be processed by comparison in short-term memory and are influential in contributing to audience response.

4 Identify conventional metaphors – the ones that a corpus shows have become a pattern such as 'beacon of hope', and where these words are metaphors between 5 and 50 occurrences in a sample of 100 lines.

5 Identify entrenched metaphors – these might have been completely invisible in the first phrase because they have become naturalized. They will occur in over half of the lines in a sample of 100.

All three types of metaphor should be identified, but for different reasons: the invisibility of entrenched metaphors can reveal the ideology behind the framing of issues in a certain way. But novel metaphors can evoke empathetic responses and contribute to powerful, heroic narratives. Where time is limited it may be preferable to focus on the extreme ends of the cline of metaphor, and paying less attention to conventional metaphors.

This is again where a corpus is useful. A method that is commonly used is to read a sample of the dataset to identify words that are often used metaphorically (referred to as 'metaphor keywords' in Charteris-Black, 2004) and then to search through the whole dataset for these (see Semino, 2008, ch. 6 for an overview of corpus methods). As Deignan (2005) explains, the collocates around metaphorical expressions in a corpus provide insight into whether they count as metaphors and will certainly assist in deciding whether they are conventional/entrenched or novel. As mentioned above, a reading of a sample of Tony Blair's speeches showed frequently used words from the semantic field of journeys (including 'journey', 'path', 'destination' and so on) and so it was then possible to search through a larger corpus of his speeches using these metaphor keywords and to categorize these as conventional or entrenched. However, this method is unlikely to be effective for novel metaphors.

A related but slightly different approach that has more potential for detecting novel metaphors is to identify a set of potential keywords from a particular semantic field *before* searching in a corpus on the basis of both intuition and previous studies; for example, a number of studies (for example, Jansen and Sabo 1994) show that war is often discussed in terms of sport (and vice versa: Charteris-Black, 2004) so it would be possible to draw up a set of words from sports ('team', 'race', 'tactics' and so on) and search for these in a corpus of speeches relating to war. In the case of Blair's use of 'beacon' we could draw up a list of words such as 'light', 'dark', 'torch', 'flame', 'shadow' and so on from the semantic field of light and dark and then use these as search terms in a corpus. For example, Ritchie (2013) identifies a metaphor used by Obama – 'incendiary' language, when he was referring to the controversial nature of statements by his pastor, Rev Jeremiah Wright; the metaphor implies both emotional intensity and the potentially destructive effect of fire – as when arson is committed during race riots. When we search a corpus such as COCA we find the ten most common collocates in the position after 'incendiary' are as shown in Table 8.1.

There is clear evidence from this limited search of collocations that numbers 4, 5, 8 and 9 are used as metaphors. As these patterns characterize around 30 per cent of the most common collocations we have some empirical evidence to classify 'incendiary language' as a conventional metaphor.

It is not always necessary to identify *every* metaphor in a text unless the approach is entirely quantitative. A number of factors will influence this decision: the length of the text, the time available for the analysis, and above all the research questions: if these are concerned with metaphor frequency or distribution, then all metaphors need to be identified. Where

Table 8.1   The ten most common collocates
in the position after 'incendiary'

1	☐	DEVICES	27
2	☐	BOMBS	23
3	☐	DEVICE	22
4	☐	RHETORIC	19
5	☐	REMARKS	8
6	☐	BOMB	8
7	☐	MATERIAL	7
8	☐	LANGUAGE	7
9	☐	COMMENTS	6
10	☐	FIRES	5

Source: Corpus of Contemporary American English
(COCA).

informants are available, insights can be gained into whether metaphors are short- or long-term mental representations. Words and phrases for which there is general agreement regarding their classification as metaphors are likely to be novel metaphors that are cognitively active in forming short-term representations, whereas those for which classifications diverge are likely to be entrenched metaphors which contribute to long-term mental representations and hence ideology.

8.3   Case Study 1: identification of metaphor in Obama's first inaugural address

Initially I distinguished between novel metaphors that are likely to be identified as such by the majority of informants – many on their first analysis – and conventional metaphors over which there will be variation. I also distinguish between conventional metaphors – the ones that are readily identifiable as metaphors – and entrenched metaphors – those for which the majority of an audience is unlikely to recognize as metaphors because they are processed entirely by categorization. This addresses critical linguistic concerns about naturalized used of language – when a particular perspective becomes habitual so that its assumptions are no longer evident. Table 8.2 (on p. 184) summarizes my analysis of metaphor in Obama's inaugural address according to psycholinguistic criteria.

At the start of Obama's speech (the text of the speech can be found at the end of Chapter 1) there is a very evident metaphor in 2.3: 'Yet, every so often the oath is taken amidst gathering clouds and raging storms'. Why might most analysts classify this as a novel metaphor? First, because these words occur in the context of a discussion of economics and international relations. Then, from the extralinguistic context, we know that the speech was not delivered in stormy weather, which allows us to identify semantic incongruity because he is not actually describing the weather. We also know that the genre of the inaugural address is too formal to permit a discussion of the weather – unless humorously – which clearly this is not. So this is a novel metaphor because it contributes to the author's intended purpose of bringing to the audience's attention an awareness of America's considerable current economic problems (the full extent of which he was probably unaware of prior to his election). It is interesting because of its potential rhetorical effect in arousing the emotion of fear or anxiety in the audience.

However, 'America has carried on' in 2.4 is likely to be processed differently by different individuals. Why is this? First, because 'America' could be treated as a metonym based on a relation of GEOGRAPHICAL PLACE FOR PEOPLE THAT LIVE THERE, and – related to this – because it is convenient and economical to talk about nation states as if they were people. However, it is a metaphor in the sense that nation states and geographical areas cannot physically move, so they cannot be the subject of a verb of motion.

I would suggest that individuals vary in the extent to which the expression activates a visual or concrete image of a person struggling heroically through bad weather. Highly patriotic Americans might not process this as a metaphor at all, as for them 'America' automatically means 'the people in America' who they visualize in a concrete way as physically struggling – so when they hear 'America', they think 'Americans', because this is entrenched in their long-term mental representations (van Dijk, 1987). Those who take a more critical stance towards the nation state might process this as a metaphor because they create a distinction in their minds between an abstract concept of the nation state and embodied human beings. 'America carries on' is not therefore independently classifiable as a metaphor, since this will depend on the cognitive schema of the individuals hearing the phrase – their values, their beliefs and perhaps their political orientations, but to the majority it is invisible and evidence for this is in the very high frequency of metaphors that represent the nation as a person in American political rhetoric. I therefore classify it as an entrenched metaphor.

Of course, identifying such entrenched metaphors is still useful for critical approaches, because the invisibility of this metaphor questions the assumption that the audience readily identify themselves as part of 'America'. We could use this as proof of an ideology: a long-term mental representation in which the nation state is primary. Distinguishing between novel metaphors that are cognitively active in short-term memory and entrenched metaphors therefore contributes to interpretation and explanation.

Table 8.2   Psycholinguistic analysis of metaphor in Obama's first inaugural speech

Novel	Conventional	Entrenched
	sacrifices borne by our ancestors (1.1)	
rising tide of prosperity (2.2)		vision of those in high office (2.4)
still waters of peace (2.2)		America has carried on (2.4)
gathering clouds (2.3)		
raging storms (2.3)		
the ways we use energy strengthen our adversaries and threaten our planet (3.5)	far-reaching network (3.2) a new age (3.3)	jobs shed (3.4) collective failure to make hard choices (3.3) economy is badly weakened (3.3)
a sapping of confidence (4.2)	a nagging fear (4.2)	
next generation must lower its sights (4.2)		
		a short span of time (5.3)
have strangled our politics (6.2)	worn out dogmas (6.2) we have chosen hope over fear (6.1)	
to carry forward that precious gift (7.2) that noble idea, passed on from generation to generation (7.2) choose our better history (7.2)	to pursue their full measure of happiness (7.2)	a young nation (7.1)
who have carried us up the long, rugged path towards prosperity and freedom (8.5)	our journey has never been one of short-cuts or settling for less (8.3) It has not been the path for the faint-hearted (8.4) in search of a new life (9.1)	

Exercise 8.1

Access your findings for Exercise 7.1 on metaphors in the speech by Michael Foot. Classify these metaphors into the following categories: novel, conventional and entrenched. Use the British National Corpus to assist with identifying these metaphor types.

8.4   Interpretation: approaches to the classification of metaphors

The first stage in interpretation can be facilitated by a very insightful distinction made by Cameron (Cameron and Low, 1999) between local, global and discourse systematicity, which can be summarized as follows:

◊ Local systematicity involves identifying patterns of metaphor in a particular speech.
◊ Discourse systematicity is when we examine metaphors in a collection of political speeches from a particular genre – say, inaugural speeches, or eulogies.
◊ Global systematicity is when we examine metaphors in a large general corpus such as the British National Corpus.

In critical metaphor analysis, I suggest we are primarily interested in discourse systems – how issues, actors and social groups are typically discussed in political speeches; however, to classify and interpret metaphors we also need to examine them in individual speeches (local systems) as well as in a representative sample of general language (global systems).

For this reason, the research design often involves compiling a set of speeches with a shared discourse feature, either because they are related to a similar topic (for example, immigration or domestic violence) or to a particular political grouping (for example, the far right). However, global systems are important because a general corpus provides insight into whether a word is likely to be processed by categorization or comparison, as it provides evidence on whether its *typical* use is metaphoric. Similarly, local systems are insightful in revealing the persuasive strategies of a particular speech. Allusions – as when the metaphors of Obama echo those of Kennedy or Martin Luther King – show the transition from local systems to discourses.

When interpreting metaphors, researchers seek to identify a pattern in the metaphors they have identified – this could be according to the mode of thinking or cognitive processing involved with reference to general conceptual representations that may link what happens in an individual's mind (on hearing a metaphor) with normative social meanings. The first stage in establishing conceptual categories is to choose between one of two approaches: identifying metaphor patterns on the basis of 'source' domains or 'target' domains, as follows:

◊ As we saw in the Chapter 7, the 'source-based' approach uses the basic, literal meanings of words that are employed metaphorically as the basis for metaphor categories – so words such as 'path', 'route' or 'guide' are classified as 'journey metaphors'; it is linguistically oriented as it proposes a linguistically superordinate term.

◇ The 'topic-based' approach considers *what the metaphor is about* rather than what the words of the metaphor normally mean when used literally – it is oriented to discourse, or meaning in context.

I shall now explain each of these in more detail.

Source-based approach

The first stage in moving to a conceptual categorization is by grouping metaphors together to establish a more general category. As we saw in Chapter 7, 'beacon' could be classified with other words such as 'glow', 'shine' and 'torch' as a 'light' metaphor. Evidence from conventional metaphors in a corpus can assist in identifying common semantic fields such as 'light', 'plants', 'animals', 'weather' and 'landscape'. There will be difficult decisions over the naming of these semantic fields as this can be done by using more or less inclusive terms. For example, 'plants' and 'animals' could both be included in a category named 'animate entities', and 'weather' and 'landscape' could both be included in a category named 'environment'. Further, all the semantic groups just mentioned (light and so on) could be subsumed under the more general notion of 'nature'; similarly 'path' and 'journey' could be integrated as 'motion' metaphors, and 'health' and 'disease' could be grouped under the more general category of 'human body'. If we are too specific, some metaphors may fit into more than one category – for example, 'beacon' could be analysed as 'fire' or 'light'. But if we are too general, the category can become too remote from its members to be meaningful – for example, 'nature' could include the human body, weather and animals. There are no hard and fast rules when we identify semantic fields from metaphor analysis, but it is the first stage in moving from the words themselves to what they might mean; that is, from language to thought: most researchers use the categories or semantic fields proposed in previous research as a starting point.

Topic-based approach

An alternative approach is to group metaphors according to their topic or tenor – that is, what it is that the metaphors are used to talk and think about; for example, Martin Luther King's major political concern was racial segregation and used metaphors from various source domains such as illness, prisons and slavery to discuss this. So it makes more sense to classify metaphors according to what he used them to talk about – racial inequality – because analysis of the context tells us that this is relevant. Critical analysts will often begin with particular issues of concern – these are typically social issues such as immigration, unemployment, war or pollution, and the classification will initially be with reference to these topics, so that *only* metaphors that refer to these topics will be of interest. However, it is not always clear what determines the selection of 'issues of concern', and these are often not formally stated by researchers, emerging instead from their own unspecified ideological view of the world. It may depend on our point of view, and life experience, as to whether we see, for example, divorced fathers or single mothers as 'vulnerable'.

The research questions should govern the approach chosen; for example, if the questions concern the sorts of metaphors that are used in particular political situations such as elections, financial crises or the build-up to war then the initial classification is likely to be by source domain. Similarly, if our questions concern a particular politician or group of politicians – whether defined by political orientation or national background – we will be interested in *all* the metaphors they use rather than just those that address a particular issue. If we are interested in the life history of a metaphor (for example, 'rogue state') or a group of metaphors ('family metaphors') we will already have determined the source domain of the metaphor(s) and be interested in the topics it/they are used to describe, and how they do this. Quite often, the process of metaphor grouping works recursively, so that if from a sample reading of a body of speeches it is found that a particular metaphor is used frequently for a particular topic, then the aim of the research becomes directed towards further evidence of the pervasiveness of this way of talking about these issues. We might explore whether 'light' metaphors such as 'beacon' are general in victory speeches; whether 'flood' and 'force' metaphors are used about 'immigration' in different political cultures; if 'weather' metaphors are generally used to describe difficult circumstances in 'state of the nation' speeches; or if 'war' metaphors characterize election speeches. In doing this we will be moving towards an interpretation of discourse style.

8.5   Classification and conceptual metaphors

Conceptual classification is influenced by the theory of metaphor that is being used and in the case of conceptual metaphor theory (originating in Lakoff and Johnson, 1980). This has been summarized as follows:

> They identified numerous groups or families of metaphors, each organized around a common implicit metaphor. For many of these families of metaphors, they traced the underlying metaphor to a literal concept based on embodied physical experience; on this basis they claim that most conceptual reasoning is fundamentally metaphorical in that our abstract concepts are experiences and expressed in terms of embodied physical experience. (Ritchie, 2003, pp. 125–6)

Typically, research involves grouping together 'linguistic' metaphors on the basis of their source domains – the semantic field of the words in them (for example, journey, war or sports) to generate a 'conceptual' metaphor – one that connects these words with a metaphor target to which they typically refer. So the researcher goes through all the authentic, linguistic metaphors that have been identified and puts together all those that are from the same source domain (for example, SPORT). Then, when a group of these linguistic metaphors also share the same metaphor target (for example, WAR) they can be classified together.

A conceptual metaphor is then inferred from this group, so if many 'sports' words are used to refer to war a conceptual metaphor might be WAR IS SPORT. When 'sports' metaphors are commonly used in political speeches this is because competitive sports metaphors place positive associations on winning and value the attributes that make winning more likely, such as fitness, strength, organization, training, a captain, teamwork, strategy and so on. Notice how the conceptual metaphor always begins with the target domain – the concept to which the metaphors refer. The conceptual metaphor should account for the relatedness of these metaphors by implying that there is a shared cognitive representation. The conceptual metaphor is then a shadow of individual metaphors – the words from which it is formed (for example, 'war' and 'sport) are not necessarily present in the speeches themselves but they are there in their reflections on the wall of the mind's cave. The claim of conceptual metaphor theory is that these reflections constitute cognitive representations – hence their relevance in critical metaphor analysis; evidence for this is that conceptual metaphors can *predict how metaphors might be used* on the basis of which metaphors *have already been used.*

8.6   Case Study 2: interpretation of metaphor in Obama's first inaugural address

I shall now illustrate how analysis of the metaphors in a particular speech can reveal local systematicity, and how interpretation of these metaphors provides insight into the discourse style of a particular politician. To do this I shall examine Barack Obama's first inaugural address, given in January 2009. Initially I classify metaphors in terms of the source domains identified and then consider to what they are used to refer (their target domains). Before proposing conceptual metaphors that influence cognitive representations, extensive evidence is needed from a range of speeches by the same politician. For example, a conceptual metaphor I identified for Martin Luther King was THE HISTORIC STRUGGLE FOR FREEDOM IS A JOURNEY and there is evidence of this in section 8.5 of Obama's speech: 'who have carried us up the long, rugged path towards prosperity and freedom'. When we locate allusions to other speakers we are tracing an emergent discourse metaphor. The same procedure would be used with speeches

by the political left or right, inaugural speeches, or speeches given in particular historical circumstances, such as around elections or in the lead-up to
war.

An analysis of the speech circumstances shows that the speech was given
at a time when the speaker was just becoming aware of the extent of the
financial crisis and so needed to dampen the feelings of euphoria – sometimes verging on hysteria – that surrounded Obama's election to the presidency. As a young president in his first term of office he needed, like
Kennedy almost 50 years before, to establish himself as a statesman and
show himself to be in command of a precarious situation. For Kennedy, this
had been in relation to an international crisis, while for Obama it was in
relation to a financial one that started in the USA but which came to have
global implications. Analysis of the speech circumstances will later assist us
in explaining the metaphor choices, and more detailed background on the
speech circumstances is given in Charteris-Black (2011, ch. 11).

We shall now examine how the metaphors identified in Chapter 7 might
be interpreted by providing some cognitive representations in the form of

Table 8.3   Analysis of metaphor source domains in sections 1–10 of Obama's first
inaugural address

Source domain	Examples
Various	*high office* (2.4); far-reaching network (3.2); a new age (3.3); jobs shed (3.4); the ways we use energy strengthen our adversaries and threaten our planet (3.5); a sapping of confidence (4.2); a short span of time (5.3); in search of a new life (9.1)
Human	economy is badly weakened (3.3); a nagging fear (4.2); have strangled our politics (6.2); a young nation (7.1)
Journeys and Motion	sacrifices borne by our ancestors (1.1); America has carried on (2.4); to carry forward that precious gift (7.2); to pursue their full measure of happiness (7.2); our journey has never been one of short-cuts or settling for less (8.3); It has not been the path for the faint-hearted (8.4); who have carried us up the long, rugged path towards prosperity and freedom (8.5)
Religion and Ethics	collective failure to make hard choices (3.3); we have chosen hope over fear (6.1); worn out dogmas (6.2); choose our better history (7.2); that noble idea, passed on from generation to generation (7.2)
Sight	vision of those in high office (2.4); next generation must lower its sights (4.2)
Weather/Sea	rising tide of prosperity (2.2); still waters of peace (2.2); gathering clouds (2.3) raging storms (2.3)

conceptual metaphors. Initially, I decided to classify the metaphors with reference to their source domains, because this early phase of metaphor interpretation delays making more debatable decisions about target domains (to what metaphors refer); this is because source domains are evident in the surface level of the text, while targets are present in the understanding of the speaker and audience. Where metaphors from the same source domain recur it is possible to identify this as a category, though it is useful to have a general category for metaphors that do not (at least initially) appear to be part of a patterned use of metaphor (see 'Various' in Table 8.3). Because I was interested in the distribution of metaphors I analysed the first part of the text (sections 1–10) and the last part (sections 22–28) separately; the findings are shown in Tables 8.3 and 8.4.

What we may notice is that most of the metaphors used in the text can be classified in terms of relatively few source domains; for example, the source domain of weather and the sea allows us to propose a conceptual metaphor CIRCUMSTANCES ARE THE WEATHER, which accounts for the group of weather and sea metaphors in the first and final parts of the speech. It is noticeable that several of the source domains that occur in the first ten sections recur in the final part (weather/sea, human, journeys and motion, religion and ethics). Identifying a distribution like this implies that there was an underlying rhetorical purpose in the use of metaphors from

Table 8.4   Analysis of metaphor source domains in sections 22–28 of Obama's first inaugural address

Source domain	Examples
Various conventional	moment that will define a generation (22.4); The instruments with which we meet them (24.1); the quiet force of progress (24.5); duties that we do not grudgingly accept but rather seize gladly (24.7); calls on us to shape an uncertain destiny (25.2)
Human	whisper through the ages (22.2); the year of America's birth (26.2)
Journeys and Motion	how far we have travelled (26.1); we refused to let this journey end (27.3); we did not turn back nor did we falter (27.3); we carried forth that great gift of freedom (27.3); delivered it safely to future generations (27.3)
Religion and Ethics	guardians of our liberty (22.3); spirit that must inhabit us all (22.4); the promise of citizenship (25.1)
Light and Darkness	sees us through our darkest hours (23.2)
Weather/Sea	the depth of winter (26.6); winter of our hardship (27.1); let us brave once more the icy currents (27.2); endure what storms may come (27.2)

Table 8.5   Analysis of target domains and propositions in Obama's first inaugural address

Target domain	Metaphors
Current dangers and risks (Negative social events, states and actions)	gathering clouds (2.3) raging storms (2.3); far-reaching network (3.2); economy is badly weakened (3.3); the ways we use energy strengthen our adversaries and threaten our planet (3.5); a sapping of confidence (4.2); a nagging fear (4.2); next generation must lower its sights (4.2); have strangled our politics (6.2); winter of our hardship (27.1)
Qualities of character required to contend with the past dangers and risks in American history	sacrifices borne by our ancestors (1.1); America has carried on (2.4); vision of those in high office (2.4); a young nation (7.1); to carry forward that precious gift (7.2); to pursue their full measure of happiness (7.2); who have carried us up the long, rugged path towards prosperity and freedom (8.5); in search of a new life (9.1); the quiet force of progress (24.5); Let it be told to the future world ... that in the depth of winter (26.6); we carried forth that great gift of freedom (27.3)
Qualities of character required to contend with the present dangers and risks: determination and endurance	we have chosen hope over fear (6.1); It has not been the path for the faint-hearted (8.4); sees us through our darkest hours (23.2); duties that we do not grudgingly accept but rather seize gladly (24.7); calls on us to shape an uncertain destiny (25.2); how far we have travelled (26.1); the year of America's birth (26.2); let us brave once more the icy currents (27.2); endure what storms may come (27.2); we refused to let this journey end (27.3); we did not turn back nor did we falter (27.3); delivered it safely to future generations (27.3)
Values	collective failure to make hard choices (3.3); worn out dogmas (6.2); our journey has never been one of short-cuts or settling for less (8.3); choose our better history (7.2); that noble idea, passed on from generation to generation (7.2); guardians of our liberty (22.3); spirit that must inhabit us all (22.4); the promise of citizenship (25.1)

this source domain. But once we start to consider 'purpose' – or the rhetorical plan behind the use of metaphor – we are moving on to the explanation of metaphor, which I discuss in Chapter 9.

When interpreting how metaphors work in this particular speech we may also wish to classify them by their target domains; this can help in identifying the specific themes or topics that metaphors are used to address. I have employed this approach in Table 8.5 (p. 191), in which many of the metaphors identified, initially by source domain, can then be grouped together by target domain to produce macro propositions – some of them quite similar to Ruth Wodak's content-specific topoi. The findings for this analysis are shown in Table 8.5 and in the Comments for Exercise 8.2.

In Chapter 9 I shall discuss how interpretation of these target domains contributes to an *explanation* of Obama's use of metaphor in this speech.

Exercise 8.2

Look at the metaphors in Tables 8.4 and 8.5 and attempt to formulate the wording of some conceptual metaphors (remember to put the target domain first and then the source domain).

Now consider the speech by Michael Foot (1999) 'The Red Flame of Socialist Courage' in B. MacArthur (ed.) *The Penguin Book of Twentieth Century Speeches*, 2nd edn, p. 418. Can you propose any conceptual metaphors?

8.7   Evaluating conceptual metaphors

I would guard against treating conceptual metaphors as having any special status because they are convenient ways of outlining a possible cognitive representation, but they are useful in identifying discourse features of metaphor as well as in detecting the underlying ideological import of metaphors through the type and intensity of the evaluation they convey. As Ritchie (2003, p. 143) points out, the conceptual metaphor ARGUMENT IS WAR actually emerges

> from a field of interrelated concepts, including athletic contests, games, and interpersonal quarrels as well as war and argument: The associations of each of these concepts are available for metaphorical application to the others as well as to external concepts such as business and politics.

So experiences, often from childhood, make available a whole set of entailments, images, schemas and so on that relate language to experience of struggle and conflict. In this respect, 'the propositional expression of a conceptual metaphor is but a mnemonic and to be accorded independent status' (ibid., p. 144). Conceptual metaphors emerge from a similar recursive process to the one described above when identifying linguistic metaphors: a conceptual metaphor is postulated as a working hypothesis but then modified in line with further evidence. Works such as Goatly (2007) and Charteris-Black (2011) contain an index showing the conceptual metaphors for which there was evidence in the speeches examined, but these should be taken as being subject to further modification, in line with findings from additional data on the politicians examined. It is also acceptable to group metaphors thematically *without* arriving at a stage of proposing a particular conceptual metaphor. One of the risks of proposing conceptual metaphors is that they become a reification or naturalization of a pattern of metaphor use that constrains how language will (or should) be used in the future, whereas we might hope that language would evolve and change in line with discourse shift over time. Lakoff and Turner (1989) and Lakoff and Johnston (1999) demonstrate how familiar source domains can be extended creatively, and critical metaphor analysis takes such an extension into the field of politics and political actions.

Conceptual metaphors should only be identified when there is evidence of the repeated systematic use of the same source domain for the same target in a particular discourse (this could be defined in terms of genre or individual style), not where there is only evidence of a local system (while an individual politician can develop a unique style of discourse, conceptual metaphors can access style). Then, where feasible, working out how this source domain is used for both positive self-representation and negative 'other' representation. For example, POLITICS IS SPORT typically conveys positive self-representations of political actors as possessing attributes for success: fitness, strength, health and so on, and as being equipped with the ability to plan strategy and defeat opponents through superior tactics and teamwork. Conversely, health and disease metaphors are more commonly used for negative representations of social issues or political opponents.

8.8   Summary

8.8.1   Framework for critical metaphor analysis

◇ CONTEXTUAL ANALYSIS and SELECTION OF SPEECHES
    When and where metaphors are identified (time/genre/sub-genre).
    Who uses metaphors (individuals/groups/comparison of individuals/ groups or with the general language).
◇ IDENTIFICATION STAGE
    How metaphors are identified (theory/definition).
    What types of metaphor are identified (conventional/novel and so on).
◇ INTERPRETATION STAGE
    How metaphors are classified (themes/concepts).
    What representations are implied.
◇ EXPLANATION STAGE
    Why are these metaphors used (impact)?
    How are these metaphors used (spread and discourse range)?

Metaphors typically arise from a tension between the intended sense of a word or phrase in its specific verbal context in a speech and the normal, or linguistic, senses that this same word or phrase has in the language as a whole (as established from a corpus). But over time these uses become conventionalized and entrenched in the everyday language of politicians so that they influence psycholinguistic processing. Critical linguistics is concerned with identifying evidence about intentions and purposes from a corpus of language, by examining the associations of a particular word – for example, the negative associations of 'blight' or the positive ones of 'beacon' – which allows inferences to be made about the intention of a speaker. 'Metaphor' is a metalinguistic concept and how far an individual 'sees' metaphors will vary according to the extent to which that person responds to the pragmatic or contextual meaning (evident from considering its use in a speech and the speech circumstances), the conceptual or cognitive meaning (evident from patterns of metaphor use) and the linguistic meaning (evident from a dictionary). Some types of metaphor will 'stand out', while others will not – to the extent that this questions whether we classify them as a metaphor or not.

Evidence from a corpus will be helpful in working out this interactive and dynamic relationship between the pragmatic and linguistic meaning, and assist with attributing intention and purpose – which we shall see is necessary when it comes to explanation. There is always a danger in studying something like 'metaphor', in that we reify it and start to attribute agency and purpose to the *metaphor itself* – whereas in critical metaphor analysis we should always return to questions of rhetorical purpose: Why is this a metaphor? What type of metaphor is it? Why was this type of metaphor chosen (for example, familiar or novel)? What social impact does this choice have? How else could it have been said?

In interpretation, some principle of classification of metaphor is needed; this can be according to psycholinguistic and/or corpus evidence, such as whether a metaphor is novel, conventional or entrenched. It can also be according to the notions of the source and target domains of the metaphors – the identification of these facilitates the formation of conceptual metaphors. Evidence for these can be found from previous research, and of their ability to predict linguistic metaphors in texts other than the ones analysed. However, they should be postulated tentatively and subject to revision and reformulation in their wording, always accepting that they are working hypotheses about the motivation of metaphor.

Essential reading

Cameron, L. and Low, G. (eds) (1999) *Researching and Applying Metaphor.* Cambridge: Cambridge University Press.

Charteris-Black, J. (2004) *Corpus Approaches to Critical Metaphor Analysis*. Basingstoke/New York: Palgrave Macmillan, ch. 2.

Deignan, A. (2005) *Metaphor and Corpus Linguistics*. Amsterdam: John Benjamins.

Goatly, A. (2008) *The Language of Metaphors* (2nd edn). London/New York: Routledge.

Ritchie, D. L. (2013) *Metaphor*. Cambridge: Cambridge University Press, ch. 9.

Semino, E. (2008) *Metaphor in Discourse*. Cambridge: Cambridge University Press ch. 6.

Chapter 9

Purposeful Metaphor and Social Cognition

9.1   Introduction

In this chapter I discuss two important concepts that relate to the explanation of metaphor: 'purposeful metaphor' and 'social cognition', and this will provide a theoretical context for an explanation of why orators use metaphors. I will then discuss a range of purposes for which metaphor is used by orators. When Aristotle defined metaphor as 'giving the thing a name that belongs to something else' (Aristotle 1952, Poetics), the use of 'giving' implies something that is done *intentionally* – an action where language is used with real-world purposes. Critical metaphor analysis explores the nature of these purposes by explaining *why* metaphors are used. The identification of conceptual metaphors as described in Chapter 8 interprets metaphor by showing that individual metaphors are not random but have an underlying pattern that can offer evidence of the speaker's purpose. In this chapter I suggest the term 'purposeful metaphor' to explain how and why such metaphors provide coherent representations of a story that a speaker is actively telling. It is the purposeful use of metaphor that turns a speech into a narrative, rather than a list of conceptual metaphors or other cognitive representations. I describe such narratives as 'myths', which can be defined as follows:

> Myth therefore ... engages the hearer by providing stories that express aspects of the unconscious. It provides a narrative based representation of intangible experiences that are evocative because they are unconsciously linked to emotions such as sadness, happiness and fear. (Charteris-Black, 2011, p. 22)

A closely related model to account for groups of related metaphors is the concept of a 'scenario', which Musolff (2006, p. 28) defines as follows:

> We can characterise a 'scenario' as a set of assumptions made by competent members of a discourses community about 'typical' aspects of a source-situation, for example, its participants and their roles, the

196

'dramatic' storylines and outcomes, and conventional evaluations of whether they count as successful, or unsuccessful, normal or abnormal, permissible or illegitimate etc. these source-based assumptions are mapped ... onto the respective target concepts.

Notice how metaphors offer whole storylines with dramatic roles that establish their interconnectedness. In fact, 'image schemas', 'scenarios', 'scripts' and 'context models' are not fundamentally different from 'myths' but have a different intellectual origin; the notion of a political myth originates in political science (Edelman, 1988; Flood, 1996), whereas the other terms originate in cognitive and discursive psychology. I shall discuss myths in more detail towards the end of this chapter, when analysing reasons for using metaphor in public communication, but first I will compare myth with these other related concepts.

Cognitive psychology is drawn on by van Dijk (2008b) in his concept of 'social cognition'; this is where 'social representation' contributes to 'organized clusters of socially shared beliefs'. He has developed this into a complete theory, in which he describes special types of mental models as 'contexts'. These contexts are ones where participants – drawing on episodic memory – construct unique, subjective interpretations of communicative situations. He adopts a distinction (made originally by Tulving (1983)) between episodic and semantic memory, in which episodic memory stores personal autobiographical experiences while semantic (or 'social') memory stores general, abstract and socially shared representations. So there are mental models for personal individual experiences (episodes) and for socially shared mental models, and the concept of 'social cognition' is one that mediates between the personal and the social. As van Dijk goes on to argue:

> It is not the social or political situation itself that influences text or talk, but rather the way individual participants represent, understand or otherwise construct the now – for them – relevant properties of a situation. Thus contexts are not objective, or 'out there', but subjective constructs of participants. In terms of contemporary cognitive psychology, this means that contexts are mental models represented in episodic memory: context models. (van Dijk, 2008b, p. 188)

While the theory is interesting, it is at times difficult to see why van Dijk restricts 'context models' to verbal communication (this is the only thing that distinguishes them from 'mental models': van Dijk, 2008b, p. 71). Why should contexts be purely verbal, and if they are not, how are context models different from mental ones? Metaphors and memories are often visual, in which case the distinction between 'context models' and 'mental models' is hard to maintain. The context model from van Dijk involves moving away from a situational to a cognitive account similar to that which I have referred to as 'speech circumstances' and emphasizes the need for a shared understanding of speaker intentions and goals.

In my view, metaphor influences the personal contexts while also contributing to socially shared beliefs; developing conceptual metaphors is a way of understanding and communicating social representations implied by metaphors, but does not determine unique personal cognitive representations. I suggest that metaphors are used with the purpose of influencing the 'subjective constructs of participants', and conceptual metaphors are similar to the socially shared mental models that are present in semantic memory and give rise to long-term cognitive representations that 'form the basis of all social practices, including discourse production and comprehension' (van Dijk, 2008a, p.175).

I shall illustrate how conceptual metaphors contribute to understanding van Dijk's mental models, or contexts, by taking further the analysis of Tony Blair's image of 'Britain is a beacon' (discussed in Chapter 7). I suggest he was contributing to a different version of the same long-term cognitive representation as Michael Foot when he talked about 'The red flame of Socialist courage'. The image of a beacon and a red flame were both intended to inspire positive representations of feelings of courage and hope associated with the political context of the time (courage was needed when the Labour Party was declining and hope was needed when it was being transformed). Each of these speakers and at least some of their audience shared these beliefs, and the audience would have recognized the speakers' purpose in using these images.

Conceptual metaphors such as ENTHUSIASM IS FIRE or ANGER IS FIRE offer a mental model, or context, that integrates not only embodied experience (we know that when our emotions are aroused we experience an increase in bodily temperature), but also cultural knowledge. Fire is used to burn debris and other unwanted things, and in social revolutions it symbolizes a rejection of the past order (at the time of writing, demonstrators in Athens have been burning buildings to demonstrate their anger at their government's decision to vote in favour of further economic austerity as required by the European Union). It may also tie in unconsciously with ideas originating in alchemy that are associated with using heat to purify base metals and turn these into gold, giving rise to a concept that PURIFICATION IS FIRE. The expression 'the sacred fire of human liberty' is used extensively in American political rhetoric (see Charteris-Black, 2004, pp. 100ff.) As well as strong emotions and idealism, Foot's 'red' fire, brings in another far-left symbol – red as the colour of Communism – a beacon only warns against danger whereas revolutionaries embrace a creative destruction of the old order. So 'fire' metaphors activate a shared network of associations based on underlying schemas that contribute to a long-term cognitive representation – a mental model or context – for idealistic social aspiration. Not all fire metaphors do this, but there are a sufficient number to show evidence of both a conceptual network and a purpose behind their use.

The 'career of metaphor' hypothesis (Bowdle and Gentner, 2005) proposed that, as a metaphor becomes conventionalized over time, the mode of processing changes from comparison to categorization. We saw in Chapter 7 how the metaphor 'cigarettes are time bombs' works by establishing a category of potentially lethal objects to which both cigarettes and time bombs belong. Conceptual metaphors provide cognitive representations that creative orators can exploit in novel metaphors to shift the mode of processing back from categorization to comparison. A conventional metaphor such as 'torch of freedom' can be represented cognitively as HOPE IS FIRE; in the following example, the metaphor (in italics) may be processed either by categorization or comparison: 'and there were enough instances in the past, mainly at Olympic Games where British *flames of hope had turned to ashes of despair*, for a note of caution to be sounded' (Christie and Ward, 1990). Here, in an extended metaphor, 'hope turning to ashes' and 'flames' may activate a general category of dangerous things.

I suggest that Foot's metaphor 'the Red flame of Socialist courage' re-activates a comparative mode of processing and is able to do this because there is a conceptual representation of a rich network of associations involving the metaphoric use of 'fire' words, and this interacts with the symbolism of 'Red'. Whether it is effective or not is another matter – the idea of being burnt in a fire may make socialism appear dangerous (as well as courageous) and activate a representation DANGER IS FIRE. The potential for the re-activation of comparative processing demonstrates the reality of underlying cognitive representations, and when researchers propose conceptual metaphors they are trying to present these cognitive representations as economically as possible. From the analysis of the above examples we could propose a more general conceptual metaphor: INTENSE EMOTION IS FIRE.

The notion of 'social cognition' put forward by van Dijk's provides a theory of why many language features (apart from metaphor) are persuasive; it is oriented to what takes place in the *hearer's* mind, whereas 'purposeful metaphor' is oriented to what occurs in the *speaker's* mind. But social cognition and purposeful metaphor offer complementary ways of exploring the same phenomenon – one places more emphasis on reception and the other on production. The purposefulness of metaphor is more obvious in political propaganda because there are government departments and agencies whose job it is to produce colourful metaphors – just as there are marketing departments of large corporations with a similar objective. In Chinese rhetoric, metaphors such as 'paper tiger' (something that appears dangerous but is in reality harmless) or 'running dog' (a servile lackey) invite processing by comparison when used in political contexts – though the rhetorical effect of the comparison will depend on the cultural values attached to animals such as 'tiger' and 'dog'. But purposeful metaphors such as 'rogue state' or 'failed state' invite processing by categorization because they have become part of a familiar lexicon for discussing international affairs – though from other perspectives they may also be interpreted as propaganda.

Critical metaphor analysis proposes that an important area of choice will be whether to use metaphors and, if the decision is positive, which metaphors to use, since such choices communicate an ideology by creating myths. No matter how socially entrenched metaphors become, the argument that they have been *chosen* presupposes that they are *purposeful*. So an assumption of CMA is that much language use is purposeful and its own purpose is to emancipate by raising awareness of choices that reinforce social prejudices.

The authors of metaphors such as *floods* or *tidal waves* of immigrants are drawing on quite a conventional way for the political right to think about immigrants. But once the terms are understood as metaphors that invite comparison – perhaps when they are used in a novel or hyperbolic way such as 'a tsunami of immigrants' – this raises awareness of a fear-based topos for describing the movement of people across national boundaries in this way (and perhaps suggests alternatives as well). In overt cases, such as in the discourse of the far right, there is direct evidence of the purposefulness of metaphors because they are chosen systematically from a range of domains associated with danger (for example, van Dijk, 1987; Hart, 2011; Chilton, 2004; Charteris-Black, 2006). But this is less the case with more covert metaphors – words such as *pressure* or *burden* when applied to immigration – and critical metaphor analysis aims to provide insight into the possible motivation of metaphors such as these that may be processed by categorization rather than comparison.

9.2   The purposes of metaphor

In this section I shall explain in more depth some purposes of metaphor first introduced in section 7.1 of Chapter 7; though I explain these separately, it should be remembered that these purposes interact dynamically with each other, so that when a metaphor is encountered it is not instantly ascribed a purpose. However, exploring possible motives (conscious or otherwise) that underlie the use of metaphor raises awareness of the potential scope for metaphor in public communication even though in real-time processing hearers are only aware of a general effect rather than its cause. A particular example of metaphor may often be motivated by a single predominant motive – though typically there are several – and it is beneficial to have an understanding of the full rhetorical repertoire for metaphor so as to identify potential purposes in a particular speech. I begin by summarizing the

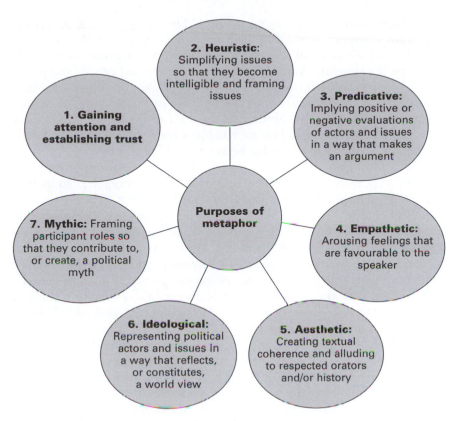

Figure 9.1   Persuasive purposes of metaphor

seven purposes in Figure 9.1 – it may help to compare Figure 9.1 with Figure 1.1 (p. 7), which shows the rhetorical means of persuasion in political speeches.

9.2.1   General rhetorical purpose: gaining the audience's attention and establishing trust

Aristotle advised orators to connect with audiences initially by attracting their attention, as this is a prerequisite for other persuasive modes such as the artistic proofs; the use of language that is colourful and memorable, such as metaphor, seems to contribute to this purpose. When gaining attention it is important to establish trust and to demonstrate that the speaker has the right intentions, so the prologue of a speech is often oriented to the speaker as he or she needs to establish ethical credentials. Notice how Michael Foot does this: 'No one is less surprised than me that this Conference has been dominated, and will continue to be dominated in my judgement, by the rising anxieties and fears and anger of our people about unemployment up and down this country.' He indexes himself as sharing the strong emotions aroused by high unemployment. Blair also points to himself and his emotional response to the situation at the start of a speech: 'It has been a long time waiting for this moment and all I can tell you is that after 18 long years of Opposition, I am deeply proud – privileged – to stand before you as the new Labour prime minister of this country.' A similar strategy was used by Earl Spencer at the start of his eulogy to his sister Diana at her funeral: 'I stand before you today the representative of a family in grief, in a country in mourning before a world in shock.'

The need to gain attention also applies to media reporting of speeches, and for this reason orators use colourful and memorable, 'soundbite' metaphors to inspire followers and arouse media interest. 'The big society', 'winds of change', 'rivers of blood' and so on are nominal metaphors that attracted attention because they were short, memorable and readily available for distribution through the media. There is also always the hope that a particularly powerful metaphor will become a catchphrase for a policy that encapsulates the predominant political perspective of a whole period – as happened with the 'war on terror'. Such metaphors become a form of shorthand and offer banners around which supporters can rally. Political advertising is no different from advertising in general – it fails completely if nobody notices it, and the more provocative the metaphor, the better from this point of view – but it also depends on political context. While 'the big society' sounded insipid, the context (a lack of a clear majority) was not one where colourful metaphors were readily available. It is generally minority parties from the political extremes that are associated most closely with a colourful use of metaphor.

9.2.2   Heuristic purpose: framing issues so that they are intelligible in a way that is favourable to an argument

Political, social and especially economic issues are abstract, complex, controversial and usually disputed, and metaphors are a way of simplifying issues to make them generally intelligible. The majority of people have only a partial understanding of these issues, especially in the case of financial matters – notice how quickly the metaphor 'credit crunch' took off to refer to the severe restriction on credit following the subprime mortgage crisis in the USA. One reason for this was that very few people knew what a 'subprime mortgage' was. A similar attempt to rename complex issues occurred when the inability of European governments to pay their debt became known as the 'sovereign debt crisis' – a term which, like 'subprime mortgage', few people probably understood in any depth. It is useful to political audiences when abstract issues are explained by image-based metaphors that make them more intelligible – though in the case of recent complex economic events the metaphors are really only a way of referring to *the effect* of economic problems rather than helping us to understand *the causes of them* (the economists themselves do not seem to understand how the problems arose). The heuristic role of metaphors concerns problems for which there may not be readily available solutions – in particular, the causes of these problems – so a metaphor such as 'wind of change' is more accessible than a concept such as 'decolonization'. As Mio (1997, 130) explains: 'Because of information-processing demands, people cannot pay attention to all aspects of political evidence. Therefore, something is needed to simplify decision-making, and metaphor and other shortcut devices (e.g. cognitive heuristics) address this need'.

Metaphor provides the mental means of accessing a concept by referring to something that is abstract, such as 'peace', using a word or phrase that in other contexts refers to a material entity, such as 'roadmap' (Semino, 2008, pp. 110–17). As we have seen, when cognitively accessible metaphors become conventionalized their status as a metaphor becomes invisible, as they are processed by categorization rather than by comparison. When metaphors become catchphrases they reveal one aspect of what they refer to but conceal another way of thinking about an issue had a different metaphor been used: they frame issues in a way that is favourable to the speaker's argument. Critical explanation of a metaphor involves working out exactly what that metaphor brings to our attention and what it obscures. Part of explaining the metaphor is to consider how we might have thought about an issue differently had a literal equivalent been used – or an alternative metaphor; for example, if another politician talked about a 'Velvet Curtain' or 'Rivers of Gold' this would reactivate the comparative processing that was originally used when Winston Churchill referred to an 'Iron Curtain' and Enoch Powell to 'The River Tiber foaming with much blood'.

Critical metaphor analysis seeks to identify both what is implied *and* the other point of view concealed by the metaphor. For example, when Harold Macmillan said: 'The wind of change is blowing through this continent: whether we like it or not, this growth of national consciousness is a political fact', he was framing the independence movements in the British colonies as a natural force and implying that independence should be accepted because it would be giving in to a natural process; it was an inevitable concession by the British government. The metaphor obscured any notion of agency on their part and its indirectness was euphemistic, because this was in reality a massive shift in political power. As the experience of the French government showed when it withdrew from Algeria in 1962, granting independence was not something that was accepted by everyone. A resistance movement – the OAS (Organisation armée secrete) – did not frame independence as a natural process to be accepted fatalistically: it was to be challenged and resisted. So 'wind of change' had a covert argument of acceptance rather than resistance. But metaphors can also be used by opponents of change: for example, when Enoch Powell used the phrase 'River Tiber foaming with much blood' he was framing immigration within a prophecy as conflict and arguing that it should be resisted, but his choice of language obscured the reality that widespread immigration into Britain was a largely peaceful process.

9.2.3   Predicative purpose: implying an evaluation of political actors and their policies

We examined the concept of predication in Chapter 6, where we found that ideological perspectives are conveyed by the traits, characteristics, qualities and features attributed to social groups. Metaphor provides a lexical resource for highlighting or concealing positive or negative features: when Hitler referred to the Jews as 'parasites' he was highlighting negative features, but when he spoke about 'the final solution' this was evidently concealing negative features of the death camps. We also saw that this often works intertextually, so that a metaphor can allude to previous uses by opponents to offer a counter-representation and contest political issues. Metaphors offer positive representations of the speaker and his supporters, and of their actions and policies, and a negative representation of opponents and their actions and policies.

While this sounds simple, how it is done by lexical choices is often much more complex. For example, Charteris-Black (2011) describes in detail how Blair and Clinton used verbs such as 'create', 'craft', 'forge' and 'shape' metaphorically to represent themselves as creative forces working for what is morally good, and proposed the conceptual metaphor POLITICAL ACTION IS CREATING WHAT IS GOOD, but these words might not at first sight be conveying any explicit evaluation. A further claim was that Blair used aggressive physical verbs such as 'stamp out', 'strip away' and so on when describing actions against negatively evaluated entities. The entities represented as warranting destruction are usually abstract entities such as the nuclear arms trade:

> We know, also, that there are groups or people, occasionally states, who trade the technology and capability for such weapons. It is time this trade was *exposed, disrupted, and stamped out.* (14 September 2001)

To capture this, I also proposed the conceptual metaphor POLITICAL ACTION IS DESTROYING WHAT IS BAD. Politicians establish legitimacy by representing themselves as upholding the moral values that bind society together by regaining control over rampant forces. Control over what is threatening is obligatory because it ensures survival of the social and moral order. Of course, the conceptual metaphor POLITICAL ACTION IS DESTROYING WHAT IS BAD *presupposes* that the speaker knows what constitutes badness and contains an argument about what should be done. Hitler thought the Jews constituted a force for social disintegration, and the metaphor of 'the final solution' was in reality an argument for the death camps.

Disease metaphors are typically used by politicians for predicative purposes. In political philosophy, the analogy between disease and social disorder demands a rational response of some sort. Early political theorists such as Niccolò Machiavelli and Thomas Hobbes recommended intervening before the disease was out of control. Susan Sontag argued that, after the French Revolution, disease metaphors became a much more melodramatic hallmark of totalitarian movements. For Hitler, the Jews were syphilitic and cancerous; for Trotsky, Stalinism represented syphilis; and in Arab polemic, Israel is represented as a cancer in the heart of the Arab world. The switch to fatal illnesses argued for much more radical cures. As Sontag (1991: 73) summarizes: 'Disease imagery is used to express concern for social order, and health is something everyone is presumed to know about.'

The main point of Sontag (1991) is that a polemical use of disease metaphors – in which disease becomes progressively represented by metaphors from the source domain of war, such as invasion, is damaging for people like herself who are actually suffering from one of these diseases. She illustrates how, when a disease is conceptualized as an invasion, it also entails a powerful moral argument, so that in the same way as it is right to end a disease, it becomes right to end whatever is metaphorically represented as being disease-like. Once the enemy is effectively demonized by disease metaphors, it becomes a moral obligation to destroy him.

Margaret Thatcher represented social problems and political opponents as illnesses, which implied that regaining control required surgical intervention. In these right-wing metaphors the politician is represented as a doctor, and his or her solutions to social and moral problems as remedies – with milder conditions treated with medicine while more drastic ones require intrusive surgery with the aim of restoring balance. For Thatcher, I proposed the conceptual metaphors: 'LABOUR POLICIES ARE A DISEASE' as in:

Labour's *real prescription* for Britain *is the disease* half the world is struggling *to cure*. (October 1989)

A Britain that was known as *the sick man of Europe* – And which spoke the language of compassion but which suffered the winter of discontent.

And 'CONSERVATIVE POLICIES ARE A MEDICINE' as in:

They dodged difficult problems rather than face up to them. The question they asked was not "*Will the medicine work?*" but "Will it taste all right?" (October 1985)

The former Malaysian prime minister, Mahathir Mohamad, developed a style of argument characterized by the systematic use of disease metaphors (see Charteris-Black, 2007, ch. 8 for a detailed account). Here is one example:

> But the deluge of immigrants which the British encouraged, and the segregation which followed, arrested this *healthy, natural process* and precipitated the problems which have *plagued* the Malays ever since, and which have undermined their rights as the definitive people of the peninsula.

To describe these, I proposed two conceptual representations: THE POLITICIAN IS A DOCTOR; and POLITICAL PRACTICE IS MEDICAL PRACTICE. Since at times a degree of force is necessary in the practice of medicine (as, say, to remove a rotten tooth or a diseased organ) this argues that similarly in politics, forceful policies are legitimate; for example, in a debate over a university merger Mahathir argued that: 'When the indications are irrefutable, amputations, however painful, must be undertaken' (Mahathir Mohamad speech, 14 July 1967). The argument here is one often used by the political right: the ends justify the means. The predicative purpose of metaphor has the same cognitive objects as the heuristic purpose: to frame political actors and issues in line with an underlying rhetorical purpose of 'being right'. But it does so more explicitly with reference to positive and negative scales for evaluation that draw on lexical semantics for good and bad embodied experience of life – health and life are inherently positive, and disease and death inherently negative. Framing an issue in way that conveys strong evaluations also contains implied arguments – ones that may not stand up in an analysis of argument structure.

Exercise 9.1

Go through the contents list of a collection of speeches such as MacArthur's *The Penguin Book of Twentieth Century Speeches*. List the titles of speeches that appear to contain a metaphor designed with the rhetorical purpose of grabbing attention.

- ➤ Select one of these speeches and analyse the heuristic role of metaphor by considering what features the metaphors that are used repeatedly in the speech bring to an audience and what they obscure. You may need to undertake some research into the speech circumstances to be able to do this.
- ➤ Identify any metaphors in this speech that convey an evaluation of some type. Make a table that shows the entities, actors or issues that are evaluated positively and negatively.   ➜

> ➢ Write a short account of how your findings framed a situation in a particular way. Try to indicate the arguments that are being made and whether these are explicit or by predication.
> ➢ Discuss how it might have been framed differently had alternative metaphors been used, and the effect this would have on any argument.

9.2.4 Empathetic purpose: to arouse the audience's feelings in such a way that they will be favourable to the speaker

The interactive dynamics between the orator and audience offer evidence of *how* metaphors evoke an emotional response; for example, if you look at the analysis of the artistic proof of pathos in Obama's inaugural address given at the end of Chapter 1, you will see that in almost every section where pathos is employed there is audible applause or cheering at the next opportunity:

> Starting today, *we must pick ourselves up, dust ourselves off,* and begin again the work of *remaking America* (CHEERS) (11.7)

> know that *America is a friend of each nation* every man, woman, and child who seeks a future of peace and dignity, and we are ready to lead once more (CHEERS and LONG APPLAUSE) (16.4)

It is worth noting how each of these metaphors encourages positive emotions of optimism and hope associated through personification: the first example creates an image of a person showing resolution and courage in recovering from being knocked over. While speaking of nation states as individual people – with the capacity for thought and action – is a conventional way of discussing national affairs, the use of the expression 'dust ourselves off' re-activates the comparison between an abstract entity, the nation state, and an embodied individual. The second example conceives of international relations in terms of personal relationships with America as a friend rather than a bully. Conceiving of abstract international relations as if they were relationships between people creates the potential for the full range of emotions that we associate with relationships – empathy towards friends and family or hostility towards enemies, criminals or villains who threaten our group.

Intertexual use of metaphor also arouses stronger emotions by transferring the emotions aroused by the historical memory of admired and loved past leaders. For example, if we look at the broader context of Obama's use of the friendship metaphor we can identify an allusion to J. F. Kennedy's inaugural address (see Chapter 3):

Obama
Those ideals still light the world, and we will not give them up for expediency's sake (3) (APPLAUSE). And so to all other peoples and governments who are watching today, from the grandest capitals to the small village where my father was born: know that America is a friend of each nation ...

J. F. Kennedy
To those peoples in the huts and villages across the globe struggling to break the bonds of mass misery, we pledge our best efforts to help them help themselves, for whatever period is required – not because the Communists may be doing it, not because we seek their votes, but because it is right. (8.1)

What evidence is there here of allusion? First, the proposition that America is offering friendship, second, the reference to 'village', and then the syntax: Obama begins 'And so to all ...' ; it is not particularly common to start a sentence in this way and it evokes the syntax of Kennedy's series of parallel phrases: 'To those old allies', 'To those new States', 'To those peoples' and so on. For Obama, allusion arouses positive emotions associated with Kennedy's memory as well as the heroic status of a young, good-looking male leader in the political culture of the American Democratic tradition. As mentioned in Chapter 1, humour also contributes to arousing the emotions, and metaphors are sometimes used humorously. Charteris-Black (2011) illustrates how right-wing politicians such as Margaret Thatcher and Ronald Reagan used humour successfully. But humour is not the exclusive preserve of the political right; Charteris-Black (2011) shows how Obama also used humour effectively. Here is a more recent example in a discussion of the debate over whether reduction in public spending would solve the financial crisis:

> And let's make sure that what we're cutting is really excess weight. Cutting the deficit by cutting our investments in innovation and education is like lightening an overloaded airplane by removing its engine. It may make you feel like you're flying high at first, but it won't take long before you feel the impact. (LAUGHTER) (Obama, 25 January 2011)

While this is closer to an analogy than a metaphor, it is visual and draws on embodied meaning to create humour and evoke laughter.

9.2.5   Aesthetic purpose: creating textual coherence

We saw in the discussion of tropes in Chapter 4 that metaphors are not evenly distributed but tend to cluster in rhetorically important parts of the speech – typically the prologue and the epilogue; this testifies to creating coherence by identifying a theme early on and indicating that a speech is approaching a conclusion when the same metaphor theme is returned to later. This is an aesthetic function that establishes the speech as being well-formed, balanced and having the aesthetic qualities of a piece of music, in which the coda is signalled by a return to a main theme. I shall illustrate this in detail in Case Study 3 (below), which explains the metaphors in Obama's inaugural address, but here I would like to illustrate a similar re-cycling of a metaphor theme in his 2012 State of the Union address. It begins with the topic of the return of American troops from Iraq and Afghanistan, the removal of Osama bin Laden as a threat, and the diminished threat of the Taliban, and contains a metaphor (in *italics*):

> For these achievements are a testament to the courage, selflessness, and *teamwork* of America's Armed Forces. At a time when too many of our institutions have let us down, they exceed all expectations. They're not consumed with personal ambition. They don't obsess over their differences. They focus on the mission at hand. They work together.

> ***Imagine what we could accomplish if we followed their example.*** Think about the America within our reach: A country that leads the world in educating its people. An America that attracts a new generation of high-tech manufacturing and high-paying jobs. A future where we're in control of our own energy, and our security and prosperity aren't so tied to unstable parts of the world. An economy built to last, where hard work pays off, and responsibility is rewarded.

Notice how in the warrant (in ***bold italics***) Obama moves effortlessly from discussing the 'teamwork' metaphor to 'the America within our reach'; that is, from a specific institution – the army – to the whole country. 'Teamwork' is a metaphor based on the concept WAR IS SPORT, which makes a positive evaluation of war. Towards the end of the speech he develops in detail the narrative of a successful American military mission:

> All that mattered that day was the mission. No one thought about politics. No one thought about themselves. One of the young men involved in the raid later told me that he didn't deserve credit for the mission. It only succeeded, he said, because every single member of that unit did their job – the pilot who landed the helicopter that spun out of control; the translator who kept others from entering the compound; the troops who separated the women and children from the fight; the SEALS who charged up the stairs …

This then leads into an analogy with America as a whole, in which elements such as teamwork, solidarity and shared purpose lead to a successful outcome:

> So it is with America. Each time I look at that flag, I'm reminded that our destiny is stitched together like those fifty stars and those thirteen stripes. No one *built this country on their own*. This Nation is great because *we built it together*. This Nation is great because *we worked as a team*. This Nation is great because we get each other's backs. And if we hold fast to that truth, in this moment of trial, there is no challenge too great; no mission too hard. As long as we're joined in common purpose, as long as we maintain our common resolve, *our journey moves forward*, our future is hopeful, and the state of our Union will always be strong.
>
> Thank you, God bless you, and may God bless the United States of America.

This is based on the conceptual metaphors SOCIAL ORGANIZATION IS A BUILDING at the discourse level, and, at the text level of this speech, SOCIETY IS AN ARMY or SOCIAL ORGANIZATION IS MILITARY ORGANIZATION, in which the roles of combined effort towards common goals are shared by both the source and target domains. The two conventional metaphors (in italics) activate the discourse metaphor SOCIAL ORGANIZATION IS A BUILDING. An extended analogy can be interpreted by forming a conceptual metaphor that offers a cognitive representation of a discourse pattern. The recurrence of the metaphor in the coda contributes to the identification of the primary theme of the speech, and establishes its coherence by drawing on the conceptual representations that contribute to social cognition.

Metaphors therefore interact with each other to create coherence – at a local textual level, but also intertextually, so that a speaker can create a particular style of discourse that forms a political identity. Charteris-Black (2011) illustrates how a number of different politicians create such identities through this stylistic of metaphor – often in combination with other linguistic features such as modality. For example, a sense of certainty and self-conviction permeates Obama's rhetorical style so that his commitment to a cause is communicated through a combination of the language of high modality, with metaphors that contribute to the coherence of his speeches. It is important that, while particular speeches may be adapted to specific occasions and audiences, there is a more enduring style that creates political identity.

9.2.6   Ideological purpose: to offer a 'world view'

In a study of political speeches, I defined ideology as: 'a coherent set of ideas and beliefs that provides an organised and systematic representation of the world' about which the holders of the ideology could agree (Charteris-Black, 2011, pp. 21–2). In Chapter 8 I mentioned a number of illustrations where ideology was at work, and I will remind the reader of a few of these. Ongoing use of 'pressure' metaphors in relation to immigration (pressure, strain, burden and so on) and the associated idea of Britain as a contained space all form part of a world view that experiences immigration as threatening. The use of crime metaphors relating to justice was an ideological motivated way of framing the 'War on Terror', and the use of plant metaphors is an ideological way of framing economic issues so that they are represented as being controllable (economic growth, the green shoots of recovery, the branches of an organization and so on). Crime metaphors cast politicians as judges and plant metaphors as gardeners, but without making explicit the role of the judge or gardener, because ideological uses of language are generally covert. These metaphor systems may be revealed by analysis of the predicates (as in section 9.2.3), but ideology may sometimes only be revealed by analysis of the systemic use of metaphor rather than merely the lexical semantics of particular words in the metaphors.

The ideological purpose of metaphor is its systematic use in such a way that it forms long-term mental representations which contribute to a particular view of the world that can be described as a political myth. An example of this is Lakoff (2002), which contrasts Republican and Democratic ideologies by contrasting a strict father and a nurturing parent. He claimed that Republicans employ metaphors that emphasize government as strength-based and as concerned with authority, while Democrats employ metaphors that emphasize the caring role of government. As Mio (1997, p. 130) puts it: 'They [metaphors] are also effective because of their ability to resonate with latent symbolic representations residing at the unconscious level.' In the conclusion of a detailed analysis of the metaphors used by American and British politicians, I claimed:

> In many cases, therefore, metaphor choice is motivated by ideology. The same notions could have been communicated in a different way had the ideology been different and the same metaphors can be employed in different ways according to ideological perspective. In politics, for example, conflict metaphors could be used either to attack an opponent's point of view or to represent the opponent as an aggressor. Different aspects of the source domain were found to correspond with different ideological outlooks. (Charteris-Black, 2004, p. 247)

The point I was making was that ideologies form world views through their use of metaphor (see Goatly, 2007). I did not discuss how deliberate this was, but assumed that linguistic decisions were purposeful. Table 9.1 summarizes some ideologies that are commonly expressed by metaphor.

Table 9.1 Conceptual metaphors and ideology in political speeches

Source domain	Positive	Negative
Human/Machine	THE IN-GROUP/NATION IS A PERSON	THE OUT-GROUP IS A MACHINE
	THE IDEOLOGY OF THE IN-GROUP IS A PERSON	OPPOSING IDEOLOGIES ARE MACHINES
Family	THE IN-GROUP IS A FAMILY	THE OUT-GROUP IS A CHILD
	RELATIONS BETWEEN NATIONS/GROUPS ARE FAMILY RELATIONSHIPS	DIFFICULTIES BETWEEN NATIONS ARE SEPARATION/DIVORCE
	RELATIONS WITHIN THE IN-GROUP ARE FAMILY RELATIONSHIPS[1]	
	NURTURANT PARENT	STRICT FATHER
Motion/Journeys	PURPOSEFUL POLITICAL ACTIVITY IS TRAVELLING ALONG A PATH TOWARDS A DESTINATION	OUT-GROUPS ARE OBSTACLES
	THE STRUGGLE FOR FREEDOM IS A JOURNEY	
	SUCCESS IS SPEED	FAILURE IS SLOWNESS
Sport and games	POLITICS IS SPORT	
	POLITICS IS A GAME	
	SUCCESS IS WINNING	FAILURE IS LOSING
	POLITICS IS FOOTBALL[2]	
	WAR IS SPORT	
War	POLITICS IS WAR[3]	SOCIAL PROBLEMS (e.g. INFLATION) ARE ENEMIES
		OPPOSING IDEOLOGIES ARE ENEMIES
	IN-GROUPS ARE ALLIES	OUT-GROUPS ARE ENEMIES
	SUCCESS IS VICTORY	FAILURE IS DEFEAT

	In-group	Out-group
Disease and Health	THE IN-GROUP'S POLICIES ARE A MEDICINE	THE OUT-GROUP IS A DISEASE
		THE OUT-GROUP'S POLICIES CAUSE DISEASE
		SOCIAL PROBLEMS ARE A DISEASE
		SOCIETY IS A SICK PATIENT
Myth	THE POLITICIAN IS A DOCTOR	THE OUT-GROUP IS A VILLAIN
	THE IN-GROUP IS A HERO	THE OUT-GROUP IS A DEATH FORCE
Creation and Destruction	THE IN-GROUP IS A LIFE FORCE	BAD GOVERNING IS DESTROYING
	GOOD GOVERNING IS CREATING[4]	
Light	THE IN-GROUP IS A SOURCE OF LIGHT	THE OUT-GROUP IS DARKNESS
Religion	THE IN-GROUP IS A FORCE FOR GOOD	THE OUT-GROUP IS A FORCE FOR EVIL
	THE IN-GROUP ARE ANGELS	THE OUT-GROUP ARE DEVILS
Animals	THE IN-GROUP IS A POWERFUL ANIMAL (BULLDOG, LION etc.)	THE OUT-GROUP IS A PARASITE/DANGEROUS ANIMAL
		THE OUT-GROUP IS A WEAK ANIMAL
		OUT-GROUP IDEOLOGIES ARE RAPACIOUS ANIMALS
		THE BEHAVIOUR OF THE OUT-GROUP IS ANIMAL BEHAVIOUR
Building[5]	SOCIAL ORGANIZATION IS A BUILDING/STRUCTURE	OPPONENTS ARE DESTROYERS

Notes:
1 See Musolff (2006) for a detailed discussion of family metaphors in debates around the European Union.
2 See Semino and Masci (1996) for a discussion of this in relation to Silvio Berlusconi.
3 See Charteris-Black (2011, ch. 7) for a discussion of how this was used by Margaret Thatcher.
4 See Charteris-Black (2011) for a discussion of this in the speeches of Bill Clinton, Tony Blair and George W. Bush.
5 See Lu and Ahrens (2008) for an interesting discussion of these in Taiwanese speeches.

Table 9.1 illustrates the findings of particular studies using conceptual metaphor theory to explain metaphors in speeches with reference to evaluation – that is, to the positive and negative representations of political actors and action, political issues, ideas and ideologies. In places, I have modified the wording of conceptual metaphors to simplify and generalize from particular speakers to concepts that characterize political speeches in general. It is not possible to list all the research but I have attempted to indicate where there is a particular source for this representation. I shall use the term 'in-group' to refer to those allied to the speaker – whether the 'we'/'us' refers to supporters who are physically present in the audience, members of a party, a region, a nation or believers in a valued ideology; and will use 'out-group' to refer to those whom the speaker represents as the other – whether 'they'/'them' refers to opponents, members of an opposition party, an enemy or subscribers to a devalued ideology.

Exercise 9.2

Put together a small corpus of speeches for a particular politician, or group of politicians, whom you think might use metaphor to make strong evaluations. Identify any metaphors used to represent the in-group positively or the out-group negatively. Where you have several metaphors that make similar evaluations for a particular social group, work out hypotheses for conceptual metaphors that express the concept or idea underlying these clusters of metaphors.

Charteris-Black (2011) proposes conceptual metaphors for the following politicians: Churchill; Powell; Thatcher; Blair; Martin Luther King; Reagan; Clinton; Bush (Senior and Junior); and Obama.

9.2.7   Mythic purpose

The mythic purpose of metaphor is to engage the hearer by providing stories that express aspects of the unconscious. Myth provides a narrative-based representation of powerful, intense, often unconsciously driven, emotions such as grief, fear, happiness and joy. Myths are purposeful but their origin is in the unconscious. I illustrate this duality in an account of journey metaphors: 'Analysis of metaphors can add to our understanding of how specific rhetorical goals are achieved through the use of metaphors that match the speaker's intentions with the audience's mental schemata and scripts for journeys' (Charteris-Black, 2011, p. 71). I emphasize the unconscious, mythic, appeal of journeys: 'In many myths going on long journeys towards some predetermined goal is an established means of taking on the stature of a hero' (Charteris-Black, 2011, p. 324). It is likely that many politicians are motivated unconsciously by a heroic ideal but will purposefully use metaphor to communicate their ideology. For this reason, 'purposeful' metaphor seems to be an explanatory term because, while it does not assume that speakers are fully conscious of their own essential motivation, it nevertheless implies that they are driven by an underlying purpose along a rhetorical path towards the anticipated outcome of political power. I shall illustrate mythic purpose at the end of my analysis of Obama's inaugural address.

9.3   Case Study 3: explanation of metaphor in Obama's first inaugural address

Look back to the findings of the analysis shown in section 8.6 and you will see that the majority of metaphors are from the source domain of journeys. These contribute to the cohesion of the text by identifying major themes, such as the difficulties that are to be overcome by American citizens, and the need for effort to contribute to social and economic progress. There is also some correlation between metaphor choice and rhetorical purpose: when the speaker is describing present difficulties there is the use of weather metaphors – these remove any possibility of blame or recrimination, since the weather is generally taken to be a given (rather than of human creation); this is in keeping with the rhetorical purpose of an inaugural speech, which is to overcome feelings of division aroused by the election campaign. When the rhetorical purpose is to emphasize agency and effort by the audience there is a shift to journey metaphors – notice how these also correlate with the use of first-person plural pronouns. Finally, we should note how metaphors of light and darkness introduce themes of spirituality and idealism – they present the speaker as a visionary with the power of 'seeing' the future, and this implies one of the attributes of a charismatic leader.

There are clusters of metaphors in the introductory and concluding sections of the speech – this is especially the case with 'weather' metaphors; this indicates the rhetorical importance of these parts of the speech as they have a high impact on the audience, and the very formal, historic occasion requires a traditional or classical rhetorical style. 'Light' metaphors introduce an important central section of the speech that highlights the ethical values of the speaker. 'Journey' metaphors are distributed more evenly through the text because of their role in identifying a major theme of effort.

We saw from Table 1.1 that Aristotle claimed that the epilogue has a high impact, since the last words the audience hears before taking a decision (in the case of deliberative oratory) are the most persuasive. He proposed that the artistic appeal that is the most persuasive for the epilogue is pathos, since it is crucial to arouse the emotions when concluding a speech. Obama uses a complex cluster of metaphors to do this at the end of the inaugural speech. The metaphors are from the semantic fields of weather ('winter', 'storms' and so on), water ('currents') and journeys ('turn back'). They arouse emotions of fear and courage that are connected to unify the audience for a common purpose. These metaphors combine for the aesthetic arrangement of the speech because these are the same semantic fields as those used in the prologue. The matching of metaphor in the prologue and the epilogue shows the aesthetic appeal of the arrangement. This aesthetic appeal is created here by metaphor to produce an elevated style that is appropriate to the main theme of his speech, which is the need for a heroic narrative of nation.

The epilogue has the purpose of arousing emotions that are appropriate to an occasion – in this case, the emotion of enthusiasm arising from the social effort that is implied by a journey in the company of others. The use of journey metaphors alludes to the heroic rhetorical style of Martin Luther King, which was also based on creating a highly persuasive messianic myth (see Charteris-Black, 2011, ch.4); and Obama had done this earlier, in his election campaign:

> And if you will join *me in this improbable quest*, if *you feel destiny calling*, and see as I see, a *future of endless possibility stretching before us*; if you sense, as I sense, that the time is now to *shake off our slumber, and slough off our fear*, and *make good on the debt we owe past and future generations*, then I'm ready *to take up the cause, and march with you*, and work with you. Together, starting today, let us finish the work that needs to be done, and *usher in a new birth of freedom on this Earth.*
> (10 February 2007)

Here metaphors are drawn from the domains of war, sleep and journeys, and personifications of 'destiny' and 'freedom'. The dense use of metaphor contributes to an elevated style intended to motivate hearers to carry out the actions necessary to bring about the anticipated outcomes, so 'war' metaphors imply struggle and effort, and sleeping is equated with inaction rather than dreaming. Metaphor is therefore a central rhetorical figure in creating the emotions appropriate for the political purpose of motivating social action. Figure 9.2 illustrates a mythic element in the circular argument structure of a speech, but with core themes (corresponding with metaphor targets) that recur at various rhetorically important parts of the speech.

If you compare this with my analysis of the mythic structure in Martin Luther King's speeches you will find many similarities (Charteris-Black, 2011, pp. 88–96). In Table 8.5 we identified the following metaphor targets in the speech: current dangers and risks; qualities of character required to

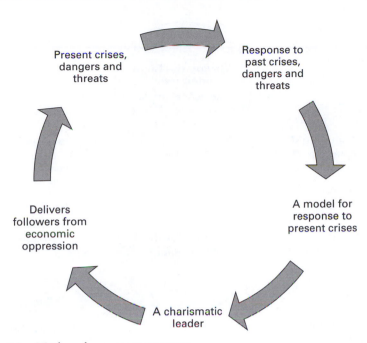

Figure 9.2   Myth and argument structure

contend with the past dangers and risks in American history; qualities of character required to contend with the present dangers and risks; and values. Figure 9.3 summarizes how all these relate to the primary rhetorical purpose of 'Being Right' through the use of metaphor.

The diagram shows how, at the level of metaphor, the model for rhetorical persuasion introduced in Chapter 1 can be applied by identifying metaphor targets that correspond systematically with underlying rhetorical purposes: this provides an explanation for metaphor choices in the speech, and more generally in Obama's style of discourse.

Exercise 9.3: Project

Assemble a small corpus of around 10–15 speeches given by a particular politician. Identify metaphors in this corpus; classify them by source domain, then by target domain; propose some conceptual representations. Consider whether they show evidence of political myth. Work out an economical way of presenting this myth. You may wish to compare your findings with those in Charteris-Black (2011).

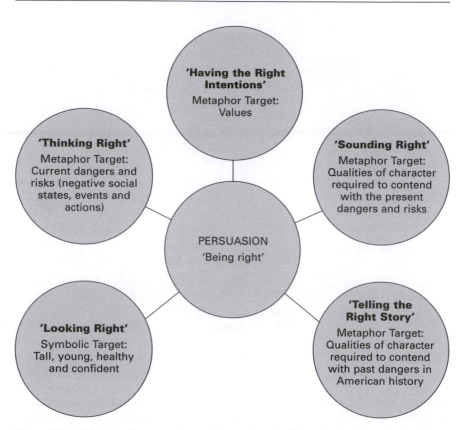

Figure 9.3   Rhetorical persuasion and metaphor in Obama's first inaugural address

Essential reading

Cameron, L. and Low, G. (eds) (1999) *Researching and Applying Metaphor*. Cambridge: Cambridge University Press.

Charteris-Black, J. (2011) *Politicians and Rhetoric: The Persuasive Power of Metaphor*, 2nd edn. Basingstoke/New York: Palgrave Macmillan.

Goatly, A. (2007) *Washing the Brain – Metaphor and Hidden Ideology*. Amsterdam/Philadelphia: John Benjamins.

Lakoff, G. and Johnson, M. (1980) *Metaphors We Live By*. Chicago: University of Chicago Press.

Musoloff, A. (2006) 'Metaphor Scenarios in Public Discourse', *Metaphor and Symbol*, 21(1): 23–38.

Ritchie, D. (2003) '"ARGUMENT IS WAR" – Or Is It a Game of Chess? Multiple Meanings in the Analysis of Implicit Metaphors', *Metaphor and Symbol*, 18(2): 125–46.

Chapter 10

Rounding up: David Cameron's European Union Speech

10.1 Introduction

As a way of summarizing the range of approaches covered in this book I shall now consider how they might be applied to an important deliberative speech by the British prime minister, David Cameron, given in January 2013, on the position of the United Kingdom within Europe. I shall consider briefly what insights the theories outlined in the previous chapters might bring to this speech. The opening section of the speech is given at the end of this chapter.

First, I shall consider the broader political context, and then the more specific context of the European debate. The 2010 election led to a hung Parliament, as the Conservatives fell 20 seats short of the 326 seats required for a majority government. As a result, a coalition was formed with the Liberal Democrats. Politically, therefore, it was essential for David Cameron to be able to establish a consensus, to ensure the survival of his government. However, given the volatility of the financial markets there has been a strong rhetorical incentive to appear strong and unified so as to ensure international credibility and avoid the cataclysm of a collapse in confidence in the UK economy. Against this background, the somewhat paradoxical rhetorical objective has been to appear strong while being in a politically vulnerable position. So, by taking a firm position in relation to Europe was a way of positioning his party towards an election strategy for 2015 by offering the prospect of a referendum on Europe – thereby stealing a march on the opposition, should they be considering offering a policy with democratic appeal. When times are tough at home, it is often politically advantageous to focus policies on abroad, and for most British people – separated by both geography and language – Europe still is 'abroad'.

The Conservative Party leader needed to address the question of Britain's membership of the European Union, because the fastest-growing party in the United Kingdom at the time was the UK Independence Party (UKIP) whose sole policy was withdrawal from Europe, and there has been an increasing division within Cameron's own party between those in favour of and those opposed to Britain's membership of the European Union. The euro crisis left the majority of British people relieved to find they had not joined the Union, and Cameron therefore saw an opportunity to redirect Europe away from its objectives of full integration and back to the original concept of a Union that was essentially economic, rather than political or social. He needed to address these issues against the immediate background of a proposed increase in the amount paid by member states to the European budget at a time when national budgets were being reduced; his aims had been to resist such an increase, and to emulate Margaret Thatcher, who had negotiated a rebate for Britain on the grounds that it benefited less from funding policies that favoured nations with large agricultural sectors. This speech presented Cameron's long-term solution to the ongoing political 'problem' of Europe: a proposal for a referendum in 2015 on continuing British membership of the EU and a promise that this proposal would be included in the Conservative manifesto for the 2015 election.

In this respect, the speech was a deliberative one because of its orientation to future policy and the promise of a referendum. He begins by taking a historical perspective on the origins of the EU in the aftermath of the Second World War, then positions Britain as a nation that is open to Europe, and himself as a leader who has a 'positive vision for the future of the European Union'. He then identifies the major problems of Europe: the euro; problems of global economic competitiveness; and democratic accountability. Having framed the EU as problematic, he then responds with a series of solutions: the need for global economic competitiveness and flexibility – by which he means allowing different degrees of membership to the EU rather than a 'one size fits all approach', thus leading to more autonomy for national governments. The speech was an appeal for a return to seeing the European Union as primarily an economic rather than a political union – with the possibility of a British withdrawal if the political overrides the economic.

10.2   Classical rhetoric: Style

The style of the speech relies primarily on the appeals of logos and ethos – as is fitting, since an appeal to pathos in a speech of the type might be interpreted as highly nationalistic and more in keeping with those committed to withdrawal from the EU. One strategy that is readily identifiable throughout the speech is Cameron's introduction of counter-arguments using refutation, and the rhetorical figure of prolepsis runs throughout the speech to introduce a series of counter-arguments; I have summarized these in Table 10.1.

This foregrounding of all the possible arguments against his policies allows Cameron to appear rational and as having considered fully a range of options before deciding on a policy. This is a style implying that the

Table 10.1   Use of counter-arguments

◇ I know that the United Kingdom is sometimes seen as an argumentative and rather strong-minded member of the family of European nations.

◇ Some might then ask: why raise fundamental questions about the future of Europe when Europe is already in the midst of a deep crisis? Why raise questions about Britain's role when support in Britain is already so thin?

◇ There are always voices saying: 'Don't ask the difficult questions.'

◇ Some will claim that this offends a central tenet of the EU's founding philosophy. I say it merely reflects the reality of the European Union today. Seventeen members are part of the eurozone. Ten are not.

◇ Some say this will unravel the principle of the EU – and that you can't pick and choose on the basis of what your nation needs.

◇ So to those who say we have no vision for Europe, I say we have.

◇ Some people say that to point this out is irresponsible, creates uncertainty for business and puts a question mark over Britain's place in the European Union. But the question mark is already there and ignoring it won't make it go away.

◇ There are some who suggest we could turn ourselves into a Norway or Switzerland – with access to the single market but outside the EU. But would that really be in our best interests?

◇ I know there will be those who say the vision I have outlined will be impossible to achieve. That there is no way our partners will co-operate. That the British people have set themselves on a path to inevitable exit. And that if we aren't comfortable being in the EU after 40 years, we never will be.

speaker is engaged in dialogue with his political opponents, and integrating their voices implies that he is aware of the range of opinion around Europe – including pro-Europeans within his own party. It therefore shows a measured respect for opponents' arguments – essential for a topic that has always been more divisive for the Conservative Party than other British parties. We hear a series of anonymous 'voices' throughout the speech and these are marked linguistically by the pattern of an indeterminate 'some' followed by a speech action verb – 'ask', 'say'; 'suggest' and 'claim'. The impression of a rational argument continues with his use of reasons to support his claim that the British are disillusioned with the EU:

Today, public disillusionment with the EU is at an all-time high. There are several reasons for this. People feel that the EU is heading in a direction that they never signed up to. They resent the interference in our national life by what they see as unnecessary rules and regulation. And they wonder what the point of it all is.

As well as a dialogical style based on reasoning and logos there is also an appeal to ethos. First, he argues that Britain does not act only in its own national interest, by alluding to British intervention in the Second World War:

Over the years, Britain has made her own, unique contribution to Europe. We have provided a haven to those fleeing tyranny and persecution. And in Europe's darkest hour, we helped keep the flame of liberty alight. Across the Continent, in silent cemeteries, lie the hundreds of thousands of British servicemen who gave their lives for Europe's freedom.

Like a marriage guidance counsellor, Cameron argues that: 'It is wrong to ask people whether to stay or go before we have had a chance to put the relationship right.' This is the metaphor of the family man grounded in moral values which, as we shall see in the next section, is reinforced by his use of modality. He represents himself as a peacemaker, and then in the epilogue of the speech – a stage when the audience will be left with their abiding impressions of the speaker, his appeal for a more flexible EU is founded in the ethos of the nation state of Britain:

> And when the referendum comes let me say now that if we can negotiate such an arrangement, I will campaign for it with all my heart and soul.

> Because I believe something very deeply. That Britain's national interest is best served in a flexible, adaptable and open European Union and that such a European Union is best with Britain in it.

> Over the coming weeks, months and years, I will not rest until this debate is won. For the future of my country. For the success of the European Union. And for the prosperity of our peoples for generations to come.

He emphasizes his personal commitment to the objective of putting country above region by repeating 'Britain', and emphasizes the personal effort he will put into saving his country. A strong patriotic style does not go amiss in political rhetoric, and he is able to combine the full range of rhetorical resources – as I hope to illustrate in the following analysis.

10.3   Classical rhetoric: Schemes and tropes

Cameron's style is articulated in an extensive range of schemes and tropes. Taking schemes first: there is evidence of anaphora (shown in **bold**):

> **More of the same will not** secure a long-term future for the eurozone. **More of the same will not** see the European Union keeping pace with the new powerhouse economies. **More of the same will not** bring the European Union any closer to its citizens. **More of the same** will just produce more of the same: less competitiveness, less growth, fewer jobs.

He also employs a version of that particular hallmark of classical rhetoric for making a powerful statement – chiasmus: 'And just as I believe that Britain should want to remain in the EU so the EU should want us to stay.' There is also parison between 'then' and 'now' in interaction with metaphor (in italics): 'What Churchill described as the **twin marauders of war and tyranny** have been almost entirely banished from our continent. Today, hundreds of millions **dwell in freedom,** from the Baltic to the Adriatic, from the Western Approaches to the Aegean.' And rhetorical questions:

In a global race, can we really justify the huge number of expensive peripheral European institutions?

Can we justify a commission that gets ever larger?

Can we carry on with an organization that has a multibillion pound budget but not enough focus on controlling spending and shutting down programmes that haven't worked?

And evidence of tricolons is found in the concluding appeal in the epilogue (see above). In this regard, the blending of tropes and schemes with an appeal based primarily on logos and ethos characterizes the choice of Isocrates' middle style – appropriate for a controversial topic addressed to a multiple audience – each element of which is intended to find something for them in it. Establishing a consensus over the process for deciding about Britain's European membership was even more important than whatever the final decision might be.

There is extensive evidence of figures of speech, but overall a preference for the simpler style of schemes over elaborate tropes. Metaphors are used sparingly – early on, when describing Britain's heroic actions in relation to Europe by using a series of colourful metaphors and descriptive language, leading up to the claim 'Healing those wounds of our history is the central story of the European Union.' Britain is a bastion of freedom and for this he uses the persuasive metaphors of light and fire that we have seen underlying the nationalist rhetoric of Blair and Obama: 'And in Europe's darkest hour, we helped keep the flame of liberty alight.' Later 'we have played our part in tearing down the iron curtain'. In this narrative, nation states are metonyms for the people that live in them, and they have living personalities rather than being abstract concepts. As in Churchill's rhetoric, Britain is a heroic warrior battling first against European forces of darkness and now against the cataclsmic effects of de-globalization that have occurred since the 2008 financial crisis. Though Europe is part of a new world, the metaphors are still those of the old world: so Britain will 'lead the charge in the fight for global trade and against protectionism' – and will not become a fortress by 'pulling up the drawbridge and retreating from the world'. We are back in the world of medieval history, with knights in castles surrounded by moats, and damsels in distress fleeing for refuge to our shores. There are a few metaphors (in *italics*) relating to economic policy:

> But when the single market remains incomplete in services, energy and digital – the very sectors that are the *engines* of a modern economy – it is only half the success it could be.

He then introduces embodiment metaphors that contrast illness – as the current state of the EU – with fitness and health metaphors to frame his vision of the future Europe, and these are located within the 'global race' frame of neo-liberal economic policy.

> And so we urgently need to address the *sclerotic*, ineffective decision-making that is holding us back.

> That means creating a *leaner*, less bureaucratic union, relentlessly focused on helping its member countries to compete.

> we should be in no doubt that a new global *race* of nations is under way today.

> a Europe that is *fit* for the challenges of the modern age.

Cameron shows an awareness of the potential for metaphors to frame arguments by explicit rejection of the transport metaphors that had frequently been used in the European media to create an argument for a single EU moving on the same tracks to the same destination:

> **Let's welcome** that diversity, instead of *trying to snuff it out.* **Let's** stop all this talk of *two-speed Europe, of fast lanes and slow lanes, of countries missing trains and buses,* and *consign the whole weary caravan of metaphors to a permanent siding.* Instead, **let's start** from this proposition: we are *a family of democratic nations,* all members of one European Union, whose *essential foundation* is the single market rather than the single currency.

Here we see intertextual allusion to a range of transport metaphors that characterized the discourse of the debate about Euro membership. Cameron indexes metaphor itself as a hallmark of this rhetoric, though he then continues by replacing the transport metaphors with another type that had characterized the earlier debate about Europe: family metaphors. The consensual style leading up to the emotionally warm family metaphor is, of course, a prelude to soften the blow later in the speech of a commitment to a referendum on British membership. Ironically, towards the end of the speech he returns to using a transport metaphor: 'If we left the European Union, it would be a *one-way ticket, not a return*' – however, it is unlikely that this would have been noticed in real time.

A metaphor he uses to encapsulate his argument for a more flexible Europe is based on the idea of liquids: 'My third principle is that power must be able *to flow back* to member states, not just away from them. This was promised by European leaders at Laeken a decade ago.' Interestingly, the same metaphor is repeated much later in the speech: 'And to those who say a new settlement can't be negotiated, I would say listen to the views of other parties in other European countries arguing for powers *to flow back* to European states.' Perhaps the systematic use of a 'sea' metaphor relates to the underlying purpose of telling a certain type of story – a story of a nation that is defined by being an island. It is likely that the choice of a metaphor based on the source domain of water in motion – of tides – evokes a cognitive schema of an island surrounded by water: a geographical and spatial reality that underlies the argument of his speech and is introduced early on:

> I know that the United Kingdom is sometimes seen as *an argumentative* and rather strong-minded member of the family of European nations. And it's true that our geography has *shaped our psychology*. We have the *character of an island nation*: independent, forthright, passionate in defence of our sovereignty. We can no more change this British sensibility than we can drain the English Channel. And because of this sensibility, we come to the European Union with a frame of mind that is more practical than emotional. For us, the European Union is a means to an end – prosperity, stability, *the anchor of freedom* and democracy, both within Europe and beyond her shores – not an end in itself.

Here, then, we see evidence of systematic metaphor use so that idea of the island nation activates the cultural schema of Britain as a ship, which is then reinforced with the 'anchor of freedom', leading up to the argument for powers to 'flow back' to these shores. So though metaphor is used sparingly, it nevertheless contributes to the coherence of the speech by articulating its central idea of an island nation that underlies so much of Britain's relation to 'Europe' and its sense of 'being apart'. However, though apart it is should not go adrift, and this he argues with a further metaphor: 'I understand the appeal of going it alone, of charting our own course', but he advises against this as the idea of a ship 'charting its own course' implies that it is setting out on a voyage across the oceans to unknown places. He supports this with the claim that 'ours is not just an island story – it is also a continental story'. His use of 'story' implies that narrative – what in other contexts we might call 'discourse' – is central to what we accept as knowledge in the form of history; as he puts it, 'We have helped to write European history, and Europe has helped write ours.' Note how this definition of European history is one that excludes British history, and this reinforces the notion of separateness that is implied elsewhere in his version of the story of Britain. For example, Britain is represented as morally different from the rest of Europe –'*a haven to those fleeing tyranny* and persecution'. These associations with freedom from corrupting influences from Europe were particularly salient soon after he gave the speech, when it emerged that a number of supermarkets had unknowingly sold horsemeat in ready meals that were labelled as containing beef, which had been sourced from various EU states.

Moving on now from the framework of classical rhetoric, metaphor and narrative, I shall consider how the speech might be analysed using more contemporary discourse approaches – first, with reference to the Hallidayan framework of agency and modality, and then the discourse-historical approach.

10.4   Social agency and modality

In a study of his most frequently used words (Charteris-Black, 2013) I show that Cameron's ability to achieve this challenging objective draws on the resources of modality, with the rhetorical purpose of establishing consensus. When issuing directives with a lower modality to emphasize the collaborative nature of his directives, he uses the more informal 'let's' as this implies willing participation on the part of the hearer. 'Let's' was not common in the *British Politician's Corpus* (see Chapter 7). For example, it was not used at all by either Powell or Churchill, and this more informal way of expressing collaboration seems to have been introduced first by Thatcher. Cameron typically uses 'let's' in conjunction with 'together', to emphasize the collaborative nature of his directives. This informal register perhaps changes the level of directness, so that his directives are represented as invitations to participate. However, more notable in this speech is Cameron's use of modal features that imply a much strong degree of commitment and legitimacy, such as 'I want', 'I know that', and in combination with other, more consensual expressions, such as 'we need to' that implies a type of moral legitimacy, and 'let's', associated with a low level of modality. Britain is construed as a dynamic and active agent in European affairs through the use of material transitive verbs, as in the following:

> Over the years, Britain has made her own, unique contribution to Europe. We have provided a haven to those fleeing tyranny and persecution. And in Europe's darkest hour, we helped keep the flame of liberty alight ... We have always been a country that reaches out. That turns its

face to the world. That leads the charge in the fight for global trade and against protectionism.

Britain is represented as a doer – an active force for change in the world. By contrast, the EU is represented as an essentially passive entity to which things happen:

> So I speak as British prime minister with a positive vision for the future of the European Union.

> There are some serious questions that will define the future of the European Union.

> The biggest danger to the European Union comes not from those who advocate change, but from those who denounce new thinking as heresy.

> More of the same will not bring the European Union any closer to its citizens.

> At the core of the European Union must be, as it is now, the single market.

> These five principles provide what, I believe, is the right approach for the European Union.

> We need to allow some time for that to happen – and help to shape the future of the European Union, so that when the choice comes it will be a real one.

The European Union is, then, not agent in its own right but an entity that is in the position of an object – something to which things happen. This essentially passive role is reinforced by the use of intransitive verbs; for example, the way that the EU is at the mercy of the eurozone crisis is conveyed through 'emerges': 'The European Union that emerges from the eurozone crisis is going to be a very different body.' And it is construed as an entity that need to change and to respond:

> So I want to speak to you today with urgency and frankness about the European Union and how it must change.

> To set out how I believe the European Union should respond to them.

Modality
The speech is characterized by a high level of epistemic and deontic modality, so that Cameron conveys a firm and unyielding point of view on Europe

Table 10.2   Deontic modality in Cameron's EU speech

So I want to speak to you today with urgency and frankness about the European Union and how it must change.

To set out how I believe the European Union should respond to them.

At the core of the European Union must be, as it is now, the single market. Britain is at the heart of that single market, and must remain so.

For just as in any emergency you should plan for the aftermath as well as dealing with the present crisis.

The EU must be able to act with the speed and flexibility of a network, not the cumbersome rigidity of a bloc.

These should be the tasks that get European officials up in the morning – and keep them working late into the night.

The second principle should be flexibility.

My third principle is that power must be able to flow back to member states, not just away from them.

By the same token, the members of the eurozone should accept that we, and indeed all member states, will have changes that we need to safeguard our interests and strengthen democratic legitimacy. And we should be able to make these changes too.

to examine thoroughly what the EU as a whole should do and should stop doing.

Nothing should be off the table.

My fifth principle is fairness: whatever new arrangements are enacted for the eurozone, they must work fairly for those inside it and out.

But that does not mean we should leave – not if the benefits of staying and working together are greater.

that is grounded in both what is certain and what is necessary. The use of the simple present tense throughout conveys facts that are known, and the use of modal verbs such as 'must' and 'should' convey strong obligation on other European actors, as summarized in Table 10.2

There is an authoritative tone throughout the speech – in keeping perhaps with the *Private Eye* magazine's satirical naming of Cameron as 'The Headmaster' – one that leaves no doubt among other European leaders as to Cameron's position, that essentially the locus of power is, and should be, with national governments: this is the primary argument of the whole speech: 'It is national parliaments, which are, and will remain, the true source of real democratic legitimacy and accountability in the EU.' What is notable in this speech is how he typically integrates the epistemic with the deontic, as illustrated in Table 10.3.

The interplay of the deontic with the epistemic pervades the speech and contributes to its overall coherence of style – there is no hesitancy or

Table 10.3   Epistemic and deontic modality in Cameron's EU speech

Text	Analysis of modality
The fact is that ours is not just an island story – it is also a continental story. For all our connections to the rest of the world – of which we are rightly proud – we have always been a European power, and we always will be.	Epistemic: use of the simple present and 'the fact' represents this as beyond doubt. There is also deontic modality, as 'pride' is represented as being necessary.
So I speak as British prime minister with a positive vision for the future of the European Union. A future in which Britain wants, and should want, to play a committed and active part.	Again, a combination of both epistemic and deontic modality; there is the naming of the communicative act and the reformulation of simple present 'wants' (epistemic) as 'should want' (deontic).
Britain is not in the single currency, and we're not going to be. But we all need the eurozone to have the right governance and structures to secure a successful currency for the long term.	A statement of certainty as regards Britain's position *vis-à-vis* the eurozone (epistemic) is followed by a 'need' statement (deontic).
We must not be weighed down by an insistence on a one size fits all approach which implies that all countries want the same level of integration. The fact is that they don't and we shouldn't assert that they do.	There is a shift from deontic modality in the first sentence, which is followed in the second sentence by the epistemic pattern 'the fact' followed by the reassertion of deontic modality.
By the same token, the members of the eurozone should accept that we, and indeed all member states, will have changes that we need to safeguard our interests and strengthen democratic legitimacy. And we should be able to make these changes too.	Again, the pattern is a statement of necessity, followed by a prediction of a future state that is in turn followed by a deontic statement of rights.

vagueness: it has the tone of a line in the sand speech that is in keeping with its political commitment to the possibility of offering a referendum on European membership – on the condition that (and here Cameron shows himself to be an astute strategist) the Conservative Party are re-elected in 2015. It is largely through the use of modality that Cameron seeks to demonstrate that he has the right intentions – for both Britain and for Europe (though clearly in that order), and that he sounds right – like a leader with a firm position on Europe. There is evidence that he uses these markers of modality more frequently than is common in British political speeches, when we compare their frequency in this speech with the *British*

Table 10.4   Deontic modality: Cameron compared with other British politicians

	Cameron (per 5,000 words)	British politicians (excluding Cameron) per 5,000 words	Level of significance
need to	16.91	7.75	P<0.1
want	18.69	8.08	P<0.01
just	14.24	8.52	P<0.1
should	17.8	7.99	P<0.1

Table 10.5   Epistemic modality: Cameron compared with other British politicians

	Cameron (per 10,000 words)	British politicians (excluding Cameron) per 10,000 words	Level of significance
will	48.95	30.28	P<0.1
believe	9.79	5.10	P<0.1
would	16.91	10.99	P<0.1

Politicians' Corpus. Table 10.4 shows the comparison for markers of deontic modality and Table 10.5 for epistemic modality.

However, as well as conveying a tone of authority, Cameron also sought to establish consensus and he used some mitigating forms implying shared purpose between speaker and audience – with, for example, the embracing 'let's' in the form of a tricolon:

Let's welcome that diversity, instead of trying to snuff it out.

Let's stop all this talk of two-speed Europe, of fast lanes and slow lanes, of countries missing trains and buses, and consign the whole weary caravan of metaphors to a permanent siding.

Instead, **let's start** from this proposition: we are a family of democratic nations

This more conciliatory or co-operative style is more typically associated with feminine language, and a study of his earlier speeches – in the period 2005–2012 – (Charteris-Black 2013) argues that he had often employed a feminine style emphasizing emotional expressivity; this was characterized by phrases such as 'I love' and intensifiers such as 'really', 'actually' and 'incredibly' that he uses more frequently than other British politicians. To 'sound right' – particularly to feminine audiences – he needed to demonstrate emotional investment appealing to feminine values. An example of a

Table 10.6   Intensifiers – Cameron's EU speech compared with British politicians' speeches

	Cameron (per 5,000 words)	British politicians (per 5,000 words)	Level of significance
entirely	2.7	0.20	P<0.01
very	11.6	4.58	P<0.01
always	6.23	2.77	P<0.1
simply	2.7	0.81	P<0.1

feature associated with women's language is the use of intensifiers in contrast to the more 'objective' and lower commitment style of men. If we compare Cameron's use of intensifiers in this speech with a reference corpus comprised of over 400,000 words from speeches by other post-war British politicians we find that these are used statistically more frequently in the EU speech; this is summarized in Table 10.6.

Looking at an example of each of these:

A vote today between the status quo and leaving would be an *entirely* false choice.

Third, there is a growing frustration that the EU is seen as something that is done to people rather than acting on their behalf. And this is being intensified by the *very* solutions required to resolve the economic problems.

we have *always* been a European power, and we always will be.

I believe in confronting this issue – shaping it, leading the debate. Not *simply* hoping a difficult situation will go away.

The style of the modern socially influential man is one in which emotional expressivity is no longer to be avoided, and politicians can represent themselves as being more human by sounding more like everyday people if they speak with an authentic level of emotional investment. However, to sound right as a leader it is also important to sound strong and we have seen how Cameron employed modality to convey strength of belief; another way he talks 'big' is through the use of powerful words that I have summarized as 'big talk' (Charteris-Black 2013); Table 10.7 shows how some examples of such lexical choices occur more in this speech than in the British politicians' reference corpus.

Finally I shall consider the speech from the perspective of the discourse-historical approach.

Table 10.7   'Big talk' – Cameron's EU speech compared with British politicians' speeches

	Cameron (per 5,000 words)	British politicians (per 5,000 words)	Level of significance
biggest	2.67	0.69	P<0.1
hundreds	2.67	0.43	P<0.1
powers	3.56	1.01	P<0.1

10.5   Discourse-historical approach

Table 10.8 illustrates and discusses examples of each of the 'topoi' associated with this approach.

There is evidence of all DHA topoi in the speech – though with a significant variation in their frequency. The European Union is represented as the cause of a number of negative social outcomes broadly related to burdens, while culture and history are important in making Britain different from the rest of Europe. Responsibility and justice also seem important – as might be expected in a speech that relies heavily on an appeal to ethos: so that Cameron constructs himself as a responsible politician for airing genuine anti-European sentiment and for proposing a more democratically accountable system of governance. But the tone of the speech is not divisive, and a major rhetorical objective is to establish consensus.

Exercise 10.1: Project and essay

➢ Select a significant contemporary political speech.
➢ Analyse its circumstances in terms of situation, and cognitive and processing factors.
➢ Analyse it with reference to each of the following approaches:

> *Classical rhetoric* – including an analysis of its style, arguments, arrangement, schemes and tropes (see Tables 2.3 and 2.4).
> *Social agency and modality* – including the analysis of syntactic (for example, transitivity and voice) and lexical choices that influence its modality (epistemic and deontic; see section 5.2.3).
> *Discourse-historical approach* – identify strategies and topoi (see Tables 6.2 and 6.5).
> *Critical metaphor analysis* – following the procedure for identification, interpretation and explanation of metaphor (see Figures 8.1, 8.2 and 9.1).

➢ Write an essay that evaluates each of these approaches with reference to their contribution in explaining the persuasive effect of your chosen speech.

Table 10.8 Topoi in Cameron's European Union speech

Topoi	Explanation/definition	Example
Usefulness	These are relatively few in number as the rhetorical purpose is not to highlight the advantages of the EU as it stands.	And while we must never take this for granted, the first purpose of the European Union – to secure peace – has been achieved and we should pay tribute to all those in the EU, alongside NATO, who made that happen.
Uselessness	This is a major topoi as there are many indications of the disadvantages of the EU as it stands.	First, the problems in the eurozone are driving fundamental change in Europe. Second, there is a crisis of European competitiveness, as other nations across the world soar ahead. And third, there is a gap between the EU and its citizens, which has grown dramatically in recent years.
Definition/naming	There are no explicit instances of naming (not surprising in a speech on this topic) but there is an interesting definition of European history as excluding British history. This differentiation was also found in his government's proposals to reform the history curriculum to place a greater focus on British history.	We have helped to write European history, and Europe has helped write ours.
Danger and threat	There are several references to the Eurozone crisis. He represents as dangers opposition to his plan to reduce the central powers of Europe, thereby turning the tables on opponents who represent his policies as a danger to European unity.	1 If we don't address these challenges, the danger is that Europe will fail and the British people will drift towards the exit. 2 The biggest danger to the European Union comes not from those who advocate change, but from those who denounce new thinking as heresy.
Humanitarianism	Britain is equated with humanitarian values such as liberty and fairness, while Europe is represented as not demonstrating these values.	Over the years, Britain has made her own, unique contribution to Europe. We have provided a haven to those fleeing tyranny and persecution.

Table 10.8 *continued*

Topoi	Explanation/definition	Example
Justice	Much of the speech is framed in the discourse that the EU has changed to become more centralized without that having been agreed by the people.	People feel that the EU is heading in a direction that they never signed up to. They resent the interference in our national life by what they see as unnecessary rules and regulation.
Responsibility	Cameron claims that it is responsible to discuss issues of concern (such as EU membership) because it is responsible to bring 'difficult' topics into the domain of politics and public debate. In Table 6.3 we saw that a similar rhetorical topoi was used by the Conservative politician Michael Howard to discuss immigration.	The result is that democratic consent for the EU in Britain is now wafer-thin. Some people say that to point this out is irresponsible, creates uncertainty for business and puts a question mark over Britain's place in the European Union. But the question mark is already there and ignoring it won't make it go away. Europe's leaders have a duty to hear these concerns. Indeed, we have a duty to act on them.
Burdening/weighting	Many EU policies are represented as burdens. The idea of a fully integrated Europe is also represented as a burden.	1 Complex rules restricting our labour markets are not some naturally occurring phenomenon. Just as excessive regulation is not some external plague that's been visited on our businesses. 2 We must not be weighed down by an insistence on a one size fits all approach which implies that all countries want the same level of integration.
Finances	The EU social spending is represented as being excessive in comparison with the income it generates.	As Chancellor Merkel has said, if Europe today accounts for just over 7 per cent of the world's population, produces around 25 per cent of global GDP and has to finance 50 per cent of global social spending, then it's obvious that it will have to work very hard to maintain its prosperity and way of life.

Reality	The Euro crisis is represented as an unavoidable reality and the catalyst for change.	The union is changing to help fix the currency – and that has profound implications for all of us, whether we are in the single currency or not.
Numbers	Few numbers are used in the speech except where they provide evidence of variation within Europe.	Twenty-six European countries are members of Schengen – including four outside the European Union – Switzerland, Norway, Liechtenstein and Iceland. Two EU countries – Britain and Ireland – have retained their border controls.
Law and Right	This topoi is not used, since one of the primary purposes is to challenge the legitimacy of European institutions.	... we need to examine whether the balance is right in so many areas where the European Union has legislated, including on the environment, social affairs and crime.
History	This topoi is quite important because much of the argument for the referendum is based on the story of a Britain that is apart from Europe – but intervenes at crucial times (as now) to help resolve its problems.	From Caesar's legions to the Napoleonic Wars. From the Reformation, the Enlightenment and the Industrial Revolution to the defeat of Nazism. We have helped to write European history, and Europe has helped write ours.
Culture	Here the character of an island people is used to indicate particular advantages of being British.	1 And it's true that our geography has shaped our psychology. We have the character of an island nation: independent, forthright, passionate in defence of our sovereignty.
	There is also a culture of entrepreneurship, which he does not identify as being within Europe but outside of it.	2 I want us to be at the forefront of transformative trade deals with the US, Japan and India as part of the drive towards global free trade. And I want us to be pushing to exempt Europe's smallest entrepreneurial companies from more EU directives.
Abuse	Abuse is discussed more in economic rather than political or social terms, so that the EU is a cause of abuse when it interferes with the operation of a free market. This is perhaps close to the topos of 'Uselessness'.	It is nonsense that people shopping online in some parts of Europe are unable to access the best deals because of where they live.

10.6   Conclusion

The preceding chapters have spanned a range of historical epochs from the classical to the contemporary, and covered a range of approaches to political discourse analysis from Aristotle's artistic proofs to contemporary discussions of how metaphors frame political situations by activating cognitive schemata to create a framework for our understanding of the social world. In the pattern of evolution there is both change and continuity at every level; in terms of communicative mode there has been a shift from direct face-to-face interaction to mediated communication, which I have summarized as a shift from oratory to public communication – but the emphasis on articulate and fluent delivery, on memory, and on engagement with an audience through performance has remained constant. There has been a shift from a belief in rhetoric as a hallmark of the educated to a largely sceptical view of politicians, as motivated by Machiavellian principles of self-interest leading to manipulation and deception, but scratch the surface and we find that suspicion of appearances was already present in the classical distinction between rhetoric and dialectic.

As the planet struggles to survive through the twenty-first century, some politicians are making appeals on the grounds of species survival – rather than on particular interest groups. The spoken word reaches ever-expanding and ever more immediate audiences, so that there is a more measurable impact between decisions made globally and their local effects, and vice versa. We are more aware of how the climate change that is associated with economic globalization impacts on local communities that are flooded or damaged by a violent storm. But the elements of persuasive language have remained unchanged: the world is dangerous, man's place in it is tenuous and temporary – and becomes more so if people are not united and states are allowed to disintegrate (as is happening in Syria at the time of writing).

Perhaps the aspect of public speaking that is most constant is the importance of telling a coherent story; since the beginning of time, the need to understand the world through stories has been a way of assuaging humanity's deepest fears and anxieties so that they do not overwhelm us. By incorporating his own life story into a political narrative, Rory Weal (see Chapter 4) was able to tell a story in which the welfare state had taken on the role of the nurturing parent he had lost, and Tory policies became symbolic of fears of isolation and loneliness in a hostile world through which he was struggling to do the best he could. As family breakdown has increased in Western society, so, paradoxically, has the rhetorical appealed to the family as a bastion of values. The definition of 'family' has become almost interchangeable with related terms such as 'community' – a network of proximate social relations. Obama's grander narrative of American patriots has similar story elements to that of Rory Weal: 'In the year of America's birth, in the coldest of months, a small band of patriots huddled by dying campfires on the shores of an icy river. The capital was abandoned. The enemy was advancing. The snow was stained with blood.' Obama was reformulating a story that runs through time and defines political rhetoric – of a people threatened by destruction who had to draw on their own resources of courage, unity and common purpose to survive. It was a variant of the story that Churchill told when Britain was threatened by Nazi invasion. and not so different from Hitler's narrative explanation for the decline of Germany. While our conceptual and linguistic metalanguage may have become more sophisticated and we may identify tropes and schemes, transitivity and modality, entrenched and novel metaphors – the persuasive power of narrative is undiminished – like a candle in a storm, it flickers but is never extinguished.

In this respect, great public speakers and great writers share this much in common: they are skilled at listening to the familiar ways through which ordinary people adjust to the world: the phrases and everyday metaphors that are recycled through the media provide the raw material for narrative. When politicians speak of a 'slippery slope' or 'the thin end of the wedge', or 'a foot in the door' we know this is an argument based on cause and effect relationships: once we allow something to happen to a minor extent – a 'small cause' – we are encouraging much worse consequences – 'big effects'. Activating this concept by using familiar commonplaces, or warrants, such as 'slippery slope' argues against whatever policy is represented as being at the bottom of the 'slope'. Once such warrants are introduced, they become arguments in themselves without providing further evidence in support of them. We know that a slippery slope leads to an unpleasant place at its bottom end, and that whatever the wedge is, the thick end is worse than the thin one. Much of this is because, what a politician seeks to do is to establish a common set of values that is shared with an audience. However, since audiences are comprised of individuals with different opinions, speakers need to overcome, or conceal, such differences by using familiar language. Ultimately, people are persuaded by instinct more than by argument: the data may be too much to absorb or the arguments are too complex to follow. Many issues facing the current generation such as climate change, nuclear power, fracking, wind turbines, urban transport systems, epidemics and so on are so complex that they require specialist scientific knowledge to understand them. The result is that politicians will go back to the old stories and the familiar ways of telling them, and their more complex and diverse audiences will do what audiences have always done: decide whether they like the story and whether it is credible.

Core text: Prologue, Cameron's European Union Speech, 23 January 2013

This morning I want to talk about the future of Europe. But first, let   1
us remember the past.

Seventy years ago, Europe was being torn apart by its second cata-   2
strophic conflict in a generation. A war which saw the streets of
European cities strewn with rubble. The skies of London lit by flames
night after night. And millions dead across the world in the battle for
peace and liberty.

As we remember their sacrifice, so we should also remember how the   3
shift in Europe from war to sustained peace came about. It did not
happen like a change in the weather. It happened because of determined work over generations. A commitment to friendship and a
resolve never to revisit that dark past – a commitment epitomized by
the Elysée treaty signed 50 years ago this week.

After the Berlin Wall came down I visited that city and I will never   4
forget it. The abandoned checkpoints. The sense of excitement about
the future. The knowledge that a great continent was coming together.
Healing those wounds of our history is the central story of the
European Union.

What Churchill described as the twin marauders of war and tyranny   5
have been almost entirely banished from our continent. Today,
hundreds of millions dwell in freedom, from the Baltic to the Adriatic,
from the Western Approaches to the Aegean.

And while we must never take this for granted, the first purpose of the   6
European Union – to secure peace – has been achieved and we should
pay tribute to all those in the EU, alongside NATO, who made that
happen.

But today the main, overriding purpose of the European Union is   7
different: not to win peace, but to secure prosperity. The challenges
come not from within this continent but outside it. From the surging
economies in the east and south. Of course, a growing world economy
benefits us all, but we should be in no doubt that a new global race of
nations is under way today. A race for the wealth and jobs of the
future.

The map of global influence is changing before our eyes. And these   8
changes are already being felt by the entrepreneur in the Netherlands,
the worker in Germany, the family in Britain. So I want to speak to
you today with urgency and frankness about the European Union and
how it must change – both to deliver prosperity and to retain the
support of its peoples. But first, I want to set out the spirit in which I
approach these issues.

I know that the United Kingdom is sometimes seen as an argumenta-   9
tive and rather strong-minded member of the family of European
nations. And it's true that our geography has shaped our psychology.
We have the character of an island nation: independent, forthright,
passionate in defence of our sovereignty. We can no more change this
British sensibility than we can drain the English Channel. And because
of this sensibility, we come to the European Union with a frame of
mind that is more practical than emotional. For us, the European
Union is a means to an end – prosperity, stability, the anchor of freedom and democracy both within Europe and beyond her shores – not
an end in itself.

We insistently ask: how, why, to what end? But all this doesn't make   10
us somehow un-European. The fact is that ours is not just an island
story – it is also a continental story. For all our connections to the rest
of the world – of which we are rightly proud – we have always been
a European power, and we always will be. From Caesar's legions to
the Napoleonic Wars. From the Reformation, the Enlightenment and
the Industrial Revolution to the defeat of Nazism. We have helped to
write European history, and Europe has helped write ours.

Over the years, Britain has made her own, unique contribution to   11
Europe. We have provided a haven to those fleeing tyranny and persecution. And in Europe's darkest hour, we helped keep the flame of
liberty alight. Across the continent, in silent cemeteries, lie the
hundreds of thousands of British servicemen who gave their lives for
Europe's freedom.

In more recent decades, we have played our part in tearing down the   12
Iron Curtain and championing the entry into the EU of those countries that lost so many years to Communism. And contained in this
history is the crucial point about Britain, our national character, our
attitude to Europe.

Britain is characterized not just by its independence but, above all, by   13
its openness. We have always been a country that reaches out. That

turns its face to the world. That leads the charge in the fight for global trade and against protectionism. This is Britain today, as it's always been: independent, yes – but open, too. I never want us to pull up the drawbridge and retreat from the world. I am not a British isolationist. I don't just want a better deal for Britain. I want a better deal for Europe too.

Comments on Exercises

Exercise 1.1 (p. 6)

There have been a number of attempts to define rhetoric; these and their authors can be summarized as below:

Rhetoric is:

◊ The art of discovering all the available means of persuasion in any given case. (Aristotle, 1952)
◊ The use of words to form attitudes or induce actions in other human agents. (Kenneth Burke, 1945)
◊ The use of language as a symbolic means of inducing cooperation in beings that by nature respond to symbols. (Kenneth Burke, 1945)
◊ Communication which helps people think alike so that they may share values, dispositions toward action, and actions. (Chaïm Perelman, 1982)

Exercise 1.2 (p. 8)

I shall leave you to work out most of these. The most debatable are (c) and (f); I would say that (c) is deliberative because decisions are likely to be taken on choice of strategies, and the orientation is towards the future, whereas (f) is more likely to be forensic, with the coach passing a verdict on the performance of particular players.

Exercise 1.3 (p. 11)

In the first paragraph he positions himself modestly with words such as 'humbled' and 'mindful'; he also avoids criticizing George W. Bush (surely a tempting proposition) by attributing to him virtues such as 'service' and 'generosity'.

In the second paragraph he refers to the presidential oath, and relates this to the vision and ideals of the founding fathers of America – appealing therefore to a shared historical identity.

Exercise 1.4 (p. 14)

When working out the major premise you need to identify the major claim that an argument is making – this is similar to identifying the main topic in a narrative. Here it is the view that young people should avoid debt. The minor premise is a second-ary topic that could be omitted, and the conclusion is about what logically follows. This is how I analysed the syllogism and enthymeme:

Syllogism

It is unwise for young people to take on large debt. (Major premise)

Going to university requires young people to take on a large debt. (Minor premise)

It is unwise for young people to go to university. (Conclusion)

Enthymeme

It is unwise for young people to take on large debt. (Major premise)

Therefore young people should choose not to go to university. (Conclusion)

Here the minor premise is omitted but will be inferred by the audience because of their everyday experience of debt repayment.

Reason and Analogy

The sort of Reason that could be introduced might be an argument based on the cost of interest, such as the following: 'After all, the more you borrow, the more interest you pay and the more you go into debt.'

The sort of Analogy that could be added might be to introduce other situations in life that are likely to incur debt, such as buying a house.

Refutation

Present a counter-position
Young people should choose not to go to university.

Refute the counter-position
If they don't go to university their life chances will be limited to servicing the needs of an economy at a relatively lowly paid level.

Offer an alternative position
By investing in their education, young people have a better chance of being fulfilled and put themselves in a position whereby they can pay back any debts they have incurred once they can afford to do so.

Exercise 1.5 (p. 15)

In the second paragraph he uses weather metaphors to reflect the emotions arising from the financial crisis. Water metaphors have been associated strongly in metaphor theory with the expression of emotions Kövecses (2003) and occur in many English expressions such as 'pouring out one's feelings'. Weather metaphors are conventionally associated with circumstances, so that the weather stands for the environment in its most general sense: economic and social conditions as well as physical ones.

There is evidence of an appeal to ethos in the following paragraphs: 1; 6–10; 13–14; 16–24; 26–27. The predominant appeal is to ethos, as the primary purpose is to establish the legitimacy of a new president through the ethical credibility of his character. But he also arouses pathos, so that a response to fears that are grounded in the reality of the economic situation is to arouse the emotion of courage. I found evidence of ethos combined with pathos in 2; 11; 18; 23.

There is some appeal to logos by analogy with a tradition of presidents of high character and ideals, and by allusion (a form of analogy) to previous examples of American history when Americans needed to show resolve – see 8–11 and 16–17. There is also logos, where he offers evidence of the current crisis (3–4) as this supports the claim. When he argues that the solution to the crisis is the work that needs to be done (see 12) he again cites proof of these public needs.

Exercise 1.6 (p. 23)

The prologue is very short – only the first paragraph – and satisfies the need to establish Obama's ethos by showing respect to his predecessor. A short narrative is effective because it arouses interest by rapidly introducing a narrative of threat and danger in 2. In 3–5 he continues to frame a narrative of crisis, and at the end of 5 he introduces his main argument – that the challenges America faces will be met. In 9 he introduces the proof of his argument: at previous periods of American history when challenges have been just as great as today, they have still been met. This is an argument by historical analogy, and it is this that sustains the momentum of the speech. In 13, the claim that 'there are some who question the scale of our ambitions' signals the prologue of a counter-argument that is then refuted. The refutation is based again on historical analogy, in 16 and 17 by referring back to America's heroic ancestors whose ambitions enabled them to overcome the challenges of their time. He continues in 18–25 with the main argument of overcoming present challenges by positive future actions but occasionally switches back to past achievement. The epilogue is paragraphs 26–28.

He creates a circular flow in the structure of the speech by oscillating between different time periods and this cyclical time orientation creates a mythical appeal. Consider how in 22, after a reference to 'those brave Americans who, at this very hour, patrol far-off deserts and distant mountains', he continues 'just as the fallen heroes who lie in Arlington whisper through the ages (2). So that instead of a linear progression from past to present to future, reflection on a present event – American soldiers on patrol in some unnamed but distant places – leads into a cycling back to the heroes of the American Civil War and other conflicts for inspiration. This cyclical flow continues in the epilogue (26) where he recounts a moving story about 'a small band of patriots huddled by dying campfires on the shores of an icy river'; notice how in 26 and 27 the focus is brought back on to fear and courage in response to fear. This related to the historical circumstances when the speech was given, following a serious financial crisis that had left America ill-resourced to continue a foreign policy based on global leadership. The message of the speech evokes the phrase Clinton used in his campaign against George Bush, Snr: 'It's the economy, stupid' – that is, the importance of the economy to the financial wellbeing of Americans.

In terms of arrangement this is similar to what I have described as messianic myth in the discourse of Martin Luther King (Charteris-Black, 2011, ch. 4). This is a narrative pattern of historical myth, which could be formulated as THE AMERICAN PRESENT IS ITS HEROIC PAST. The effect of this pattern on the arrangement is that rather than a sequence of narrative, followed by proof, followed by refutation, we find a reiterated cycle of narrative – argument – proof, narrative – argument – proof. This cyclical arrangement adds a mythic dimension to the speech that allows it to make an appeal at the unconscious level and gives it a truly aesthetic status (see Figure 9.2 on p. 217). It is a work of art, and one that we understand better by analysing its arrangement using the tenets of classical rhetoric.

Exercise 2.1 (p. 32)

The style of the current elected Mayor of London, Boris Johnson, is one that creates a tension from both the visual and verbal aspects of his style. A hallmark of his appearance is the traditional dark suit and tie of a businessman, yet this conflicts with his dishevelled hair which evokes a naughty schoolboy or public school rebel. In his verbal style there is a tension between his directness and his accent: Oxford English is quite typical of this social class, whereas directness and honesty are not stereotypical qualities of the English upper classes.

The effect of this clash between the expected and the unexpected is to give the impression of honesty and intimacy – there is a mixture between socially conventional elements – the accent and the suit, with those more individual, eccentric features of the outspoken rebel. 'Boris' is usually referred to by his first name in the media, which implies that his style evokes trust, as if we know him personally. By contrast, Tony Blair – in spite of his considerable communication skills – became simply 'Blair' in public discourse, with 'Tony' being only an echo of an earlier public persona. I am not sure that Blair was ever fully trusted by the public, though he was much admired.

Exercise 2.2 (p. 44)

There is the use of antithesis to contrast good qualities of character – fighting according to international law, magnanimity in victory and so on – with bad qualities – dishonourable behaviour and 'over-enthusiasm in killing'.

Repetition operates at the level of words, so there is 'fly' (1.2) and 'flown' (1.3); 'to liberate' (1.1) and 'to free' (1.2); in 2.1 there is 'alive at this moment' and 'not be alive shortly' (2.1). In 3 there is the use of anaphora, where words are repeated at the start of a sentence 'You will ...' (3.3. and 3.4); there is a triple repetition (tricolon) in 4.2 and 4.3. In 8.1 there is 'wish to fight', and 'aim to please'; in 10.1 'It is (not) a question of' is repeated, and 'decision' is repeated in 10.2.

Exercise 2.3 (p. 49)

Tropes

Both speeches allude to myth by using place names; Collins alludes to biblical locations and personal names in 3, while the Henry V speech alludes to the festival of St. Crispian, and in 14 and 15 aristocratic families are listed by reference to their family title.

Metaphors are used sparingly but appropriately, so in Collins' speech we have a series of metaphors related to battle as a journey (in 2.2, 3.3 and 7.1) and this is continued in 9.2 with the idea of 'deeds' following the audience through history – so the journey metaphor becomes a journey through time: not of individuals but of the effect of their actions – like the Buddhist idea of karma. There are religious metaphors in Collins' speech referring to light in 3.7 and to fire in 6.2; there are also two other metaphors: in 5.2, where the idea of death as sleep is evoked by 'sleeping bag', though this is also metonymic as it alludes to the bags in which the bodies of war fatalities are transported. In the final line there is a metaphor of business as war; though this could also be metonymic, since military combat is how soldiers earn a living. Both these metaphors seem euphemistic as they tend to reduce the threat and danger of war, though without hiding its realities.

There are fewer metaphors in the Henry V speech, only occurring in 27 where the idea of moral value as material value is present in 'hold their manhoods cheap'. There are, however, a few metonyms: in 8 and 9 the 'scars' and 'wounds' stand for the heroic acts which caused them and so imply bravery and pride, and the 'flowing cups' in 16 stand for recognition of past valour. In a sense the whole image that is evoked of a remembrance ceremony appears to stand for the heroism of the victors.

Schemes

We find two similar antitheses that underlie the messages of both speeches: first, pervading the whole structure of the Henry V speech is an antithesis between the present – the imminent battle – and the distant mythic future when it will be celebrated on Saint Crispin's day. This contrast is explicit in line 19, but is also realized lexically in the contrast between 'forget' and 'forgot' in line 10 and 'remember' in 11, 16 and 20. It is important to the purpose of the speech because only those who fight heroically will be remembered and, by implication, those who don't will be forgotten. Significantly, 'remember' also occurs in 2.4, 4.1 and 7.4 of Collins' speech.

Equally important to the cadence of both speeches is the use of repetition and parallelism. In the Henry V speech, 'Crispian' is repeated several times to enforce the mythical appeal of the speech; 'he that outlives/shall live this day' is repeated in 2 and 5; from 12–26 we have repetition of predictive clauses using 'shall'. 'Few' and 'brothers' are both repeated. Dense repetition at short intervals is important because attention is likely to be limited when the focus is on the battle and repetition aids short-term memory and facilitates processing.

Time viewpoint

In both speeches the orator takes the perspective of someone in an idealized future reflecting on an imminent battle; this rhetorical method presupposes that there will be victory because without survivors there would be no perspective for this point of view. It is also worth noting how the schemes and tropes contribute to the time orientation of both speeches: prior to combat, the focus is on a future after the victory. The use of a compressed time scale is present in both speeches, so that actions taken in the very near future will have very long-term consequences: Collins does this very explicitly in 9, where he emphasizes the shame that will attach to dishonourable conduct, whereas Henry V focuses more on the duration of honour that will accrue from victory. From this we can assume that Collins was rather more convinced of victory than was Henry V, so needed to give more emphasis to the ethical rather than the military outcome of combat.

Social relations and space viewpoint

The social relations in the Collins' speech are formal and impersonal, appropriate to the social distance between a respected officer and his men. The first person pronoun is used only once – implying detachment, but the first plural pronoun is used extensively to communicate solidarity between leader and followers.

In the Henry V speech, social relations are communicated by a contrast based on physical space between those who are close to the speaker – in line 21 'we band of brothers' and those who are remote (line 25) from the speaker and less emotionally close. This spatial contrast then becomes the basis for an appeal to ethos in a contrast between men who are worthwhile (see lines 17, 23) and men who have little value 'hold their manhoods cheap' (line 27).

Exercise 2.4 (p. 54)

In 2.2 there is interaction between several metaphors, with both parallelism and an inverted syntax (it is not 'we will not send those who do not wish to go on that journey', which would be the normal word order). In 3.1 and 3.2 we have metaphors and allusions that lead into parallelism in 3.3 and 3.4; in 4 we have a metaphor followed by a tricolon. In 5 we have parallelism and metaphor.

The analysis identified the presence of multiple schemes in both speeches, a large number of metaphors in the Collins' speech and quite a few metonyms in the Shakespeare speech; as a result, the two speeches seem to share a range of stylistic features: they both share the communicative purpose of motivation and achieve this by keeping the focus on the distant future rather than the imminent future.

They both also draw on a mythic element and in places employ an elevated style – for example, when considering honour or the outcome of the battle. But they also use a plain style with a simple and uncomplicated lexicon to express esprit de corps and solidarity in death; because of the evidence of both an elevated and a plain style I suggest that, overall, both speeches employ a middle style. The movement between high and low styles corresponds with the conflicting emotions that are likely to be experienced by the audience on such an occasion.

Exercise 3.1 (p. 57)

Coherence is the impression that a reader has of a text's unity or completeness. This impression of unity does not necessarily arise from specific linguistic features in the text, though these can contribute to such an impression. Coherence arises from the reader's awareness of the writer's communicative purpose, based on their shared background knowledge of the world and of how texts have similar communicative purposes.

Exercise 3.2 (p. 63)

Perhaps you identified exophoric reference in (11.1): 'Finally, to those nations who would make themselves our adversary'; here, the reference is to America's perceived enemy (the Soviet Union and its allies). Other examples are references to a 'generation of Americans'; these could be analysed as exophoric reference when they refer to groups of Americans who have not been mentioned previously (for example, in 3.2), but where reference is repeated, as in 21.2, the second example is endophoric. Because of its political purpose this speech probably has quite a large amount of exophoric reference.

Most people find it preferable to approach this task methodically, by analysing each of the types of deixis separately, so going through the text to identify first person deixis, then place deixis, and after that time deixis (though not necessarily in this order). Others might prefer to work in a more synthetic way by going through the text sequentially to identify all examples of deixis simultaneously. The first approach is more likely to avoid missing occurrences, whereas the second might be better for a discursive account where some examples of deixis are illustrated rather than each one.

Something to note in analysing person deixis is that second-person pronouns are only introduced towards the end of the speech; prior to that the deictic reference is impersonal but using syntactic inversion (that is bringing to the front of the sentence) – for example, 'to those states' (7.1) 'to those peoples' (8.1). This indirect form of address to the audience enhances the rhetorical effect.

Exercise 3.3 (p. 66)

You will note that pronouns are usually anaphoric references because they refer back to a noun. You will also note that the majority of cohesive ties are references – these usually account for as many as 90 per cent of all ties.

Generally, texts where there is less reliance on cognitive circumstantial knowledge will use more grammatical cohesion. For example, advertisements reduce the amount of grammatical cohesion because they rely on audience inferencing and therefore on cognitive knowledge; other types of text reduce this sort of cohesion for reasons of economy, though this is often at the expense of comprehension. The reduction of grammatical cohesion can present difficulties for the decoding of texts by younger learners; authors of children's books are particularly concerned to make cohesive relations explicit rather than relying on inferencing. Given that political speeches need to accommodate multiple audiences, they are likely to be in the mid-range.

Exercise 3.4 (p. 70)

There are a number of examples of repetition throughout the speech. The following are just some of the ones that you might have identified.

In 14–18 there is repetition of the phrase 'both sides', first introduced in 11.1.
'unite' in 15 is a repetition of 'united' in 6.2; and 'divide' is a repetition of 'divided' in 6.3.
'arms' in 16.1 is a repetition of the same word in 12.2.
'power' in 16.1 is a repetition of the same word a number of times in the speech, including 2.2, 7.3 and 9.4.
'world' in 19.1 is a repetition of the same word in 2.1, 3.2 and 10.1.

Synonyms of 'planet' (20.2) include the following lexical chain: 'world' (2.1; 3.2; 10.1; 19.1; 24.1; 24.4; 26.1 and 27.1)
'globe' (2.3; 8.1) and 'global' 23.1
'earth' (18.1; 27.1).

A synonym of 'enemies' (22.1; 23.1) is 'adversary' 11.1.

Antonyms include 'peace' (19.1), which is itself a repetition of various earlier examples is an antonym of 'war' (3.2; 10.2 and 13.1).

Overall there are probably more examples of repetition and reiteration than there are of synonyms and antonyms; however, both types of tie would seem to be equally important in forming cohesion in the speech.

Exercise 3.5 (p. 73)

Once we have identified lexical cohesion in a speech there are a number of stages of analysis we could then undertake; a simple quantitative approach would be to work out the number of each type of cohesive tie, as in the table opposite.

Summary of cohesive relations in Kennedy inaugural address

Type of cohesive tie	Paragraphs 1–13
REPETITION	60
COLLOCATION	22
SYNONYM/ANTONYM	19
TOTAL LEXICAL COHESION	101

From this we see that repetition is the most frequently used tie; and collocation, synonymy/antonymy are similar in frequency. These patterns could be different in speeches by different speakers. It is possible that, in speeches, given the greater demands on the hearer for cognitive processing, there will be more repetition than in other types of text.

We could also use cohesion analysis to identify key sentences or paragraphs of a speech; 'key' here would mean that one paragraph has multiple cohesive ties to preceding or following paragraphs. For example, paragraph 9 is linked especially closely with preceding sentences, with many lexically cohesive ties (more than a quarter of all those identified in the first half of the speech). It is particularly dense in collocations – with nearly half of all the collocations identified in this part. The following sentences refer back to it: there are 7 ties between paragraph 10 and paragraph 9, and a further 3 between paragraphs 11 and 9. So our analysis of lexical cohesion suggests that paragraph 9 identifies the major theme of the speech because of its close bonding with other paragraphs. Hoey (1991) argues that paragraphs with a high density of cohesive ties can be used to produce a précis of the whole text; there seems to be support here for his analysis, as paragraph 9 presents Kennedy's main arguments that:

1 America welcomes allies, especially from recently independent nations.
2 America threatens those nations (such as Cuba, though that is only implied, since Cuba is to the south of the USA), who make alliances with the USSR, by implication, against the USA.

Paragraph 9 could be taken to predict the Cuban missile crisis that occurred in October 1962 and the USA response to the Soviet strategy of moving nuclear missiles to Cuba. Lexical cohesion is central in contributing to the coherence of a speech and analysis – combined with analysis of the arguments – enables us to identify what constitutes persuasive oratory.

Exercise 4.1 (p. 85)

A definition of power: power is when an individual or social group, A, forces another social group or individual, B, to do things that are in A's best interests and prevents B from doing things that are in B's best interest.

Legitimate uses of power: the authority of a legitimate court; the authority of a parent over a child when acting in the child's best interests; the authority of a teacher or lecturer over a pupil or student acting in the pupil's or student's long-term interests.

Illegitimate uses of power: the force used by an illegitimate source of power such as the Mafia. The physical or sexual abuse of children or young people by those in positions of authority over them. The use of a position of authority to collect illegal payments.

Exercise 5.1 (p. 113)

The normal level of modality in political speaking is high:

Cameron is emphasizing the necessity of his actions with a moral claim that they are right.

He uses 'promise' (in (2)) – a verb that like 'swear' strongly commits himself to a position; it gives what he is saying the status of the speech act known as a 'commissive' because it *commits* the speaker to a future action.

He emphasizes that this is his personal view 'I want to say' (in (2)) followed by the simple present tense to make a factual claim that this is the truth.

He repeats the personal emphasis with 'I tell you what' (in (3)). Using speech verbs such as 'say' and 'tell' heighten the rhetorical commitment to what he is saying by pointing to what he is going to say next.

He uses the form 'must not be allowed' (in (5)) which emphasizes negative permission – a concept closely related to obligation and necessity.

He finishes (from (7)) with some firm promises about the future effects of reductions in government spending. The use of the predictive future expresses a high level of modality – the pain he is describing is represented as both obligatory and necessary, as if there were no other policy options available.

Exercise 5.2 (p. 119)

There are, of course, many changes and modifications made from the Joint Intelligence Committee assessment that was prepared for a specialist audience and that produced by political advisers for the general public and Members of Parliament. I summarize the main ones in the following table.

	Published dossier	Commentary
1	Title: Iraq's Weapons of Mass Destruction	The development of the generic name 'Weapons of Mass Destruction' not only sounded more frightening but also deliberately left it vague as to whether or not Iraq was developing nuclear capability. There was more evidence of chemical weapons programmes than of other weapon types – but to put them all into a category of 'destruction' was rhetorically persuasive.
2	This chapter sets out what is known of Saddam's chemical, biological, nuclear and ballistic missile programmes, drawing on all the available evidence.	The JIC was clear that it had little concrete evidence of current weapons programmes; the phrase 'all the available evidence' concealed the fact that the evidence was very limited in nature.
3	The intelligence picture ... is extensive detailed and authoritative. (Blair in House of Commons)	The phrase 'judgement and assessment' emphasized the essentially subjective nature of the evidence; however the use of a new set of adjective clearly increases the level of epistemic modality.
4	Intelligence shows that Iraq has covert chemical and biological weapons programmes, in breach of UN Security Council Resolution 687.	The verb 'shows' is an interesting choice as it makes a strong epistemic claim: if something is 'shown' it is available for all to 'see' as well as to know.
5	Intelligence also shows that Iraq is preparing plans to conceal evidence of these weapons, including incriminating documents, from renewed inspections.	The use of the phrase 'conceal evidence' implies an intention to deceive that fits with the general idea of deception that was felt rhetorically essential in winning the argument for invasion. If Saddam wilfully misled, then there was no reason ever to trust him.
6	... intelligence indicates that as part of Iraq's military planning Saddam is willing to use chemical and biological weapons.	Again the use of 'is willing to use' heightens the threat posed by Saddam. It is a highly significant shift from 'to defend the regime from attack' as it implies his potential to launch an attack – just as he had done in Kuwait in 1991.

➡

Published dossier	Commentary
7 We judge that Iraq has developed mobile laboratories for military use, corroborating earlier reports about the mobile production of biological warfare agents.	The nominal phrase 'mobile production' is from a semi-technical register that implies a degree of scientific sophistication that again raised the perception of threat.
8 The Iraqi military are able to deploy chemical or biological weapons within forty-five minutes of an order to do so.	The replacement of the modal 'could' by the use of the simple present 'are able to' significantly changes the level of epistemic modality from something that is possible to something that is certain.
9 What I believe the assessed intelligence has established beyond doubt is that Saddam continues in his efforts to develop nuclear weapons (PM forward)	The use of 'established beyond doubt' clearly raises the level of epistemic modality from possibility to certainty.

Exercise 6.1 (p. 126)

Fields of action 1, 7 and 8 – Speeches in a political assembly with legislative powers. Speeches given in the High Court or Court of Appeals could also be relevant.

Fields of action 2 and 6 – Inaugural speeches, televised speeches during election campaigns by politicians; speeches made in prime ministerial debates, but also comments and statements made on the radio, on television or via blogs. Increasingly, speeches and statements given via digital media, either through politicians' own websites or through blogs. For example, at the time of writing, the black Labour politician Diane Abbot has been forced to apologize for a comment she made via Twitter: 'White people love playing divide and rule.' Though she said in her defence that 'I think the tweet has been taken out of context and some people have misinterpreted it maliciously', it was considered by her opponents to be contributing to a stereotypically negative view of white people as being racist.

3—(a) Speeches given at party conferences and other political meetings. Acceptance of candidacy speeches.
4—(b) Speeches given in public debating arenas or in political legislatures.
5—(c) Speeches given on overseas visits, for international occasions, such as Nobel prize acceptance speeches, speeches to the nation or even declarations of war.

Your list might have included anything from the Del Hymes' (1972) model for the context of situation to that proposed by Normal Fairclough (2003). Wodak and Meyer (2009, p. 93) identify four 'levels' of context for a particular discursive practice:

1 The other language in the text, or co-text of the practice.
2 The evocation of other texts leading to intertextual and interdiscursive relation-ships as it is often similarity between utterances in different contexts that creates genres and discourses.
3 The particular extralinguistic context of situation as in Hymes' sense (such as the institution where this discursive practice occurs).
4 The broader sociopolitical and historical context of the practice.

An analysis of the context for public communication includes aspects of the setting, such as the time when and the location where a speech was given, the occasion of the speech and its audience. We would identify the sex, age, profession, educational level, ethnic, regional, national or religious affiliation of the speaker. Similar generic characteristics of an audience might also be identified. We would identify the partic-ipants' roles, shared knowledge, intentions and goals.

Exercise 6.2 (p. 132)

In terms of class rather than ethnic identity, 'chav' is used in South-East England to refer to those who wear 'bling' (large earrings and garish jewellery) and behave in a socially irresponsible way – smoking, drinking, speaking loudly, exhibiting promiscuity and so on; chavs speak with a strong Estuary English accent; they may be from a lower social class background. As a discursive strategy, 'chav' could be analysed as nomination and predication as it is a name associated with negative traits relating to social irresponsibility and is used by people who do not consider themselves within this category. 'Chav' is productive in contemporary colloquial English as it has a verb form meaning 'to steal' as in 'you have chaved my pencil case'.

An interesting pair of names in British culture refers to people leading itinerant lifestyles without established home bases (for example, working with a funfair) – sometimes with origins in gypsy culture. A pejorative name is 'gypo', while a posi-tive name is 'traveller'; 'gypo' marks an ethnic identity whereas 'traveller' refers more to a particular lifestyle that involves moving from place to place. Here are two examples from the British National Corpus:

> ... arrested six of them all they found all bits and bobs off hundreds and hundreds and thousands of pounds worth of cars, and four wheel drives they specialize in and off to the Continent with it. Yeah, it's all organized, it's *not* like the *gypos* will be doing like this, Oh yes! Yeah, this is all organized bloody down to! Oh yes, all yeah! They handled something like a thousand pounds worth of cars that they did. (BNC)

> We have already significant contact through the international Save The Children alliance partners in Europe and we have representation on the European forum for child welfare. On particular issues, such as work with refugee children and work with *traveller* and gypsy *families*, there is already established European collaboration. (BNC)

In terms of the discursive strategy of naming, 'gypo' is a name used to position a people who do not live in conventional houses as an out-group that is associated with negative traits such as stealing scrap metal, whereas 'traveller' is used an in-group marker or as a sympathetic term towards an out-group.

Exercise 6.3 (p. 146)

The table below shows a possible analysis of the second part of the speech using Wodak's categories.

Analysis of topoi in second part of Howard's immigration speech

	Analysis of topoi
17	Uselessness of the present system for monitoring immigration.
18	Uselessness of system for work permits.
19	Law and right would be re-established by Conservative government. Numbers – small number or prosecutions.
20	Uselessness + Burdening that immigration puts on publish services and housing.
21	Usefulness and Humanitarianism.
22	Numbers of work permits issued. Numbers of those with work permits who then apply for settlement.
23	Responsibility of governments for limiting work permits.
24	Uselessness of asylum system.
25	No definition of the difference between 'those claiming asylum', 'genuine refugees' and 'failed asylum seekers' – as if they all belong to the same category.
26	Justice: illegality of asylum seekers exposes them to danger of people-smugglers.
28	Justice: Conservative government will impose justice in accordance with international law.
30	History shows that people can integrate successfully.
31	Usefulness of controlled immigration.
32	Usefulness of controlled immigration but uselessness of uncontrolled immigration.

There is an implied argument in the analysis of lexical cohesion in the speech that the asylum seekers referred to in 25, 26 and 27 can be equated with 'failed asylum seekers' (10, 14 and 25) (lexical repetition) and that 'illegal immigrants' (13, 16 and 19) can be equated with 'immigrants' 2, 7, 11 29 and 31. This draws on the discursive strategy of predication because it attributes failure and criminality to immigrants and asylum seekers. The process of negative association that underlies the perspective is motivated by a synecdoche in which a part of a group (the 'failed asylum seeker', the 'illegal immigrant') represents the whole group (*all* asylum seekers; *all* immigrants). It is therefore also a form of intensification.

Exercise 6.4 (p. 150)

The topoi in the second edition that do not feature in the first edition include: 'topos or fallacy of frightening'; ' topos or fallacy of authority'; 'topos or fallacy of nature'; 'topos of technological progress'; 'topos or fallacy of consequences of wealth to environment'; 'topos or fallacy of pressure'; 'topos or fallacy of wasting'; 'topos of fallacy of freedom'; ' topos or fallacy of thrift'; 'topos of uncertainty'; 'topos or fallacy of compulsion' and so on.

Other topoi in the second edition appear to be renamed topoi from the first edition; for example, 'topos/fallacy of pressure/compulsion' is similar to 'burdening and weighting'; 'topos or fallacy of frightening' is similar to 'danger and threat'; 'topos of costs' and 'topos or fallacy of thrift' both appear similar to 'finance'; finally, 'topos or fallacy of moral duty' is similar to 'Humanitarianism'.

Here is a possible analysis of section 20:

There do not appear to be any data that support the claim made here; in fact, it seems to contradict another claim made in section 31: 'Immigration is good for Britain – we are a stronger and more successful country because of the immigrant communities that have settled here.' This claim could be considered to be supported by the evidence of personal experience offered in 30: 'Everything I have I owe to this country. My family came here with very little and made a life for themselves'. This could be analysed as follows:

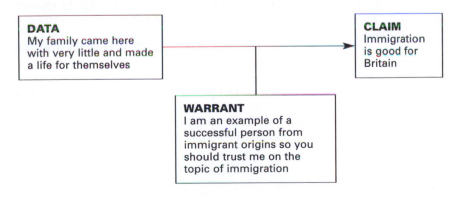

The warrant here appears to be the assumption that the speaker is an example of a successful immigrant and so one should trust his arguments all the more. This does not seem to correspond closely with a topos – the nearest is perhaps 'History'; but it is an argument where a general proposition 'immigration is good when accompanied by effort' is supported by a specific example – himself, so it is really family history. This seems to work in a way similar to synecdoche in that it is a part/whole relationship in which a single case, the speaker's family, stands for a general category of successful immigrants. However, it could be analysed as a Category Error because Howard is not a typical immigrant. I would therefore suggest a warrant of 'Category Error'.

The use of claims without data is identified through the analysis of argument structure. The corresponding topos for 20 was 'Uselessness'; 31 was analysed as 'Usefulness of controlled immigration' so the fallacious argument of making contrary propositions is reflected by a contrast between the two topoi. The use of an argument based on synecdoche or family history does not appear to be covered by topoi as they are presently formulated, but could be if a warrant of Category Error was introduced.

Exercise 7.1 (p. 162)

Some background to the speech is given in *The Penguin Book of Twentieth-Century Speeches* (MacArthur, 1999, p. 418). There are many candidate metaphors, including:

> to muster all our energies (1.4)
> to get the levers of power again, the whips would be changed to scorpions for our chastisement (3.1)
> the scourge of unemployment (6.1)
> we can face an economic typhoon of unparalleled ferocity (7.1)
> the red flames of Socialist courage

One way of grouping the metaphors might be according to their level of intensity; for example, those I have listed above seem more intense than others such as: 'full panoply of socialist measures' or 'stifling dissent'. Another way might be by whether they make positive or negative evaluations (though it seems there are many more of the second type).

I would say the main purpose for using these metaphors is to intensify the force of his emotional commitment to encourage support for the Labour government of the time. In my view they are effective in heightening the impression of passionate commitment to socialism, and that a party conference is an arena where leaders can safely express powerful emotions about ideological issues. While some of these metaphors may sound too impassioned by current-day standards, at the time the speech was given it was more acceptable to use an ornate oratorical style.

Exercise 7.2 (p. 170)

There is variation among researchers as to whether they provide sufficient information about the source of their data to allow their research to be replicated. This is especially the case for researchers into 'discourse' – who are interested in how metaphors may pervade a whole way of talking and thinking. However, there can be difficulties in accurate generalization from sets of data that mix up quite different types of speeches; for example, in the above papers, Lu and Ahrens (2008) are very specific about the source of speeches and controls for the genre of speech; this is less the case with the other two papers, who use general categories of 'speeches by New Labour' and 'speeches given in the European Parliament', though this may be because of their interest in identifying discourse characteristics of these entities. Reisigl (2008a, 2008b) have an overview of types of political speeches that would allow researchers to control for the variable of genre and generally this allows findings to be stated more confidently.

Exercise 7.3 (p. 172)

We should first recall that psycholinguistic approaches typically invite some form of empirical enquiry to gain insight into cognitive processing; without this it is, of course, difficult to know what takes place in the human brain. There is also likely to be individual variation in the responsiveness to active metaphor, so some individuals tend to 'hear' more metaphors than others; we are aware of this when learning idiomatic expressions in a second language, where the learner may be more aware of the comparisons because they are new and unfamiliar than are native speakers of the language.

The following are simply hypotheses about the types of processing that may occur:

1 Here, 'recipe' seems to be used as a general term for a plan and does not activate an idea of cooking in particular, therefore processing is likely to be by categorization.
2 The human body is being used as a general term for an organization, so 'heart and soul' are again probably processed by categorization.
3 While there is a general way of talking about economic affairs with reference to the weather (for example, 'a stormy day on the markets'), extreme weather events such as typhoons, or more recently, tsunamis, are likely to activate some type of comparison between economic affairs and such an extreme event.
4 'Forge' is often used as a general term for some types of political action, and it is unlikely that there is any image of a blacksmith or other concrete event activated, so processing is by categorization. We find similar references by political actors to their actions in verbs such as 'craft', 'shape' and 'knit'.
5 Here the metaphor seems to invite comparison between the colour red – symbolizing the political left since the time of communism – and fire, so it is likely that processing is by active comparison. We saw from the analysis of Blair's 'beacon' metaphor how fire is a rich source domain for metaphor. It draws on a wide range

of everyday human experience. It is a vivid metaphor that came to be used to refer to the speech.

I emphasize again that the above are simply illustrations based on introspection as to the type of processing that may occur; an empirical approach would require some source of data on how different individuals respond to these metaphors.

Exercise 8.1 (p. 184)

The table below summarizes my findings for the first part of the speech (section and sentence numbers in brackets)

Psycholinguistic analysis of metaphor in Michael Foot's conference speech

Novel	Conventional	Entrenched
scorpions for our chastisement (3.1)	levers of power (3.1)	deepest instinct (2.1)
insidious attack (2.4)	muster all our energies (1.4)	crisis should be faced (2.1)
is part of an affliction (1.3)	rising anxieties (1.1)	I shudder to think (2.2 and 2.3)
	closest alliance (2.1)	
	Western world is gripped (1.3)	
	If we were to fall apart (2.2)	

The novel metaphors identified in the first phase were then classified with reference to the British National Corpus (BNC). For example, intuitively I classified 'levers of power' as novel but on finding 17 instances of this phrase in the corpus I re-classified it as conventional. However, I classed 'insidious attack' and 'part of an affliction' as conventional but as I could find no such collocations in the corpus, then re-classified them as novel. Words that a dictionary shows as having a more basic meaning, but where the metaphoric meaning is much more frequent, are classified as entrenched. For example, the most common verb preceding the word 'crisis' is 'face' (the only other high frequency verb preceding 'face' is 'resolve') so the idea of 'facing a crisis' is entrenched; the expression 'shudder to think' occurs 20 times in the corpus, which is enough evidence to classify this embodied meaning as entrenched. Originally I classified 'closest alliance' as entrenched; however, I did not find this collocation at all in the BNC, and other adjectives such as 'strategic', 'holy', 'unholy' and 'Islamic' occurred. However, it did not intuitively seem novel and we have to remember that while the corpus was collected between the 1970s and 1993 it may be skewed towards the 1980s and early 1990s. We may notice that conventional metaphors occur more frequently than the other types. We shall see in

Chapter 9 that conventional metaphors are more likely to yield conceptual metaphors.

Exercise 8.2 (p. 192)

A number of metaphors seem to personify the Labour movement, such as 'faced and surmounted by/Labour government', 'the heart and soul of our Labour movement', 'a Labour movement that tries to dodge', 'the Socialist imagination', 'socialist courage'. These show evidence of the conceptual metaphor THE LABOUR MOVE-MENT/SOCIALISM IS A BRAVE PERSON. This would fit quite well with some of the conceptual metaphors I proposed for Margaret Thatcher: SOCIALISM IS A DEATH FORCE; SOCIALISM IS A DISEASE; SOCIALISM IS AN IMMORAL PERSON (Charteris-Black, 2011, p. 181).

Exercise 9.1 (p. 206)

Here are a few obvious ones:

Harold Macmillan – 'The winds of change' (1960).
Martin Luther King – 'I have a dream' (1963).
Robert Kennedy – 'A tiny ripple of hope' (1966).
Enoch Powell – 'I seem to see the River Tiber foaming with much blood' (1968).
Michael Foot – 'The red flame of Socialist courage' (1976).
Edward Kennedy – 'The dream shall never die' (1980).
Prince Charles – 'A monstrous carbuncle' (1984).
Jesse Jackson – 'Keep hope alive' (1988).

Further Reading and References

Anderson, R. D. (2004) 'The Causal Power of Metaphor: Cueing Democratic Identities in Russia and Beyond'. In A. Beer and C. De Landtsheer (eds), *Metaphorical World Politics*, pp. 91–110.

Aristotle (1952). In W. D. Ross, *The Works of Aristotle*, Vol. XI *De Poetica*, trans. I. Bywater. *Rhetoric* (Oxford: Clarendon Press).

Beer, A. and De Landtsheer, C. (eds) (2004) *Metaphorical World Politics. Rhetorics of Democracy, War and Globalization* (East Lansing, MI: Michigan State University Press).

Bernstein, B. (1990) *Class, Codes and Control*, Vol. IV *The Structuring of Pedagogic Discourse* (London/New York: Routledge).

Billig, M. and MacMillan, K. (2005) 'Metaphor, Idiom and Ideology: The Search for "No Smoking Guns" Across Time', *Discourse & Society*, 16(4), 459–80.

Bowdle, B. F. and Gentner, D. (2005) 'The Career of Metaphor', *Psychological Review*, 112(1), 193–206.

Burke, K. (1945) *A Grammar of Motives* (Berkeley, CA: University of California Press).

Cameron, L. and Low, G. (eds) (1999) *Researching and Applying Metaphor* (Cambridge: Cambridge University Press).

Carver, T. and Pikalo, J. (eds) (2008) *Political Language and Metaphor: Interpreting and Changing the World* (London: Routledge).

Charteris-Black, J. (2004) *Corpus Approaches to Critical Metaphor Analysis* (Basingstoke: Palgrave Macmillan).

Charteris-Black, J. (2006) 'Britain as a Container: Immigration Metaphors in the 2005 Election Campaign', *Discourse & Society*, 17(6), 563–82.

Charteris-Black, J. (2007) *The Communication of Leadership: The Design of Leadership Style* (London/New York: Routledge).

Charteris-Black, J. (2009) 'Metaphor and Gender in British Parliamentary Debates'. In K. Ahrens (ed.), *Politics, Gender and Conceptual Metaphor* (Amsterdam/Philadelphia: John Benjamins), pp. 196–234.

Charteris-Black, J. (2011) *Politicians and Rhetoric: The Persuasive Power of Metaphor*, 2nd edn (Basingstoke/New York: Palgrave Macmillan).

Charteris-Black, J. (2012) 'Forensic Deliberations on Purposeful Metaphor', *Metaphor and One Social World*, 2(1), 1–21.

Charteris-Black, J. (2013) 'Political Style – A Study of David Cameron'. In P. Stockwell and S. Whiteley (eds), *The Cambridge Handbook of Stylistics* (Cambridge: Cambridge University Press).

Chilton, P. (1996) *Security Metaphors: Cold War Discourse from Containment to Common House* (New York: Peter Lang).

Chilton, P. (2004) *Analysing Political Discourse* (London/New York: Routledge), ch. 7.

Chilton, P., Reisigl, M. and Wodak, R. (2009) 'The Discourse-Historical Approach'. In R. Wodak and M. Meyer (eds), *Methods of Critical Discourse Analysis*, 2nd edn (London: Sage), pp. 87–121.

Christie L. and T. Ward, (1990) *Linford Christie: An Autobiography* (London: Arrow Books).

Coates, J. (1983) *The Semantics of the Modal Auxiliaries* (London: Croom Helm).

Davies, M. (2004) BYU-BNC (Based on the British National Corpus from Oxford University Press). Available online at http://corpus.byu.edu/bnc/

Davies, M. (2008) 'The Corpus of Contemporary American English: 450 million words, 1990–present'. Available online at http://corpus.byu.edu/coca/8/

De Braugh, M. (2007) 'The Parts of Speech'. In I. Worthington, *A Companion to Greek Rhetoric* (Chichester, UK: Wiley-Blackwell), pp. 187–252.

Deignan, A. (2005) *Metaphor and Corpus Linguistics* (Amsterdam: John Benjamins).

De Landtsheer and De Vrij (2004) 'Talking about Srebrenica: Dutch Elites and Dutchbat. How Metaphors Change during Crisis. In F. A. Beer and C. De Landtsheer (eds), *Metaphorical World Politics*, pp. 163–92.

Drulák, P. (2008) 'Identifying and Assessing Metaphors: Discourse on EU Reform'. In T. Carver and J. Pikalo (eds), *Political Language and Metaphor: Interpreting and Changing the World* (London: Routledge), pp. 105–18.

Edelman, M. (1988) *Constructing the Political Spectacle* (Chicago/London: University of Chicago Press).

Edwards, P. (2009) *How to Rap: The Art and Science of the Hip-Hop MC* (Chicago, IL: Chicago Review Press), p. 88.

Fairclough, N. (ed.) (1989) *Critical Language Awareness* (London: Longman).

Fairclough, N. (1995) *Critical Discourse Analysis: the Critical Study of Language* (London: Longman).

Fairclough, N. (2003) *Analysing Discourse: Textual Analysis for Social Research* (London: Routledge), pp. 1–18, 105–20, 164–90.

Fairclough, N. (2006) Global Capitalism and Critical Awareness of Language. In A. Jaworski and N. Coupland (eds), *The Discourse Reader*, 2nd edn (London: Routledge).

Fairclough, N. (2010) *Critical Discourse Analysis: The Critical Study of Language*, 2nd edn (London: Longman).

Ferrari, F. (2007) 'Metaphor at Work in the Analysis of Political Discourse: Investigating a "Preventive War" Persuasion Strategy', *Discourse & Society*, 18(5), 603–25.

Flood, C. G. (1996) *Political Myth: A Theoretical Introduction* (New York/London: Garland).

Flowerdew, J. (2002) 'Globalization Discourse: A View from the East', *Discourse & Society*, 13(2), 209–25.

Flowerdew, J. and Leong, S. (2007) 'Metaphors in the Discursive Construction of Patriotism: The Case of Hong Kong's Constitutional Reform Debate', *Discourse & Society*, 18(3), 273–94.

Foot, M. (1999) 'The Red Flame of Socialist Courage'. In B. MacArthur (ed.), *The Penguin Book of Twentieth-Century Speeches*, 2nd edn (London: Penguin), p. 418.

Fortenbaugh, W. W. (2007) 'Aristotle's Art of Rhetoric'. In I. Worthington, *A Companion to Greek Rhetoric* (Chichester, UK: Wiley-Blackwell), pp. 107–23.

Gee, J. P. (2011) 'Discourse Analysis: What Makes it Critical?' In R. Rogers, *Critical Discourse Analysis in Education* (New York: Routledge), pp. 23–45.

Gentner, D. and Bowdle, B. F. (2001) 'Convention, Form, and Figurative Language Processing', *Metaphor and Symbol*, 16(3/4), 223–48.

Glucksberg, S. and Keysar, B. (1993) 'How Metaphors Work'. In A. Ortony (ed.), *Metaphor and Thought*, 2nd edn (Cambridge University Press), pp. 401–24.

Goatly, A. (2007) *Washing the Brain: Metaphor and Hidden Ideology* (Amsterdam: Benjamins).

Goatly, A. (2008) *The Language of Metaphors*, 2nd edn (London/New York: Routledge).

Gregg, R. B. (2004) 'Embodied Meaning in American Public Discourse during the Cold War'. In A. Beer and C. De Landtsheer (eds), *Metaphorical World Politics*, pp. 59–74.

Gunderson E. (ed.) (2009) *The Cambridge Companion to Ancient Rhetoric* (Cambridge University Press).

Halliday, M.A.K. (1994) *An Introduction to Functional Grammar*, 2nd edn (London: Edward Arnold).

Halliday, M. A. K. and Hasan, R. (1976) *Cohesion in English* (London: Longman).

Hart, C. (2011) 'Force-interactive Patterns in Immigration Discourse: A Cognitive Linguistic Approach to CDA', *Discourse & Society*, 22(3), 269–86.

Herbeck, D. A. (2004) 'Sports Metaphors and Public Policy'. In A. Beer and C. De Landtsheer (eds), *Metaphorical World Politics*, pp. 121–40.

Hoey, M. (1991) *Patterns of Lexis in Text* (Oxford: Oxford University Press), ch. 3.

Holmgreen, L. L. (2008) 'Biotech as Biothreat? Metaphorical Constructions in Discourse', *Discourse & Society*, 19(1), 99–119.

Hymes, D. (1972) 'Models of Interaction of Language and Social Life Directions'. In John Gumperz and Dell Hymes (eds), *Sociolinguistics: The Ethnography of Communication* (New York: Holt) 35–71.

Jansen, S. C and Sabo, D. (1994) 'The Sport/War Metaphor: Hegemonic Masculinity, the Persian Gulf War, and the New World Order', *Sociology of Sport Journal*, 11, 1–17.

Jones, R. (2012) Section B2: 'Cohesion and Coherence'. In R. H. Jones, *Discourse Analysis: A Resource Book for Students* (London/New York: Routledge).

Kienpointer, M. (1992) *Alltagslogik* (Stuttgart-Bad Cannstatt: Frommannholzboog).

Konstan, D. (2007) 'Rhetoric and Emotion'. In I. Worthington, *A Companion to Greek Rhetoric* (Chichester, UK: Wiley-Blackwell), pp. 411–26.

Kövecses, Z. (2003) *Metaphor and Emotion: Language, Culture and Body in Human Feeling* (Cambridge: CUP).

Kress, G. (1992) 'Critical Discourse Analysis', *Annual Review of Applied Linguistics*, 11, 84–99.

Lakoff, G. (1991) 'The Metaphor System Used to Justify War in the Gulf', *Journal of Urban and Cultural Studies*, 2(1), 59–72.

Lakoff, G. (2002) *Moral Politics*, 2nd edn (Chicago/London: University of Chicago Press).

Lakoff, G. and Johnson, M. (1980) *Metaphors We Live By* (Chicago, IL: University of Chicago Press).

Lakoff, G. and Johnson, M. (1999) *Philosophy in the Flesh: Embodied Mind and Its Challenge to Western Thought* (New York: Basic Books).

Lakoff, G. and Turner, M. (1989) *More than Cool Reason: A Field Guide to Poetic Metaphor* (Chicago/London: University of Chicago Press).

Lancaster, S. (2010) *Speechwriting*. London: Robert Hale.

Leith, S. (2011) *You Talkin' To Me? Rhetoric from Aristotle to Obama* (London: Profile Books).

L'Hôte, E. (2010) New Labour and Globalization: Globalist Discourse with a Twist?, *Discourse & Society*, 21(4), 355–76.

Lu, L. W. and Ahrens, K. (2008) 'Ideological Influence on BUILDING Metaphors in Taiwanese Presidential Speeches', *Discourse & Society*, 19(3), 383–408.

Lyons, J. (1977) *Semantics* (Cambridge University Press).

MacArthur, B. (1999) *The Penguin Book of Twentieth-Century Speeches*, 2nd revd edn (London: Penguin).

Mancroft, Lord (1967) *Reader's Digest*, February.

McEntee-Atalianis, L. J. (2011) 'The Role of Metaphor in Shaping the Identity and Agenda of the United Nations: The Imagining of an International Community and International Threat', *Discourse & Communication*, 5(4), 393–412.

Mio, J. S. (1997) 'Metaphor and Politics', *Metaphor and Symbol* 12(2), 113–33.

Mio, J. S. and Lovrich, N. P. (1998) 'Men of Zeal: Memory for Metaphors in the Iran-Contra Hearings', *Metaphor and Symbol*, 13(1), 49–68.

Mullany, L. and Stockwell, P. (2010) *Introducing English Language: A Resource Book for Students* (London/New York: Routledge), pp. 20–3.

Musolff, A. (2006) 'Metaphor Scenarios in Public Discourse' *Metaphor and Symbol*, 21(1), 23–38.

Musolff, A. (2010) *Metaphor, Nation and the Holocaust: The Concept of the Body Politic* (Abingdon, UK/New York: Routledge).

Nash, W. (1989) *Rhetoric: The Wit of Persuasion* (Cambridge, UK: Blackwell).

Palmer, F. R. (1986) *Mood and Modality* (Cambridge Universty Press).

Perelman, C. (1982) *The Realm of Rhetoric* (Paris: University of Notre Dame Press).

Pragglejaz Group (2007) 'MIP: A Method for Identifying Metaphorically Used Words in Discourse', *Metaphor and Symbol*, 22(1), 1–39.

Reisigl, M. (2008a) 'Analyzing Political Rhetoric'. In R. Wodak and N. Krzyżanowski (eds), *Qualitative Discourse Analysis in the Social Sciences* (Basingstoke: Palgrave Macmillan), pp. 96–120.

Reisigl, M. (2008b) 'Rhetoric of Political Speeches'. In R. Wodak and V. Koller (eds), *Handbook of Communication in the Public Sphere* (Berlin/New York: Mouton de Gruyter), pp. 243–69.

Reisigl, M. and Wodak, R. (2001) *Discourse and Discrimination, Rhetoric of Racism and Antisemitism* (London and New York: Routledge).

Richards, I. A. (1936) *The Philosophy of Rhetoric* (New York/London: Oxford University Press).

Richardson, J. E. (2007) *Analysing Newspapers* (Basingstoke: Palgrave Macmillan), ch. 1.

Ritchie, D. (2003) ' "ARGUMENT IS WAR" – Or Is It a Game of Chess? Multiple Meanings in the Analysis of Implicit Metaphors', *Metaphor and Symbol*, 18(2), 125–46.

Ritchie, D. L. (2013) *Metaphor* (Cambridge University Press), ch. 9.

Rogers, R. (2011) *Critical Discourse Analysis in Education* (New York: Routledge).

Rosati, J. A. and Campbell, A. J. (2004) 'Metaphorical Thinking during the Carter Years'. In A. Beer and C. De Landtsheer (eds), *Metaphorical World Politics*, pp. 217–36.

Santa Ana, O. (1999) ' "Like an Animal I Was Treated": Anti-Immigrant Metaphor in US Public Discourse', *Discourse Society*, 10(2), 191–224.

Semino, E. (2008) *Metaphor in Discourse* (Cambridge University Press), ch. 6.

Semino, E. and Masci, M. (1996) 'Politics Is Football: Metaphor in the Discourse of Silvio Berlusconi in Italy', *Discourse and Society*, 7, 243–69.

Shimko, K. L. (2004) 'The Power of Metaphors and the Metaphors of Power'. In A. Beer, A. and C. De Landtsheer (eds), *Metaphorical World Politics*, pp. 199–216.

Sontag, S. (1991) *Illness as Metaphor and AIDS and Its Metaphors* (London: Penguin).

Steen, G. (2008) 'The Paradox of Metaphor: Why We Need a Three-Dimensional Model of Metaphor', *Metaphor and Symbol*, 23(4), 213–41.

Stenvoll, D. (2008) 'Slippery Slopes in Political Discourse'. In T. Carver and J. Pikalo (eds), *Political Language and Metaphor* (London: Routledge), pp. 28–40.

Straehle, C., Weiss, G., Wodak, R., Muntigl, P. and Sedlak, M. (1999) 'Struggle as Metaphor in European Union Discourse on Unemployment', *Discourse & Society*, 10(1), 67–99.

Thomas, L. (2004) *Language, Society and Power*, 2nd edn (London and New York: Routledge), ch. 1.

Toulmin, S. E. (2003) *The Uses of Argument* (Cambridge University Press).

Tulving, E. (1983) *Elements of Episodic Memory* (Oxford: Oxford University Press)

van Dijk, T. (1987) *Communicating Racism. Ethnic Prejudice in Thought and Talk* (Newbury Park, CA: Sage).

van Dijk, T. (1990) 'Discourse and Society: A New Journal for a New Research Focus', *Discourse & Society*, 1(1), 5–16.

van Dijk, T. (1998) Ideology (London: Sage).

van Dijk, T. (2008a) *Discourse and Power* (New York: Palgrave Macmillan), ch. 1.

van Dijk, T. (2008b) *Discourse and Context. A Sociocognitive Approach* (Cambridge University Press).

van Hulst, M. J. (2008) 'Love and life in Heartless Town or the Use of Metaphor in Local Planning. In T. Carver and J. Pikalo (eds), *Politics, Language and Metaphor*, pp. 212–24.

Vertessen, D. and De Landtsheer, C. (2008) 'A Metaphorical Election Style: Use of Metaphor at Election Time'. In T. Carver and J. Pikalo (eds), *Politics, Language and Metaphor*. (London: Routledge), pp. 271–2.

Widdowson, H. G. (1998) 'The Theory and Practice of Critical Discourse Analysis', *Applied Linguistics*, 19(1), 136–51.

Wodak, R. (2006) 'Review Focus: Boundaries in Discourse Analysis', *Language in Society*, 35(4), 595–611.

Wodak, R. (2011) *The Discourse of Politics in Action: Politics as Usual* (New York: Palgrave Macmillan).

Wodak, R. and Krzyżanowski, M. (eds) (2008) *Qualitative Discourse Analysis in the Social Sciences* (Basingstoke: Palgrave Macmillan).

Wodak, R. and Meyer, M. (eds) (2001) *Methods of Critical Discourse Analysis* (London: Sage).

Wodak, R. and Meyer, M. (eds) (2009) *Methods of Critical Discourse Analysis*, 2nd edn (London: Sage).

Worthington, I. (2007) *A Companion to Greek Rhetoric* (Chichester, UK: Wiley-Blackwell).

Žagar, I. Ž. (2010) 'Topoi in Critical Discourse Analysis', *Lodz Papers in Pragmatics*, 6(1), 3–27.

Glossary

agent: the person or entity that performs an action described by a verb, or a process.

allusion: a rhetorical figure in which there is indirect evocation of another text that is recognised as having some status, as in 'But what the people heard instead – people of every creed and color, from every walk of life – is that in America, our destiny is inextricably linked. That together, our dreams can be one' – Obama alludes to Martin Luther King's 'I have a dream' speech.

analogy: a parallel or similar instance, referred to because it helps the process of explanation – 'Cutting the deficit by cutting our investments in innovation and education is like lightening an overloaded airplane by removing its engine' – Obama creates an analogy between the economy and an aeroplane.

anaphora: repetition of syntactically similar clauses at the start of a section: '*It's a promise that says* each of us has the freedom to make of our own lives what we will, but that we also have the obligation to treat each other with dignity and respect. *It's a promise that says* the market should reward drive and innovation and generate growth, but that businesses should live up to their responsibilities' (Obama).

anaphoric reference: when a word refers back to another word previously used in the text, as in 'And so this afternoon, I have a dream. It is a dream deeply rooted in the American dream' (King); 'it' is an anaphoric reference to 'dream'. (See also cataphoric reference.)

antithesis: a rhetorical relation of opposition or contrast – 'We need a President who can face the threats of the future, not keep grasping at the ideas of the past' (Obama) relies on an antithesis between future and past.

antonymy: a sense relation expressing the meaning of oppositeness, as in 'the black man will have whip hand over the white man' (Powell); 'black' and 'white' are antonyms.

autonomasia: a figure of speech in which a person is referred to indirectly without using their name.

backgrounding: the linguistic means for deflecting something away from the audience's attention.

cataphoric reference: when a word refers forward to another word used subsequently, as in 'So I've got news for you, John McCain. We all put our country first.' The word 'news' is a cataphoric reference to the whole of the second sentence.

chiasmus: a rhetorical figure of two parts in which the word order of the second part is the reverse or near reverse of the word order in the first part; for example, 'Some people use 'change' to promote their careers; other people use their careers to promote change' (Sarah Palin).

265

circumlocution (or **periphrasis**): the use of more words than is necessary to express a meaning, as in 'And it is that promise that 45 years ago today, brought Americans from every corner of this land to stand together on a Mall in Washington, before Lincoln's Memorial, and hear a young preacher from Georgia speak of his dream.' Obama avoids referring directly to Martin Luther King.

coherence: the impression a text makes of being unified – though without explicit linguistic evidence of how this sense of unity arises.

cohesion – the impression a text makes of being unified that can be traced to the effect of specific lexical and grammatical relations within it.

collocation – the habitual co-occurrence of individual lexical items, such as 'markets' and 'global' or 'bankers' and 'bonuses'.

colloquialism: the use of informal and non-standard coinages such as 'Eurowimpishness' – said of a politician expressing his support for the euro in a weak manner.

connotation The connotations of a word are the associations it creates; for example, the connotation of December, within British and North American culture would be 'cold', 'dark nights' and 'Christmas parties'. Connotations are either personal or cultural.

conviction rhetoric: a persuasive way of speaking in which a speaker's views are expressed with a very high level of personal emotional investment.

corpus: an electronically searchable database of language.

counterposition: an argument that is held by an opponent and which the speaker seeks to refute.

deixis: where meaning arises by referring to some aspect of the context in which words are spoken. It is sub-divided into person (for example, 'he'); place (for example, 'here') and time (for example, 'now').

deliberative speech: a speech given to a decision-making or policy-forming body.

delivery: the vocal means through which a speech-maker communicates.

denotation: the literal, dictionary definition of a word.

deontic modality: the linguistic means available to a speaker for conveying how necessary or desirable it is that something has happened, is happening or will happen.

dialectic: a mode of persuasion that emphasises the importance of logic and reason by arriving at a balanced and truthful perspective after considering every point of view.

direct speech: the use of an actual utterance, without grammatical modification, as part of a narrative. The term contrasts with **indirect speech** (also called **reported speech**), which is speech that is reported with grammatical modifications.

discourse-historical approach: an approach developed by Ruth Wodak to interpret power relations in discourse with reference to their social and historical context.

ellipsis: a sentence where part of the structure has been omitted, for reasons of economy, emphasis or style. Typically, the omitted element can be recovered on close scrutiny of the context; for example, as in 'On November 4th, we must stand up and say: "Eight is enough" (Obama). The word 'years' is omitted.

embedding: when one clause is contained within another.

emotive language: language whose primary function is the expression of emotion; also called **expressive language.** The clearest case is the use of swearing, but other emotive utterances include involuntary responses to art or scenery, expressions of fear or affection, and the outpourings found in a great deal of poetry.

endophoric reference: when a lexical item refers to something that is within the text.

enthymeme: a type of argument structure in which there is a single premise and a conclusion (an incomplete syllogism).

entrenchment: a mode of processing metaphors where is no longer any active comparison, as what was originally a metaphor has established a category meaning of a word. For example, 'blight' has taken on a general meaning of 'harmful entity' rather than a specific disease affecting potatoes.

enumeration: a listing which brings more force to an argument or vividness to a description. For example: 'Here files of pins extend their shining rows, Puffs, powders, patches, bibles, billet-doux' (Alexander Pope, 'The Rape of the Lock').

epilogue: the closing part of a speech.

epiphora: repetition of syntactically similar clauses at the end of a section: 'This country of ours has more wealth than any nation, *but that's not what makes us rich.* We have the most powerful military on Earth, *but that's not what makes us strong.* Our universities and our culture are the envy of the world, *but that's not what keeps the world coming to our shores*' (Obama).

epithet: a word or phrase which characterizes a noun and is regularly associated with it: the 'Iron Lady' became an epithet for Margaret Thatcher.

epideictic speech: a speech given at a ceremonial occasion with the purpose of building consensus.

epistemic modality: the linguistic means available to a speaker for conveying the truth, accuracy or certainty of what he or she is saying.

ethos: one of the three artistic proofs in which an argument is based on an appeal to the character of the speaker and the values that he or she shares with the audience.

euphemism: the use of a vague or indirect expression in place of one that has an unpleasant association, thus '9/11' became a euphemism for the terrorist attack on the World Trade Center in 2001.

exophoric reference: when a lexical item refers to something that is outside the text.

expressive: descriptive of any use of language which displays or affects a person's emotions. Poetic language is usually highly expressive, as is the language of prayer, political speaking and advertising.

figurative: where words are used in a non-literal way to suggest illuminating comparisons and resemblances; also called **figures of speech.** Literal language, by contrast, refers to the usual meaning of a word or phrase. (See also **hyperbole, imagery, irony, litotes, metaphor, metonymy, oxymoron, paradox, personification, rhetoric, simile, synecdoche, zeugma**).

foregrounding: the linguistic means for bringing something to the audience's attention.

forensic speech: a speech given to an assembly whose duty it is to arrive at a decision about guilt or innocence as regards a crime.

genre: a traditional sense refers to an identifiable category of artistic composition (for example, poetry, drama, novels, science fiction as well as a song, sermon or conversation). More recently, genre has taken on a wider meaning that has lost its literary connotations and refers to any body of texts (literary or non-literary) that share a communicative purpose.

hedge(s): words and phrases which soften or weaken the force with which something is said; for example, 'kind of', 'sort of', 'by any chance', 'as it were', 'admittedly'.

heurisis: the phase of working out the most persuasive arguments.

humour: a use of language that evokes amusement or laughter, as in 'If I am a mop, David, you are a broom – a broom that is cleaning up the mess left by the Labour government', where Boris Johnson alludes humorously to David Cameron's reference to him as 'a mop' (that refers humorously to Johnson's famous 'mop of hair') and Johnson uses a 'broom' to refer to Cameron, alluding to the proverb 'a new broom sweeps clean'.

hyperbole: a figure of speech which involves emphatic exaggeration, as in 'We meet at one of those defining moments – a moment when our nation is at war, our economy is in turmoil, and the American promise has been threatened once more' (Obama).

hyponym: a lexical item that is a specific member of a more general class of lexical items; for example, 'saxophone' is a hyponym of 'musical instrument'.

hypotaxis: when one clause is subordinated to another by using, for example, 'because', 'when' 'which' and so on. This creates a distinction between a main and a subordinate clause.

imagery: words or sentences which produce clear or vivid mental pictures; concrete nouns, for example, are highly visual, whereas abstract nouns are not. The use of metaphors, similes and other figures of speech contributes to the imagery in a passage.

inaugural address: a speech given by an American president following his/her election and marking the beginning of his/her presidency.

irony: figure of speech where the meaning conveyed contrasts with that implied by the literal meaning of the words, usually for humorous or dramatic effect. A contrast is often drawn with **sarcasm**, where words are also used with a contrasting meaning but here the intention is to ridicule or wound.

isocolon: figure of speech containing two equal and syntactically balanced parts.

juxtaposition: the placing of two items side by side. Authors and speakers can achieve humorous or telling effects by the judicious juxtaposition of opposing, unusual or incongruous terms.

kairos: a sense of timing so that a particular argument is introduced at the moment it is most likely to be persuasive.

litotes (pron. lieTOEtease): a figure of speech where something is understated; the word comes from the Greek, meaning 'simple, meagre'. An everyday example is 'Not bad', when said of something the speaker considers to be very good.

logos: one of the three artistic proofs in which an argument is based on an appeal to reason and rationality.

mental model: a term associated with van Dijk, referring to the ongoing subjective representations of participants when processing discourse in episodic memory.

metaphor: a figure of speech in which words are used with a sense that is different from their primary or basic sense, as in 'America, in the face of our common dangers, in this *winter of our hardship*, let us remember these timeless words. With hope and virtue, let us *brave once more the icy currents*, and *endure what storms may come*.' Obama uses three expressions whose primary sense relates to the weather to describe economic and political difficulties.

Several kinds of metaphor have been recognised. A **conventional metaphor** is one that forms a part of our everyday understanding of experience and is processed without effort, such as 'to lose the thread of an argument'. **Novel metaphors** are those that have not been extensively adopted in a language community. **Conceptual metaphor** is the shared implied meaning that organises a family of metaphors; for example, ARGUMENT IS WAR underlies metaphors such as 'I attacked his views'; 'he retorted with a salvo' (Lakoff and Johnson, 1980).

metonymy: a figure of speech in which the name of an attribute of an entity is used in place of the entity itself. In 'So we must be ready to fight in Viet-Nam, but the ultimate victory will depend upon the hearts and the minds of the people who actually live out there', Lyndon B. Johnson used 'hearts' in place of 'feelings' and 'minds' in place of 'rational thought'.

modality: the linguistic means for expressing certainty and conviction by conveying what the speaker holds to be true, necessary or desirable.

narrative: in classical rhetoric this was the part of the speech in which the main arguments were introduced.

oratory: the practice of formal persuasive speaking in public.

oxymoron (pron. oxyMOREon): a figure of speech that combines words of incongruous or contradictory meaning. Oxymora are usually identified in literary contexts such as the poet Milton's 'living death' (in *Samson Agonistes*), but they are often to be heard in everyday conversation; for example, describing a toddler as 'a piece of charming wickedness'. (Sometimes terms like 'fun run' and 'military intelligence' are referred to ironically as oxymorons.)

paradox: a statement that is contradictory or absurd on the surface and thus forces the search for a deeper level of meaning: 'War is peace. Freedom is slavery. Ignorance is strength' (George Orwell).

parallelism: a scheme in which two or more clauses share the same syntactic pattern: 'America, *we are better than* these last eight years. *We are a better country than* this' (Obama) (similar to isocolon but more linguistically marked by some form of repetition).

parataxis: when clauses are connected by co-ordinates such as 'and' so that the relation between each clause is equal.

parison: a figure of speech where two entities are compared; for example, 'then' and 'now'.

participants: the people involved in a process.

pathos: one of the three artistic proofs in which an argument is based on an appeal to emotion.

periphrasis: the use of more words than is necessary to express a meaning.

personification: a type of metaphor in which human qualities are ascribed to non-human entities. In 'know th*at America is a friend of each nation* and every man, woman, and child who seeks a future of peace and dignity, and we are ready to lead once more' Obama personifies America, a nation state, as a person.

persuasion: a sustained effort to influence the point of view of an individual or a group.

process (verbal): what actually happens and is indicated by verbs.

prolepsis: the anticipation and answering of an objection or argument before one's opponent has put it forward.

prologue: the opening section of a speech.

proof: the part of a speech where the speaker works out which of the artistic proofs (ethos, pathos and logos) to employ for a particular argument.

quotation: the repetition of language that has previously been encoded. In 'I have a dream that one day this nation will rise up and live out the true meaning of its creed: "We hold these truths to be self-evident: that all men are created equal"' Martin Luther King quoted the American Declaration of Independence.

reference: the grammatical relationship of identity between grammatically related lexical items; for example, a pronoun refers to a noun or noun phrase.

refutation: the part of a speech that attacks an opponent's anticipated arguments.

register: a variety of language defined according to its use in social situations. Examples include 'the scientific register' and the 'formal register'.

reification: a figure of speech in which a word that has a literal concrete meaning is applied to an abstract concept, as in 'To repair our broken society, it's not more of the same we need, but change' (Cameron); 'broken' usually has a concrete meaning but is applied here to 'society'. Reification is often used when coining political slogans; for example: 'the winds of change', 'the domino theory', 'the big society'.

reiteration: a form of repetition where there is some variation (of word form or syntax) of the repeated forms.

repetition: when an identical lexical item recurs.

rhetoric: the study of all the means that could be used for effective persuasion.

rhetorical question: a question for which no answer is expected because it is already assumed to be known.

scheme: a figure of speech where some modification is made in the sequence of words (for example, chiasmus).

semantic field: a group of words which are related in meaning, normally as a result of being connected with a particular context of use. For example 'chop', 'sprinkle', 'salt', 'dice', 'wash', 'simmer', 'boil', 'herbs' are all connected with the semantic field of cookery.

simile: a figurative expression which makes an explicit comparison, typically using *as* or *like*, as in 'Yes, I have a dream this afternoon that one day in this land the words of Amos will become real and "justice will roll down like waters, and righteousness like a mighty stream"' (King).

speech: a coherent stream of spoken language that is usually pre-prepared in written form and delivered by an individual speaker to an audience on a particular occasion with a purpose that corresponds with that occasion.

style: the means through which an individual expresses his or her identity.

substitution: the process of replacing one lexical item with another.

superordinate: a lexical item that represents a general class containing a number of specific lexical items; for example, 'musical instrument' is the superordinate of 'saxophone' and 'trumpet'.

syllogism: a type of argument structure that contains a major premise, a minor premise and a conclusion.

symbolic: Something is symbolic when it suggests associations rather than refers to something directly.

synecdoche: a figure of speech in which the part is used for the whole or the whole is used for the part. In 'to put their hands on the arc of history and bend it once more toward the hope of a better day' (Obama), 'hands' is used in place of 'American people'.

synonyms – words that have equivalent meanings. For example, 'cheap' and 'inexpensive'.

transitivity: the relationship between participants in a process and indicates who does what to whom.

tricolon: figure of speech containing three equal and syntactically balanced parts (for example, *veni, vidi, vici*: I came, I saw, I conquered).

trope: a figure of speech where words are used with senses other than their normal ones (for example, metaphor).

Index

Abbot, Diane, 128
abuse, 135, 235
aesthetics, 208ff
African-American rhetoric, 51ff
agency, 101ff, 227
allusion, 46, 208
analogy, 12
anaphora, 40, 42
anaphoric reference, 63ff
antithesis, 40, 44
antonymy, 69
Arab spring, the, 33, 161
argument, 44, 151, 217
   content, 133, 149
   fallacious, 146ff
   form 133, 149
appearance, 96
Aristotle, 5, 196
arrangement, 16ff
autonomasia, 46

backgrounding, 102
Berlosconi, Silvio, xvii
'Big Society'/'big talk', xvii, 202, 231, 232
Blair, Tony 108ff, 114ff, 155, 177, 204
blogs, 96
burdening/weighting, 135, 232, 234

'call and response' 52
'calm to storm', 43
Cameron, David, xvii, 103, 219ff
career of metaphor, 199
cataphoric reference, 64ff
categorization, 171, 200
category error, 147
causation, 136ff, 237
chiasmus, 40, 223
Churchill, Winston, 237
Cicero, 49
claim, 137, 139
Clinton, Bill, 204

cognitive circumstances, 57, 86, 88
cognitive schema, 158, 236 (*see also* frames *and* schema)
coherence, 55, 159, 210
cohesion, 57ff
   grammatical, 58
colligation, 177
Collins, Tim 34ff
collocation, 67, 7ff
communication, 3
conceptual metaphor, 158, 187ff, 190, 192, 199, 210, 212ff
conjunction, 65ff
context, 86ff, 167, 168, 174, 194
conviction rhetoric, 108
corpus methods, 148, 166, 178ff, 181
'credit crunch', 202
critical discourse analysis, 83ff
critical metaphor analysis, 155ff
Crosby, Lynton, 141
culture, 135, 232, 235

danger/threat, 134, 143, 233
data, 137, 139
dataset design, 164
definition 134, 143, 233
deixis, 60
   person, 60ff
   place, 61
   time, 62
delivery, 30, 90
dialectic, 4, 236
dialogical style, 221
dictionary, use of, 170
discourse-historical approach, 123ff, 232ff
discriminatory rhetoric, 127, 129, 132
disease/illness metaphors, 205, 224
dominance, 127
dossier (dodgy), 111, 120ff

ellipsis, 40, 65
Eminem, 32

Printed and bound by CPI Group (UK) Ltd, Croydon, CR0 4YY